THERAPISTS CHALLENGING RACISM AND OPPRESSION
The unheard voices

Edited by
Neelam Zahid &
Rachel Cooke

Foreword by
Dwight Turner

First published 2023
Product safety code – 012025200

PCCS Books Ltd
Wyastone Business Park
Wyastone Leys
Monmouth
NP25 3SR
United Kingdom

contact@pccs-books.co.uk
www.pccs-books.co.uk

This collection © Neelam Zahid and Rachel Cooke, 2023
The individual chapters © the contributors, 2023

All rights reserved.

No part of this publication may be reproduced, stored in a retrieval system, transmitted or utilised in any form by any means, electronic, mechanical, photocopying or recording or otherwise, without permission in writing from the publishers.

The authors have asserted their right to be identified as the authors of this work in accordance with the Copyright, Designs and Patents Act 1988.

Therapists Challenging Racism and Oppression: The unheard voices

British Library Cataloguing in Publication data: a catalogue record for this book is available from the British Library.

ISBNs   paperback – 978 1 915220 29 5
         epub – 978 1 915220 30 1

Cover design by Jason Anscomb
Cover illustration © Susan Cousins @susan_cousins_author
Typeset in-house by PCCS Books using Minion Pro and Myriad Pro
Printed in the UK by CMP, Dorset

This product has been assessed as low risk and can be used safely without safety information.
The manufacturer's authorised representative in the EU for product safety is:
Easy Access System Europe – Mustamäe tee 50, 10621 Tallinn, Estonia
gpsr.requests@easproject.com

Praise for *Therapists Challenging Racism and Oppression*

Therapists Challenging Racism and Oppression: The unheard voices is bold, passionate, clear and unapologetic in its challenge to oppression. It marks another historical turning point in the evolution and decolonisation of the psychotherapeutic profession. With each chapter illuminating lived experiences of racism, oppression or trauma through the authors' personal stories in the therapeutic realm, the book inevitably takes a critical yet necessary stance. I found it gripping but also very painful to read. I have struggled to write praise for it not because I don't think it is brilliant but because the very fact that such a book needs to be published speaks to the pain of many (as well as my own). I wish things were different and that we didn't need this book. But make no mistake – these voices will not remain unheard! The book's value is not confined to just therapists interested in anti-oppressive and anti-racist practice within the profession. Rather, it speaks to all those committed to upholding the values of equality, social justice and human rights and combating both conscious and unconscious racial discrimination at a personal and a professional level.
Divine Charura, Professor of Counselling Psychology, York St John University

This thoughtful and reflective, intersectional book shares vulnerability and visceral experiences. A courageous, tangible plethora of voices previously hidden embody and analyse experiences that highlight the duality of being inside identity while in training and practice. This is a bold contribution that addresses resistance and liberation, freeing who we really are. Secrets are revealed and transparency and collective catharsis open wide systems of oppression. Silence about traumatic learning is broken to expose the rawness of racism. Decolonising and a breakthrough in personal, political and psychological aspects of therapeutic connection are encouraged. The authors question power relationships and hierarchies, racial dynamics and shaming in the field of counselling and psychotherapy. Most importantly, the book offers recommendations for safeguarding people of colour in the professions and institutional, personal and professional justification for more ethical training, practice and supervision.
Dr Isha Mckenzie-Mavinga, psychotherapist, lecturer and author of *Black Issues in the Therapeutic Process* **and** *The Challenge of Racism in Therapeutic Practice*

Here is a book that is both timely and a treasure trove, full of lived experiences of therapists of colour in practice and training. Its chapters prompt reflections about anti-racist practices in the face of everyday experiences of racism that many black, brown and people of colour encounter in their training and, sadly, throughout their working life. The editors and writers bravely and boldly speak truth to power and call powerfully for change to challenge the ongoing performative allyship across settings. This book generates necessary thinking about anti-racist practices and the importance of decolonising therapy, so it becomes truly inclusive and safe for all.

Anthea Benjamin, group analyst, supervisor and organisational consultant

How I wish this book was around when I was training to be a therapist. I remember regularly feeling, after sharing my lived experiences of anti-blackness, difference and homophobia to others at this time; that they were being downplayed, discounted, gaslighted or ignored. Now I have a collection of fearless, incisive, forensic and necessary writing that proves that my feelings and thoughts are valid. I highly recommend this book to all students, clients, practitioners and supervisors who are committed to making their work, trainings, organisations and practice more robust and fit for purpose for life in 21st century UK.

Dennis Carney, therapist, facilitator, trainer and member of BAATN Leadership Team

This brave book boldly calls on us to summon the courage to speak out for ourselves as therapists and for our clients who suffer under oppression. Each contribution serves as a reminder that oppression is a global issue that affects the majority, and that it is imperative for us to respond holistically as therapists to a system that impacts nations, societies, and humanity as a whole. The book disrupts and unsettles the reader, encouraging us to collaborate outside of therapy through peer dialogue, advocacy and allyship. And without explicitly stating so, it inspires our clients to become active citizens and change agents. If the writers are suggesting that authentic, empathic dialogue, guided by deep acceptance and a thirst for knowledge, is the key to defeating the systems of oppression, then we must take the necessary risks and engage in meaningful dialogues within our profession about race, racial difference and intersectionality. This is essential for our personal growth as therapists and for the betterment of society as a whole.

Rotimi Akinsete, therapeutic counsellor, clinical supervisor, training & organisational development consultant and mentor

These 'unheard voices' constellate a healing well from which readers can draw nourishment in the face of what ails when systemic oppressions intersect. Interwoven personal and professional reflections enable practitioners, trainees, training institutions, assessors and professional bodies to deepen dialogue and inform action in the cultivation of a therapeutic craft that robustly engages with social justice. Rather than offering performative, surface-level, dogmatic offerings about doing and saying 'the right thing', these authors courageously foreground the messiness and often-unresolved nature of meaning-making within psychotherapeutic discourse. Readers are invited to engage with rich opportunities for transformation that are evoked through supposed mistakes, rupture and repair, relationally and systematically. From the realms of silence, each reflexive chapter provides much-needed language to articulate unconscious, somatised states, re-imagining and renewing practice. Relevant, relatable and overdue, these unheard voices offer pertinent insight and challenge for troubling times.

Joel Simpson, psychotherapist, writer, presenter and celebrant

Required reading for all counselling professionals, this is a book that speaks from personal, political and psychological perspectives while also making it clear that racism is not a 'private problem' but a structural and societal encounter. Exclusion and marginalisation lurk in counselling training, practice and delivery in real-life situations. This is a vital and essential collection of work focusing on the authors' journeys and the lived stories that provide us with constructive notes to inform our work towards anti-oppressive practice where action is needed. Each chapter focuses on the author's journey and neatly applies intersectionality as a lens for further examining all systems of oppression and how they operate in the field of counselling and psychology. The authors have provided us with powerful and disturbing descriptions that invite us to delve deeper and challenge previously held beliefs. These are stories we have not heard before, but they are stories we need to hear.

Susan Cousins, author and Senior Advisor, Race, at Cardiff University

CONTENTS

	Foreword Dwight Turner	ix
	Introduction Neelam Zahid and Rachel Cooke	1
1	What's in a name? Why names matter for people of colour Neelam Zahid	11
2	Cultivating intersectional nuance within the dissociative confines of capitalism Rachel Cooke	30
3	Attending to self, attending to others: the impact on the Black therapist of client presentations of racial trauma Ohemaa Nkansa-Dwamena	62
4	Call me by my name Anita Gaspar	77
5	A need for deep learning – not training Joanna Traynor	90
6	Racism and coercive control in an NHS counselling service Anya Amrith and Roshmi Lovatt	105
7	Confronting the colonial history of transphobia Sam Hope	123
8	(Inter)racial transference: A case of projective identification Jaspreet Tehara	138
9	Diunital healing: A multi-dimensional approach to therapy Oye Agoro	154
10	My journey to visibility: Using congruence to explore racial microaggressions within the supervisory relationship Rajita Rajeshwar	175
	About the contributors	193
	Name index	197
	Subject index	202

About the editors

Neelam Zahid is an integrative counsellor, psychotherapist and clinical supervisor accredited by BACP. She has practised as a therapist since 2003, having previously worked in higher education for more than a decade, and currently has her own private practice. She is also deputy course leader for the Foundation year at the Minster Centre and teaches on the Introduction to Counselling Skills course. In addition, she is currently a visiting lecturer at the University of Westminster, teaching on the BSc Psychology and Counselling and Introduction to Counselling Skills courses. Her areas of interest are intersectionality, difference and diversity, and she has contributed to several publications, including *The Handbook of Transcultural Counselling and Psychotherapy* (2001) and *Black Identities + White Therapies: Race, respect + diversity* (2021).

Rachel Jane Cooke (she/they) is a queer, integrative psychotherapist, supervisor and educator from Ireland, in practice since 2009. She is based in London, runs an online therapy platform (p-therapy.com), consults to charities and social enterprises, and has a longstanding weekly radio segment on sex and relationships, where she often discusses identity, privilege and oppression. She regularly speaks on podcasts and hosts talks and workshops for the public, for therapists and for organisations, on topics such as intersectionality, trauma, attachment, health and wellness under neoliberalism, embodiment, feminist therapy and gender, sexuality and relationship diversity. Rachel is passionate about training therapists committed to social justice, particularly through embodied and relational practice. You can read more about her work at racheljanecooke.com

Acknowledgements

Neelam Zahid

There are so many people I'd like to acknowledge and thank for making this book possible and for being on this journey with me, through all its trials and tribulations. So here are just a few of them.

To the contributors of this book, thank you so much for sharing your stories, working so hard and taking a risk in breaking the silence. To PCCS Books, for giving us all the opportunity to share our stories and voices. To Pretish Raja-Helm and Anita Gaspar, for listening to me when I went through hardships through this journey – you listened wholeheartedly with care and warmth. To my supervisor, who believed in me through this whole process and who has supported me to believe in myself. To my co-editor Rachel, who has worked so hard alongside me with her gentleness and rigour to compile such an amazing piece of work.

To my family: my daughters, Diya and Inaayah, who have shown me patience, understanding and love throughout this process – I could not have done this without you, my loves. To my sister, Firdous, for believing in me and being there for me unconditionally through thick and thin – I love you with all my heart. To my mum, who is no longer with us, for her wisdom, strength and courage – I would not be the woman I am without you, Umee Jee.

And last, to my creator, the Almighty, for giving me the strength to be unapologetically me in this complex yet beautiful world.

Rachel Cooke

Many people, other creatures and environments have supported me, cheered and spurred me on during the making of this book. I appreciate every moment and relationship of warmth, grounding, compassion, clarity, insight, gentle yet firm probing and much more.

Thank you to all the contributors, whose mettle and openness has awed me. It's been an honour and privilege to work with you, your stories have touched me profoundly.

Thank you to PCCS Books, specifically to Catherine Jackson, for expressing her passion for the topic and the project from the get-go, as well as her enthusiastic, dexterous direction.

To Neelam, with whom I felt a kinship from when we first met, who knows this journey has been difficult and tangled at times, as well as immensely meaningful. Your honesty, thoughtfulness and solidarity has brought so much to the book and to my experience.

To everyone who submitted proposals and pieces of writing: your voices, stories and ideas are valuable and have helped shape what the book has come to be.

To my encouraging, brilliant, patient, wise friends and partners, who supported me through the project: particularly Joe Wild, Dora Darvasi and Kelly Field – your care and humour scooped me up. You have my heart.

To my parents, for encouraging curiosity, speaking up and embracing nonconformity.

To my supervisors, for holding, challenging and inspiring me when I felt emboldened and when I felt lost.

To my clients, for radically enriching my life, year after year. Therapeutic relationships continue to imbue me with hope and purpose, sharpening and expanding my vision of a better future.

Thank you also to the people, courses, institutions and systems that have painfully provoked me to become more deeply connected to my values and principles, as well as regularly confronting me to investigate, re-evaluate and update them.

Foreword

Dwight Turner

I first want to give some background to why I felt it was important to take on the writing of this foreword and why I believe that the stories in this book need to be seen, heard and learned from.

I am a massive fan of comic books. Some of my favourite are those about the X-Men, created in 1963 (Saunders, 2011). The creators, Stan Lee and Jack Kirby, didn't want to write regular comic books about superheroes from another planet who come to Earth to save us from imminent annihilation (Russell & Leslie, n.d.). They wanted to use the medium to communicate important messages about civil rights. Their Professor X and his one-time friend and now enemy Eric Lershnerr, otherwise known as Magneto, can in many ways be seen as the Martin Luther King and Malcolm X of the comic book world.

This was a time when stories about Blackness were rarely told or heard. Very few Black characters were allowed to exist in the comic book realm – even Charles M. Schultz had to fight to include one Black character, Franklin, in his *Peanuts* strip cartoons (Jenkins, 2018). The tales and the horrors of what it was to be the racialised other in America during that time were often hidden under the rug of Whiteness – suppressed, repressed, hidden away, a distinctive bump on the floor of White supremacy. What Stan and Jack did by giving a voice to the racialised other in the comic book realm was to reach a substantial number of Black readers, like me and many of my peers, and provide affirmation and comfort through the images and narratives about people who had been left to the side and marginalised. That these stories are still so prevalent and powerful today says an awful lot about just how far (or not) we have come along this racialised path towards a just and compassionate world.

This is the backdrop to my reading of and response to this book. I want also to state how touched I was to receive and be invited to read these stories.

The tales here, of the misuse and mispronunciation of names, of experiences of racism on counselling courses and in practice, with colleagues and with clients, and of the struggles of White practitioners to recognise their own complicity within the structures of White supremacy, have rung bells for me around my own experiences of what it was like to transverse a training in psychotherapy – indeed, to transverse every educational setting I have endured since I was a child.

Not long ago, I gave a presentation on privilege and otherness in counselling at a university in the North of England. At the end, I was approached by a woman of colour of maybe 40 years of age. She had tears in her eyes, and I asked her if she was alright and whether she would like to sit with me if she needed to talk. After a few minutes of small talk, the woman told me that my presentation was the first time she had ever received a lecture from a person of colour, male or female, while in training to become a counsellor. In fact, she said, this was also the first time she had been taught anything about Blackness by anyone of colour in her whole educational career. Her tears were a deep-seated reflection of the pain of realising that she had not been seen or represented for so many years; that her otherness, her racial difference, had been so marginalised. It was a privilege to have been able to be that first for her.

Experiences of racism and exclusion are sadly still commonplace on training courses, be they psychotherapy, counselling or psychology. What often gets left out of our understanding of these experiences is that part of the pain inherent in them comes from the silencing of the racialised other. For me, that is the beauty of this book. In any drive towards equality or equity, the first stage is always going to involve hearing the voice of the other. In these cases, the voices of the racialised other, their pain, their wisdom and their abilities to reflect, are crucial in carving out a space and building a platform for others, who also see themselves marked out as the racialised other, to come after.

This first stage in any initiative towards re-establishing equity should not be underestimated. There are other stages, I believe, along this path towards inclusion, decolonisation, equality and equity, but this first one is perhaps the most difficult. Having a voice means you may be seen. The double-bind, or the internalisation of the supremacist's narrative that we, as a racialised other, should be silent, often has to be fought against and pushed through in order for us to inscribe our voices in black ink and on pages as white as these.

The bravery of these authors who have challenged the normativity of academia by writing about their own positioning not only challenges the White supremacist within and the White supremacist without; it also runs counter to the academic norm of supposed objectivity. What these stories also do is reach into a more diasporian (by which I mean anyone from Asian, African,

Caribbean backgrounds) presentation, whereby learning and knowledge is not just about what is written on the page; it is also about the ability to tell a story, and for that story's metaphors and lessons to become a huge part of the experiences and healing of the racialised other.

What I am saying ultimately is that wisdom comes in forms like this – in the lived stories and experiences of those who have been marginalised, othered and racially harmed and hurt as they have tried and fought to make sense of their experiences. The facing up, standing up and speaking up of all those authors will, I hope, lead to other persons of racial difference feeling able to stand up and tell their stories, be it on their training courses, in their lectures, in their essays, on their blogs, or in books that follow on from this one.

I urge the reader to reflect on the wisdom and pain in each and every chapter. Note what touches you, why it touches you, and how it touches you. I also urge you to actually sit with and learn from the pain of each of these stories. You will not find this wisdom or this pain in mainstream academia. I believe these stories will inspire new generations of counsellors and psychotherapists to be the X-Men, X-Women, X-People of their profession.

These stories blaze a new trail for others to follow. They deserve to be known.

Dr Dwight Turner
Senior lecturer, Brighton University, and author of *Intersections of Privilege and Otherness in Counselling and Psychotherapy*

References

Jenkins, B. (2018). *The inspiring true story of Franklin, 'Peanuts' 1st black character.* www.inspiremore.com/charles-schulz-franklin/

Russell, C. & Leslie, P. (n.d.). Heroic moments: A study of comic book superheroes in real-world society. *Explorations: Social Sciences*, 121–131.

Saunders, B. (2011). *Do the Gods wear capes? Spirituality, fantasy and superheroes.* Bloomsbury Academic.

Introduction

Neelam Zahid and Rachel Cooke

Neelam Zahid

This book has been in the pipeline for a couple of years now. It started out as a blog, which transitioned into an article, which now forms part of this book. This transitory process feels important to name as it illustrates the metamorphosis of 'going public' with the racism I experienced in training workshops over the past decade. The experiences of racism I write about in this book caused great harm to me, and each time I found my racial and relational trauma being re-activated, taking me to a young, delicate place of vulnerability and fragility. It's not often I go back there these days, after years of therapy, personal development and healing. For many of you who know this feeling, it is a scary place, where often no light shines. The most recent time I experienced racism in my professional life, I got angry, I got mad. It was then that I made a decision to stop running. I made a decision to face the ugly truth of what I had experienced and show up for myself and give myself a voice. I had been silenced for far too long. I chose to speak up. And I recognise that in this book I have the privilege to speak up. I feel empowered by the other voices in this book and feel a sense of solidarity with the contributors, while also feeling sad that so many of us continue to experience harm because of the colour of our skin.

My going public about this racism has been met with many obstacles on many fronts, too numerous to name, which has felt like conscious and unconscious silencing by the perpetrators. This has been powerful, often immobilising, and painful. It has also been a frightening process that lays bare the reality of racial abuse within our world of psychotherapy, which often gets overlooked, hidden or minimalised.

For me, speaking out about the painful experiences of racism in this book was, and still is at times, paralysing. In the final stages of completing the book,

I noticed myself spiral into a place of fear and shame, questioning the validity of what we were doing, gaslighting myself into asking myself, 'Are we making a fuss about nothing?' It's something that I think Black and Brown therapists experience as a constant when we are trying to decide whether to go public with our experiences. Too often we are silenced by that fear and shame, and fear too of being shamed professionally by accusations of breach of confidentiality of the therapeutic space, whether it is in training contexts or in our therapy rooms.

This process feels typical of an abusive cycle where the perpetrator intimidates their victim to stay silent about their abuse. Certainly, the experiences in this book have had to be carefully managed and anonymised so that the individuals written about could not identify themselves or be identified and client confidentiality is preserved. There is no question that we are rightly bound by our professional ethical frameworks to keep confidential what happens in the therapy room between us and our clients. However, I ask, where do we draw the line of confidentiality in situations between peers and in professional contexts such as education and training and CPD workshops? Research repeatedly shows that racism – overt, large-scale but also the so-called microaggressions that are described in these chapters – causes immense psychological and physical harm. What protection do our professional ethical frameworks offer against this? What come-back is there for those who perpetrate it intraprofessionally, in interactions with colleagues, students, trainers and professional bodies?

The BACP and UKCP ethical frameworks clearly state our responsibilities as practitioners to protect clients from harm and emphasise the importance of the confidentiality and privacy of our clients. However, neither of these accrediting bodies explicitly names or has a procedure for dealing with incidents when there is racism towards practitioners either from clients, colleagues/peers, supervisors or from training institutes and professional organisations themselves. Most professional bodies have a complaints procedure for clients when practitioners are deemed to have done something unethical or harmful to them, but there is nothing in the frameworks about when harm is done to us as therapists by our clients or fellow practitioners. Harm is mentioned in the BACP *Ethical Framework* 19 times (BACP, 2018) and five times in the UKCP *Code of Ethics and Professional Practice* (2019), but not once in relation to harm caused to the practitioner. UKCP does refer to challenging 'questionable practice in yourself or others' (para.37) but again only in reference to clients.

There are pitifully few points in the BACP *Ethical Framework* that are relevant to this. For example:

We share a responsibility with all other members of our professions for the safety and wellbeing of all clients and their protection from exploitation or unsafe practice. We will take action to prevent harm caused by practitioners to any client. (2018, para.11)

On respect:

We will take the law concerning equality, diversity and inclusion into careful consideration and strive for a higher standard than the legal minimum.

We will challenge colleagues or others involved in delivering related services whose views appear to be unfairly discriminatory and take action to protect clients, if necessary. (2018, paras.23, 24)

And for trainees:

Trainees working with each other will:

a. relate respectfully to others and endeavour to support each others' learning
b. follow good ethical practice when working with each other, for example when practising skills or in personal development. (para.81)

For trainers, the framework states:

Trainers and educators will model high levels of good practice in their work, particularly with regard to expected levels of competence and professionalism, relationship building, the management of personal boundaries, any dual relationships, conflicts of interest and avoiding exploitation. (2018, para.79)

And:

Trainers and educators will encourage trainees to raise any concerns at the earliest opportunity and have processes and policies for addressing any trainee's concerns. Trainers and educators are responsible for providing opportunities for trainees to discuss any of their practice-related difficulties without blame or unjustified criticism and, when appropriate, to support trainees in taking positive actions to resolve difficulties. (2018, para.80)

These ethical principles go some way towards addressing harm that may have been inflicted upon the practitioner but, as you can see, the word 'harm' has not been mentioned once.

Similarly, when both ethical frameworks refer to equality, diversity and inclusion, this is with reference to the client and the personal development of the practitioner. It does not stipulate a procedure for when these ethical principles are breached by clients, supervisors, training bodies, educational institutes or professional associations, although the latter two will have internal procedures of their own to address racist practices in accordance with the law.

The Equality Act (2010) and other related legislation such as the Human Rights Act (1998) protect people from discrimination and harm in the workplace and in wider society, including places of education. Both the professional associations I have mentioned here state that confidentiality can be broken if required by law, but again this is in reference to protecting the client. If a client or a colleague/peer/trainer in a training group is racist towards a therapist of colour, we find ourselves in a double bind. Are these accrediting bodies contravening legislation when practitioners are required to keep the confidentiality of the perpetrator regarding the harm in question? And the matter becomes even more complex if the training organisation or training is not accredited by any recognised accrediting body.

As you can see, the matter of confidentiality and harm is complex, and I would implore the major accrediting bodies to review their ethical framework, considering what has been written here and in light of the harm described in this book by the contributors. It is, in my opinion, unlawful to uphold the principle of confidentiality if harm has occurred to any practitioners regarding matters of racism and other protected characteristics.

How many other unheard voices of therapists of colour are out there? How many practitioners feel paralysed by the ethical principle of confidentiality and fear of professional shaming when they consider reporting when harm has occurred? I bear witness to the powerful accounts in this book and am reminded of why I wanted to create a book where therapists share their stories of racism within the therapy field. It was because I wanted to create a space for these therapists to have their voices heard. I wanted our stories of racism to take centre stage so that the power and agency lost and abused in these experiences could be reclaimed. The power of telling my stories of racism within safe professional environments helped me breathe and grow; it helped me feel validated in my experiences and able to sit with the harm that had been caused. This was essential for me, so that I could finally speak out and start the healing from racism, white supremacy and the structural inequality I grew up in. Even as I write this, I have a visceral feeling in my body of letting go, with a sigh of relief and a loosening of the tension in my neck, shoulders and stomach.

I learnt about the concept of recognition trauma (Mckenzie-Mavinga, 2009) from a workshop run by Isha Mckenzie-Mavinga a few years ago. She defines it as 'the awakening of hurtful experiences related to racism'. I feel this book is an attempt to recognise and display the racial trauma we therapists of colour have had to endure during our training and in our work as practitioners. Giving a voice to these awakening experiences through this kind of narrative is an attempt to heal the individual telling the story and to start the process of healing in the wider society in which it took place.

This book is also a response to an increasing awareness of the context of structural racism, as well as other oppressions and inequalities experienced by therapists of colour, and against the backdrop of the murders of George Floyd, Breonna Taylor and Mohammed Hassan, to name just a few, and the inequalities experienced by Black, Asian and minority ethnic people throughout the coronavirus pandemic. It is also a response to the epidemic of global capitalism and consumerism, which perpetuates the toxic legacy of slavery, colonialism and indentured labour and is rapidly destroying our planet before our eyes.

Our book advocates for the Black Lives Matter movement and upholds the values of equality and human rights within the psychotherapeutic profession. Our intention is to engage readers through emotive storytelling to raise awareness of, as well as develop empathy for, the pervasive imbalance of power within racial dynamics in the therapy arena. We strive to draw attention to harmful practice, to bring more conscious awareness to that which is unconscious and so contribute to the dismantling of white supremacy within the profession.

For this reason, it was important to us, as editors, that the majority of the chapters here should be written by therapists of colour, and that they include different intersections, where possible. Although this book is primarily about race and racism, it is important not to ignore that we bring intersecting identities that will impact how we experience our racial identities within the wider world.

Each chapter relates a personal story of experiencing, inflicting or witnessing racism (as well as other forms of prejudice and discrimination) in the therapeutic realm. This is followed by an analysis of the incident, and ideas and action points for reflection and self-development to address and combat both conscious and unconscious racial discrimination at a personal and professional level. The experiences of racism described in each of these chapters are powerful, emotive and traumatic.

I understand the cost of asking therapists of colour to tell their stories of racism to the world and reconnect with these horrific and painful experiences. It's not easy at all. In fact, one of the concerns I had when putting this book together was the risk of therapists of colour feeling re-traumatised by telling their stories and then having to dissect them and analyse them. We did not want to cause further harm. I was aware of what we were asking our contributors to do, and the potential cost of connecting with these painful experiences. I am eternally grateful to each contributor for sharing their stories. Thank you all for your bravery and courage in speaking out about your experiences of racism and going deep into the depths of your discomfort and pain. I felt humbled, sad and my own deep pain when editing these chapters. The process of carrying the trauma of other people of colour was heavy and at times activating for me, as I am sure it was for the writers. These wounds are collective and, as you read through this book, I am certain that you will identify with aspects of the trauma being written about. Perhaps through this collective identification we can start to gain the necessary impetus to make the changes we all so need.

Some final thoughts

As I was writing this introduction, my co-editor Rachel asked me what my hopes were for the future, for me and for other therapists of colour. Did I think healing from racial trauma was possible? Did I believe there was hope for the world while we still live under oppressive systems but continue to strive to make changes for those who continue to suffer? The answers to these questions are not easy. It is difficult to have hope when we continue to inflict pain on each other and continue to deny the harm it causes. What I know for now is that we need to continue to speak up, and the rest will follow. I trust the innate wisdom of humanity to take us along the path we need to walk. As we continue to challenge racism and oppression in all its forms, we do not need to know where it will take us. Through the process of destruction there is rebirth; through pain there is connection, and through connection we can heal.

Rachel Cooke

The process of working with the contributors and putting this book together with Neelam has been deeply moving, humbling and enriching for me. It's been a privilege to work alongside so many engaged, reflective, heartful people who trusted us to support and guide their stories and ideas. The book has transformed many times over the course of its writing; it required us to embrace its remarkably elastic unfolding. From its conceptual birth as a consequence of a series of racist, unacceptable experiences with a training organisation here in the UK in 2020, to publishing this year, I have become increasingly solid in my conviction of how much, and what, has still to change in relation to race and intersectionality in the field of therapy.

There were people who feared this book's premise represented exploitation of people of colour's pain and trauma. Others were exasperated by the prospect of another anti-racist lecture telling people of colour what they already know, or imploring, cajoling or pleading with white people to do better. There were some contributors who dropped out along the way, when they found that the process brought to the surface unmanageable levels of past trauma. Others withdrew at the point at which we encouraged them to explore the emotional and somatic aspects of their experience more deeply; when we invited them to de-intellectualise their approach to their writing of these deeply personal and vulnerable chapters.

This book hovered and shifted between styles and approaches. In the beginning, Neelam and I had expected the book to focus on anti-oppressive practice – for authors to share personal practices and rituals they find stabilising, community practices that help discharge trauma and ground people in a shared sense of belonging and meaning, as well as suggestions for training organisations, institutions and the government to (often radically) change their policies, to decolonise and operate more ethically and anti-oppressively. What we discovered was considerable initial reticence to share such ideas and knowledge. I was in touch with many people's deep sorrow, often the understandable fear of putting their head above the parapet, and profound fatigue in dredging up past experiences. Most contributors laughed wryly when we suggested that they share a single experience in their chapter. 'Just one? I've so, so many,' came a chorus of responses.

I hope these accounts and essays will make the topics of racism, intersectionality, power, positionality, cultural criticism and theory, anti-oppressive practice and the future of therapy more significant and compelling to you. I hope they will precipitate expansive change in how you think about, engage with and practise therapy, and support your sense of responsibility to the field, along with empowerment to take action. Some of the ideas and experiences in these chapters may seem (and may even be) conflicting. I invite you to allow yourself to savour the details, the contradictions, the richness of variety and multiplicity, as well as the friction you may feel, where possible.

Some people have been curious about and understandably wary of my involvement in the project, as a white person, and it feels important to be transparent about that journey. It was a hefty compliment to be invited by Neelam to support and collaborate with her. There was synchronicity in the timing: I had witnessed the damage, denial and delusion of racist and otherwise oppressive ways of being and operating on far too many occasions and was in a place to be able to speak out in a more substantive way. I was very fortunate to have time, enough health, energy and stability and much desire to help bring this book into being.

I also believed I would be able to engage and communicate with contributors in a way that would ensure that racist (and otherwise prejudiced and oppressive) patterns would not be replicated, that it would be a supportive and safe enough environment. Despite my efforts to address and flatten any power dynamics as much as possible, to offer the right amount of transparency and assistance, I felt uncomfortable with my position as a White editor at many points. The contributors were patient, gracious and kind throughout. I can only imagine how complex and tiring the process of sharing their stories was for many, if not all of them. I want to say to them all that being alongside you has been a challenge and a great pleasure. Thank you.

What I've written is enriched and limited by my lived and inherited experience. I'm a white, Irish, non-disabled, neurodivergent, queer, middle-class woman, living in London. I am very aware of how my White privilege, sighted privilege and literacy privilege, among other privileges, reduced the structural and logistical barriers to my participation in the project.

My own chapter and perspective have shifted substantially along the course of the project. I began with a focus on personal mistakes in relation to race in my role as therapist – my own racist clangers that I had sometimes believed weren't racist because they were 'benevolently' intended ('But sir, I had good intentions!'). As I began hearing and reading more about the racism, intersectional oppression and despotism enacted in institutions and therapy training environments, I shifted to a focus on institutional errors I've witnessed, and in some cases been complicit in. Over the course of the past two years, while reading chapter proposals and then chapters, and editing and offering support to the contributors, I was also speaking to dozens of therapists through delivering training and facilitating workshops, engaging in peer supervision groups and working with supervisees. I heard so many practitioners express their disillusionment and hopelessness in relation to the field of therapy. This led me to redirect my focus to describing more of the contextual environments for therapists, clients and wider afield.

I believe that therapy has not done nearly enough to grasp and incorporate the social and environmental aspects of how we live. There is also still a great need, on our part as therapists, for deeper awareness and solidarity that often comes through empathising with adversity, which I hope the book will stir in you. I'm excited by the prospect of this book doing more than encouraging you to take individual action – that you will be inspired to collaborate, prioritise, strategise, vision and organise for collective impact. I invite readers to see this work as a noticing that has the capacity to shape our next steps, as more tributaries joining the river; to see it as a way to become more aware of the knowledge and wisdom we have so far, so that we can move forward with intentionality from here. I want to encourage readers to take what's useful and leave or redefine areas, based on your own knowledge and experience; to provide a springboard for consideration and discussion as part of fostering solidarity, collective care, widespread change, maybe even revolution. The quotes and citations are from people and work in which I've found sustenance, stabilisation and illumination. I hope they do some of the same and more for you.

There are increasing numbers of spaces for people of colour to talk about their experiences, but many therapists still don't have adequate outlets and support for the particular set of challenges, indignities and trauma that can result from training and working in white-dominated, white-originated organisations and institutions. We wanted to be very cognisant of the potential for this book to be seen as a form of trauma porn, created not for the marginalised group but for the consolation or entertainment of the non-marginalised group. It could have been exploitative or emotionally provocative for unethical and unhelpful reasons; it could have lacked respect and compassion. It could also have been patronising, under the guise of being didactic, at the expense of the wellbeing of people of colour. Marginalised people are keenly aware of the issues they face – the impact of acute and chronic stress, the death rates, day-to-day discrimination and other hazards that come from existing outside of the default:

> To talk about pain without expressing pain is to expect a human to recall information like a robot. When you insist that BIPOC talk about their painful experiences with racism without expressing any pain, rage, or grief, you are asking them to dehumanize themselves. (Saad, 2020)

We want to call to mind and heart that people of colour are more than stories of suffering, and that people racialised as 'white' are not only defined by oppression, while maintaining our commitment to the themes of racism and intersectional oppression herein. Most of all, I want, without defaulting to colour-blindness, to humanise us in our desire for safety, respect, support, love and equity for our fellow therapists, our clients, ourselves and everyone else. We wanted to hold a deep awareness of the people who will be impacted by engaging with this book. We didn't want another book solely telling white therapists to reform, or one aimed at therapists of colour when the onus of responsibility to change is not on them. We hoped it would abound with stimulating, undeniable calls to action rather than simply emphasise pain of therapists of colour. It is of course up to you to decide whether we have accomplished this.

A note on race capitalisation

There are diverse considerations and perspectives that strive to be anti-racist on capitalising only Black, or Black, Brown and Indigenous, whether to include White as well, or whether to keep them all lower case. As editors, we have reflected on whether to encourage consistency across the book or to acknowledge and support contributors' individual decisions. Since this is a book about individual voices and deeply personal stories about race, we've chosen to honour each contributor's preference.

Invitation for self-care

As soon as we get into the detail of trauma, there is the possibility of it bringing up challenging sensations and emotions. Although we have sought to limit the amount of traumatic (and potentially retraumatising) material, while maintaining the heart and viscerality of these stories, it may be activating or triggering for some. We urge readers to take care of yourselves as you connect to these accounts of injustice, oppression and abuse from people who've experienced trauma. Use practices to stay as grounded as possible; call on friends, family or other support if you need to and can; take breaks if that is helpful, or skip over anything that feels too much and return to it if and when it feels more possible.

References

BACP. (2018). *Ethical framework for the counselling professions*. BACP.

Mckenzie-Mavinga, I. (2009). *Black issues in the therapeutic process*. Palgrave Macmillan.

Saad, L. (2020). *Me and white supremacy: How to recognise your privilege, combat racism and change the world*. Quercus.

UKCP. (2019). *Code of ethics and professional practice*. UKCP.

1. What's in a name? Why names matter for people of colour

Neelam Zahid

This chapter is dedicated to every person of colour who has had their name anglicised, shortened, mispronounced, forgotten or ridiculed.

My name is Neelam, pronounced *Nee*-luhm. Not Nee-*lamb* or Ni-lam or any other way you might wish to pronounce it. My name means sapphire in Sanskrit and, coincidentally, my favourite colour is blue. My name holds meaning; it is part of my identity. I love my name now, and I would not want to be called anything else. But this has not always been the case. I remember when I was about five years old, I used to pretend my name was Ruby. I did not quite understand back then why I wanted to change my name, but now I do. It was partly because I liked the name Ruby, but it was also because I wanted to fit in. I wanted to have a 'normal' name, just like everyone else. I still sometimes use the name Ruby as my alias; perhaps it's the name of my alter ego. Now that's a whole different chapter!

I consider myself a Londoner, born and bred. However, I do not consider myself to be English, as both my parents are from Pakistan and I have brown skin. Having a non-English name in England has been challenging since I was young. In childhood, my name was quite often mispronounced, forgotten, shortened and sometimes ridiculed by both peers and teachers. At primary and secondary school, I remember feeling I could not correct people who mispronounced my name, and quite often I laughed with the other children when they made fun of it. Young children can be very cruel to each other. Even now, as I write this, I can feel the pain and a deep shame within my gut. I feel small, bruised and disempowered as I recall those memories.

It was the same when I went to college and then university. People no longer made fun of my name, but they did forget it or mispronounce it, and I very rarely corrected them. When I did correct people, I felt embarrassed and insignificant, as though I was making a big deal out of nothing. When, around my mid-20s, I started my psychotherapy training, I once again experienced tutors and peers forgetting or mispronouncing my name. Sometimes, they'd call me by another Brown student's name, which for me reinforced the stereotype that 'We all look the same'. This phenomenon is called 'misidentification', which really speaks to the homogenisation of Brown people and not seeing us as individual people (see Anita Gaspar's chapter in this book (Gaspar, 2023)).

When I completed my training and then went on to practise as a psychotherapist, my frustration with the name mispronunciation and amnesia grew. I was left with the thought that, if self-awareness and honesty are at the core of psychotherapy training, why did I feel that I could not challenge tutors and peers with *their* difficulties around my name? I felt like the problem was mine: *I* could not challenge people because of *my* lack of confidence. I did not even consider that it might be because structural racism is designed to gag minority groups to oppress and silence them.

Gradually, through my work with people of colour and my own self-development, I became more confident to correct people when they got my name wrong. As I learnt more about my own experience as a Brown, female, Muslim psychotherapist, I began to feel I was entitled to have my name remembered and pronounced correctly. To this day, I sometimes feel that 'I'm making a fuss' when I do this, but I am more able to soothe the young child who feels too unimportant to correct others.

'What's in a name? That which we call a rose by any other name would smell as sweet'

In this chapter, I directly challenge this quote from Shakespeare's play, *Romeo and Juliet*. Names matter, especially if you are from a minority community. Hirsch, in her book *BRIT(ish)* (2018), tells a story about her grandfather, who fled to Britain to escape the Nazis:

> When it comes to identity, names matter. When my father's father, a Jewish teenager in Berlin, boarded a train in 1938 that would carry him out of Nazi Germany, to safety in Britain, the first thing he did was change his name. 'Hans' became John, and with it, he sought to recraft his identity into something British. 'Hans' was buried forever, along with the blissful ignorance of not knowing what it's like to bear a heritage that is grounds, all on its own, to be put to death. (2018, p.30)

These powerful words remind us that names carry our identity, history and stories. They remind me that people getting my name wrong does matter and that this is why I was compelled to write this chapter to tell my story.

In it, I will describe a psychotherapy workshop where I experienced a microaggression (a term I will go on to discuss in more detail later in the chapter) in relation to my name. The incident I describe is fictionalised in that it is a composite of several such incidents that happened to me in various organisations. I have done this to protect the identity of those organisations and the people involved, but what I describe is true to my experience, if not to the precise contexts.

I will explore and discuss what I feel was being acted out by me, the tutor and the other training group members, and how these fit into the larger puzzle of racism.

The demonstration

I was taking part in a psychotherapy drama workshop. As a Brown Asian woman, I was in a minority, although not the only person of colour in the group. I had volunteered to take part in a role play with the trainer to demonstrate a particular technique. They asked me to sit opposite them in the centre of the room, with the rest of the group sitting around us, watching. We took our seats, and the trainer then paused, looked distressed and confused, and said, 'Oh dear, I can't seem to remember your name.' It wasn't clear to me if this was for real or part of the role play. I was confused and a bit shocked, so said nothing and waited to see what would happen next. The trainer then asked if it was a problem for me that they had forgotten my name. In that moment, I was unsure whether to be honest or to play it safe. Playing it safe felt insincere in that context; being honest carried the risk of being seen to be 'difficult'. I took a risk. I said that I felt irritated, upset and angry. I said I felt had already been feeling invisible in the group before we started the role play, which is why I had volunteered for the demonstration. I went on to say that it was not uncommon for people to forget my name, so it did not surprise me that the trainer had also forgotten it.

The trainer responded defensively, saying that forgetting my name was not about them not seeing me and that, while they had forgotten my name, they did 'see me'.

They spoke as if the forgetting of my name was of no significance, so long as they could claim to 'see' me. When I replied that I didn't feel they were taking responsibility for forgetting my name, and that at least they might apologise, the trainer retorted, 'I was always told to stand up for myself'. This astonished me, as it positioned them as the victim and me as the aggressor.

The trainer then moved us on to the actual role play exercise and, when it was finished, I carried my chair back into the circle with the other participants.

The trainer then turned to the whole group and asked them what they felt about the interaction about my name. There was a silence for a few minutes. Then a handful of white people spoke up, saying things like:

> People get my name wrong all the time and it's never a problem.
>
> It's quite common to forget names. I don't know what the fuss is about.
>
> I would have just told you my name. (Said to the trainer.)
>
> I don't know why it's important for names to be remembered – I don't know why people get so upset by it.

As I listened, I became acutely aware that most of the members of the group were effectively reaching out to rescue the trainer. I felt an overwhelming shock, dismay and confusion about what had just happened. I sat, frozen and unable to comment. Yet again, it was as though I had done something wrong; I had shamed this poor white person for forgetting my name. The familiar feeling resurfaced – I was the problem, not the other.

A final comment came from a white man who said to the trainer (and I'm paraphrasing here):

> I'm aware of the power dynamics within the demonstration that just took place – a person of colour was sitting opposite you, a white person who then forgot her name – I'm curious about that and wonder if you can be too?

The trainer came back at him straight away, saying: 'I didn't forget her name because of her colour and race.' They then shut down the discussion and moved us on to another exercise.

This time, a white person volunteered. The trainer told them to choose a group of people to tell a story from their life. The volunteer chose a handful of people, including me. The volunteer gave us all a script and a scene to act out and started to allocate the roles. When they came to me, they asked me to lie on the floor at the feet of the others. I felt humiliated, confused and defiant and remained silent in a moment of shock, not knowing what to say or how to respond. I did not lie down and the exercise continued.

After that, I could not fully engage with the group and the material being taught. I felt hurt, demoralised, humiliated and outraged by what had happened and the harm I had experienced by the trainer not being willing or open to acknowledge and address the racism that was clearly in the group. So why didn't I challenge it at the time? In part, because I felt silenced by the group and the trainer; in part because I was not going to take the risk again of having my feelings as a Brown woman denied, shut down and rejected. I was not going to be a victim of gaslighting.

That night, I dreamed I was sitting on a bus full of people. At the back of the bus, I could see a group of white men and I felt cautious and afraid. At that moment, a South Asian man came and sat next to me, so right up close to me that his body touched mine. I felt squashed and uncomfortable and in an annoyed tone asked him if he could move away and not sit so close to me. This man then suddenly changed to a white man. I did not seem perplexed by this and began to sing: 'You are being racist. Do you not know how I feel? You only care about yourself and do not care about how you are affecting me.' The white man was indifferent. Everyone else on the bus was silent and just looked on as this was happening.

Microaggressions

The term 'microaggressions' was first coined by Professor Chester M. Pierce, who defined them as 'subtle, stunning and often non-verbal exchanges which are put downs' (Pierce et al., 1978, p.66). Sue and colleagues (2007) built on this definition to describe racial microaggressions as:

> brief and commonplace daily verbal, behavioural, or environmental indignities, whether intentional or unintentional, that communicate hostile, derogatory, or negative racial slights and insults towards people of colour.

Sue and colleagues (2007) go on to say that microaggressions can take three forms:

- *Microassault* – an explicit racial derogation characterised primarily by a verbal or non-verbal attack meant to hurt the intended victim, such as name-calling, avoidant behaviour or purposeful discriminatory actions.
- *Microinsult* – characterised by communications that convey rudeness and insensitivity and demean a person's racial heritage or identity. They may be in the form of subtle snubs, frequently unknown to the perpetrator but clearly conveying a hidden insulting message to the person of colour. They can also be non-verbal, such as not seeing a person of colour or making statements such as: 'I believe that the most qualified person should get the job, regardless of colour.'

- *Microinvalidation* – communications that exclude, negate or nullify the thoughts, feelings or experiential reality of a person of colour, such as: 'I don't see colour,' or, 'You're being oversensitive.'

In the demonstration I described, I experienced a microinvalidation. The trainer forgot my name, which might not be racist but became a microinvalidation when they adopted a position of indignation at what they perceived to be the injustice of my response and refused to hear my upset and anger. They also failed to acknowledge the impact of this happening in front of the whole group, and how humiliating and belittling that was for me. They also set an example to the rest of the workshop participants that it was fine to forget a person of colour's name and then to deny the harm and hurt it caused.

When I talked about what had happened within the group with another Asian peer, he accurately pointed out that forgetting my name was not the same as forgetting a white person's name:

> It *is* about race. When a white person in 'power' forgets a BAME individual's name, the impact is different.

Names hold charge and great importance; they carry a history of our family origin and ethnicity (Wykes, 2017). In the South Asian diaspora, most given names are intentionally chosen for their specific meaning, and many of us are very aware of that meaning (as am I). When we are young, our identity and concept of self is developed through our family's repeated use of our name (Sears & Sears, 2003). We begin to understand who we are from our parents' accent, intonation and pronunciation of our name. Our names carry cultural and family significance, and can often connect us to our ancestors, country of origin or ethnic group and have deep meaning or symbolism for our parents and families. For example, my surname, Zahid, means pious or devoted to God – an identity that my father strongly holds onto. However, when a name is mispronounced or changed, it can negate all this thought, care and significance, and thus deny the identity of the individual. Kohli and Solorzano (2012) write:

> This happens for white and non-white children alike. However, the fact that this experience occurs within a context of historical and continued racism is what makes the negative impact of this experience so powerful for students of colour. (p.444)

They go on to say that non-English names are frequently anglicised, shortened, mispronounced, forgotten or ridiculed and conclude that mispronunciations of names are microaggressions, with heightened impact on children:

... daily insults that, as a form of racism, support a racial and cultural hierarchy of minority inferiority. Furthermore, enduring these subtle experiences with racism can have a lasting impact on the self-perceptions and worldview of a child. (p.441)

Ali Michael (2015) blogs how, during an educator's event, a white teacher said, 'I get everybody's name wrong. I get my own children's names wrong! Names are hard for me, and they get harder as I get older.' Michael identifies this dismissiveness as the true root of the problem. Teachers can:

> justify the microaggressions they commit a thousand times over with what they believe are legitimate excuses (busyness, age, sheer exhaustion), good intentions (almost always positive, loving, caring), and logical explanations (I do this with everyone).

This is what happened in the workshop I have described; the trainer and the white participants could not accept that it was even important to remember my name and denied the impact of this. Michael reminds us that such microaggressions 'are actual microcosms of our bias and our conditioning'.

The power of names

I was moved by a powerful story told by Kohli and Solorzano (2012) of a student called Nitin. Nitin's teacher named him 'Frank' (the teacher's own name) because he could not pronounce his real name:

> As a joke, he crossed my name out of the gradebook and told the class he was renaming me 'Frank'... after himself. Everyone thought it was pretty funny and the next day at school, everyone kept on calling me 'Frank'. I soon grew used to the name and within a few months, I was introducing myself as 'Frank'. I went to school for 6 years – seventh through 12th grade. By the time I graduated, I firmly thought of myself as 'Frank', so much so that at college, I introduced myself as 'Frank' to everyone, including other South Asians. (2012, p.451)

When I read this story, I felt incredibly sad. It triggered so many memories of teachers at school saying nothing to my fellow students who ridiculed my name. I have carried this internalised message throughout my life that it was okay for my name to be ridiculed. Similarly, Nitin internalised his teacher's microaggression and the impact lasted for years. This also highlights the importance of recognising that teachers hold power that can influence a student's sense of self and worldview (Kohli & Solorzano, 2012). This power dynamic can then be re-enacted by those in positions of authority later in life, be they managers, supervisors or tutors. They are not the originators of racial inequality, nor the root cause of institutionalised racism, yet they uphold the racial inequality that already exists in the system. It is also important to note here that some cultures may hold teachers in particular high esteem (Hofstede et al., 2002), making it even more difficult for a child to challenge them. My parents would tell me that my teachers were like parents, and we needed to respect them as such.

Allport (1937) writes that a person's name is the most important anchor point of their identity. Walton (1937) considered one's name to be a determining factor in personality development. Changing, forgetting or ridiculing a person of colour's name clearly will have long-lasting effects, especially in the historical contexts of slavery, indentured labour and colonialisation (Zitkala-sa, 1921; Irons, 2002). Palsson (2014) reminds us that slaveholders routinely gave slaves new names, and often used similar names to those they gave their livestock and pets. For slaves, being renamed symbolised the erasure of their history and identity.

Research indicates that racial microaggressions have potent psychological effects. They can undermine the emotional wellbeing of people of colour, triggering suicidal ideation, depression, anxiety and lowered self-esteem (Nadal et al., 2014; O'Keefe et al., 2015). In addition, they can lead to lower energy levels, poorer emotional wellbeing, impaired social functioning, sleep disturbance and greater sensitivity to pain (Nadal et al., 2017). Therefore, mispronouncing, forgetting or changing a person of colour's name is not a harmless mistake: it is a racist microaggression, with a significant impact on our mental health.

I never really considered the longstanding impact of teachers, peers, friends, colleagues, and associates getting my name wrong before I explored it for this chapter. Yes, it was hurtful and painful, but I did not really connect it with the internal damage it could cause when there is a repeated exposure to it from a very young age. Up until I experienced the race-related name amnesia in the workshop, I had given very little thought to how this had contributed to shaping my self-confidence and self-esteem, and how I carried shame around my name. Addressing it now has enabled me to work through this shame, to name it and to reclaim the power I had lost.

I don't see colour

Even though the trainer insisted that they had 'seen' me, because they did not acknowledge the significance of forgetting my name, *I did not feel seen*. In that moment, there was a denial of my experience, feelings and of my colour, race and heritage. Cousins and Diamond (2021) discuss the microaggression in statements such as 'I don't see colour' and 'We are all the same'; it is a 'tension-filled interaction where your skin colour is swept underneath the carpet and our racial and cultural heritage denied' (p.20). They go on to argue that this erasure of colour is due to several different factors, which I summarise here:

- People do not want to walk into a conversation about race.
- People do not want to acknowledge or 'see' your race because they feel they have moved beyond race or are somehow above it.
- There is a suggestion that you are no different to anyone else and certainly not special.
- People want you to believe that they meant no harm.
- People want to disarm you of your life experiences.

I would like to add to this important list that mostly all this takes place unconsciously. I am relatively confident that not many people are aware of these underlying defences when they claim not to see colour. When the trainer said, 'I didn't forget her name because of her colour and race,' they clearly did not want to get into a conversation about race, for any/all of the reasons above.

Intersecting identities

When writing this chapter, I started to reflect on what was going on for the trainer. Why had they asked me how I felt about them forgetting my name? What did they think I was going to say? And even when I shared my honest feelings with them, they did not explore what I said in the way I would expect a person with psychotherapy training to do. They seemed surprised by what I said and reacted as if caught off guard. If they did not want to know my honest feelings, why did they ask me? I can only conjecture, and as a woman of colour, I will be bringing to this question a few assumptions of my own. If I look at this incident through an intersectional lens, I am a Brown woman in an educational establishment, interacting with an older white person who I assumed to be middle class. Kaur (2022), in her book *Brown Girl Like Me*, points out that the stereotypical Brown girl or woman is quiet, compliant and passive, inanimate even (as when Muslim women who wear the burqa are compared to 'letterboxes'), and both oppressive and ridiculous. Kaur says:

> We live in a world where the brown girl is consistently being ignored by every establishment, whether it's schools, universities, the workplace, the media, or the government. Or rather we aren't being completely

ignored. These institutions have played a key role in the construction of our identities. The state and media's interest, or should I say obsession, with young brown girls has only ever reinforced negative stereotypes. Characterizing our cultures and traditions as oppressive, and associating us only with forced marriages, 'honour' crimes, FGM and grooming – these so-called brown problems that we need 'saving' from. (p.52; italics in original)

She goes on to argue that, 'within schools, Brown girls are seen as hard-working, but teachers ultimately tend to characterise them as quiet and passive, beliefs that stem from outdated historical assumptions about Asian cultures' (p.52). Apparently, we are too quiet and not confident enough (Archer, 2008), and our 'lack of freedom' in our cultures has bred us into submission (Kaur, 2022, p.53).

This reminds me of when I was in primary school, aged around 9 or 10, and the teacher announced there would be netball trials after school, where they would choose two teams of girls to play for the school. My hand went up straight away because I wanted to be chosen, I wanted to play. One by one, other girls in my class were chosen to take part in these trials, while I was completely ignored. Feeling embarrassed, disappointed and humiliated (as I later felt at the workshop), I put my hand down, not knowing what next to do.

I don't know what came over me, but I decided at the end of class to go up to one of the PE teachers and ask if I could play at the trials. She reluctantly agreed. When lessons finished, I made my way to the playground, nervous and excited, wishing and hoping I would be chosen for the teams. When I got there, the teacher once again proceeded to choose two netball teams from the girls sitting next to me and did not choose me. I was told to sit on the bench and be a reserve. I was gutted. Literally. I felt my stomach turn and I wanted to cry. I feel quite emotional as I write this now. I sat on the side, waiting, and after about half an hour, one of the players hurt her leg and I was invited to take her place. I walked onto the netball court, head held high, knowing in my heart that I would smash it – and I did. I smashed every single game I played and from that moment on I was given one of the best positions – Goal Attack (for those of you who know!) – and won every single game for the school. This was the start of my netball reign, which led on to me playing for the borough – I still have the local newspaper cuttings to prove it. Success aside, this is a perfect example of teachers assuming that Brown girls are not 'good enough' for certain activities, such as sports, because we are too quiet and unassertive. I have lost count of the number of times I have been told by teachers, employers and those in positions of power that I am 'different' to other Brown girls because they see me as assertive and vocal.

Going back to the workshop trainer, I wonder whether they expected me to be vocal and honest about my experience or they assumed I would fit the stereotype of the quiet and submissive Brown woman and not say anything to challenge them. I also believe that age was relevant in this interaction. The trainer was an older person, and from what I could ascertain from their relationship with a few of the other 'ethnic minority' students, they had established a clear parent/child dynamic. Hofstede and colleagues (2002) point out that, in more collective societies, teachers and elders are accorded higher status and more power, and therefore some people of colour may be reluctant to question the authority of those they perceive to be 'elders', or to challenge them. Was this also being played out? Did the trainer expect me to slot into that kind of relationship of deference with them? So, race, age and gender may all have contributed to the playing out of this dynamic.

The non-verbal conversation about race

The trainer was a very experienced psychotherapist and yet they missed the potential for causing racial trauma by their response to me. Was this a sign that something else was happening beneath the surface that they were unable to access? Was their own racial trauma also being activated in this moment?

The part of the interaction when the trainer said 'I was always told to stand up for myself' really stood out for me. I would never dream of saying this to a client or trainee if they felt I had got something wrong. What did they mean by this? And why would they need to 'stand up' to me? For me, this part of the interaction indicates that the trainer probably went into a fight or flight response – they needed to stand up to me because they perceived me as a threat. This is in line with what Menakem (2017) refers to as the 'reptilian' or 'lizard' brain, more formally known as the amygdala, which has a primary role in the processing of memories, decision-making and emotional responses such as fear, anxiety and aggression. The amygdala activates a person's fight-or-flight response in response to a real or perceived threat of danger. So, the tutor was potentially like an animal in the wild whose hair stands on end, or that stands up on their hind legs, like a bear, to appear larger to potential aggressors – they literally 'stand up' to the threat.

If my hypothesis is true, then I am curious to know why their flight-or-fight response was triggered. In his excellent book *The Race Conversation*, Ellis (2021) explores how the pain and suffering of racism lives in our bodies, for Black, Brown and white people alike, and how neuroscience can explain what happens to our nervous system when conversations about race take place. Menakem (2017) has also discussed this in his book, *My Grandmother's Hands*. Menakem says:

> The traumas that live in white bodies, and the bodies of public safety professionals of all races, are also deep and persistent. However, their origins and nature are quite different. The expression of these traumas is often an immediate, seemingly out-of-blue flight, flee, or freeze response, a response that may be reflexively triggered by the mere presence of a Black body – or sometimes, by the mere mention of race or the term *white supremacy* or *white-body supremacy*. (p.16; original italics)

Although race was not explicitly mentioned in the initial interaction between me and the trainer, I believe that racial trauma was being enacted in the interaction, as it centred around my name, which is not an English name. I wonder whether the trainer would have become defensive in the same way with a white person with a more traditional Western name? Would the wider group still have gone into a process of 'rescuing' the trainer after the incident? Would they have reacted in the same way if I had been white?

I can't answer these questions but what feels evident is that something was being acted out by both me and the trainer, and I hypothesise that, for both of us, it was our racial history and trauma. As Ellis (2021) says:

> The race construct carries within it the shadow of dehumanising, traumatising and brutal acts inflicted on both victims and witnesses. From birth, both people of colour and white people would have had their expectations and assumptions about themselves, and others influenced and shaped by racism, both inside and outside the home. There is also the transmission of unresolved trauma, passed on from one generation to another. This generational transmission of racial trauma within families needs far more attention that it receives and holds an important key for understanding the challenges of the race conversation. What I am proposing is that difficulties in the race conversation are a direct result of the relational trauma in the past that has been passed on intergenerationally and then triggered in the present. (p.39)[1]

Not only was the tutor's racial trauma being triggered, but so was the group's racial trauma as a racially mixed group. This is what made them retreat into their 'white fragility' and attempt to annihilate me by denying my racial identity.

---

1. Ellis defines relational trauma as 'where an individual is traumatised… by other people who have who have primary roles in their lives' (2021, p.37).

White fragility

So, what about my peers? What part did they play in this unconscious racism? They sought to rescue the trainer by their comments because they could not tolerate their own anxiety and the trainer's discomfort. Me vocalising my anger and upset triggered the white fragility of the white majority in the group. I was left silenced, intimidated and shamed.

DiAngelo (2019) describes white fragility as follows. By 'we', she means white people:

> Socialized into a deeply internalised sense of superiority that we either are unaware of or can never admit to ourselves, we become highly fragile in conversations about race. We consider a challenge to our racial worldviews as a challenge to our very identities as good, moral people. Thus, we perceive any attempt to connect us to the system of racism as an unsettling and unfair moral offense. The smallest amount of racial stress is intolerable – the mere suggestion that being white has meaning often triggers a range of defensive responses. These include emotions such as anger, fear, and guilt and behaviors such as argumentation, silence, and withdrawal from the stressed-inducing situation. These responses work to reinstate white equilibrium as they repel the challenge, return our racial comfort, and maintain our dominance within the racial hierarchy. I conceptualise this process as *white fragility*. Though white fragility is triggered by discomfort and anxiety, it is born of superiority and entitlement. White fragility is not a weakness per se. In fact, it is a powerful means of white racial control and the protection of white advantage. (pp.1–2; original italics)

As demonstrated in the training, white fragility is so powerful that it shuts down any conversation about race. And of course, this is not the first time this has happened to me in group settings and conversations with individuals. For example, a white colleague told me that they knew what racism felt like because they had olive skin and, as a child, they were often called 'P**i'.[2] Another white person told me that she knew what racism felt like because her mixed-race children were also called 'P**i' at school. I was speechless and stayed in shock for quite some time after. In those moments, my reality and experience of racism were trivialised, even though this was not their conscious intention. These comments were unconsciously intended to shut down the conversation about racism and protect white privilege and supremacy. The comments

---

2. I have not used the racial slur for a Pakistani person here as I believe racial slurs should never be repeated.

also reduced my experience of racism to a single racial slur and did not take into account the long history of oppression and racism a person of colour experiences, or the histories of their ancestors.

Similarly, the large group in the workshop could not tolerate the discomfort of witnessing the unconscious racism that the trainer was demonstrating. Just like my dream, the bystanders on the bus watched 'the performance' between me and the trainer and then became an ally to the trainer in denying my hurtful and difficult experience through their defensive comments. What I haven't explained is that issues around race, power and safety had come up before in the same group with the same trainer, and they too were not addressed. I was still holding this unconsciously, unaware that, for me, it was percolating beneath the surface. So, just like in my dream, I performed; I 'sang' about my experience of racism within the role play because it was within a 'safer' staged framework. The South Asian man in my dream represented my race and the part of me that was feeling irritated, uncomfortable, and angry. I was being 'rubbed up against' and violated, just like I was harmed and bullied in the group.

When the second exercise was staged, the unconscious racism continued to play out, completely undetected by the trainer or the group. The white volunteer asked me, the only Brown person in the exercise, to lie at the feet of the other white people in the group. This felt to me like the volunteer continued to carry the group's unconscious racism. It was an extension of what was already being played out in the room and felt to me like an explicit, but arguably unconscious, attempt to 'keep me in my place' – down on the floor, at the feet of white people. It could also have been a display of the group's anger with me for upsetting the equilibrium of the group and shaming the white trainer.

I feel angry about what I lost in terms of the learning enjoyed by all the other participants in this workshop; the disadvantage I experienced is something that white people will not experience in the same way. As a person of colour, I feel exhausted with having to be the one who brings up the issues of race and racism into the arena. And then, when I do, my experience is invalidated, ignored or brushed aside. The learning there for all the white participants is also devalued, brushed aside and ignored.

Aftermath – an opportunity for repair

I have experienced so many such incidents of racism in my counselling training: from being penalised for voicing the racism I experienced, to being accused of breaking confidentiality when sharing my experience anonymously with others. There isn't space to include them here, and there is still a part of me that is afraid to speak out. However, I will include an extract from one letter I received after one such event, from a white peer who witnessed the racism in the room (again, it has been anonymised and details changed). It speaks to the power of racism within the classroom and why breaking the white silence is so important. It speaks to the impact this has on everyone, not only people of colour. It speaks to the reflection and work that is required when making changes and taking responsibility for racism. It is not enough to just be anti-racist; action is also needed to become a true ally. I reproduce it here with the writer's permission.

Dear Neelam,
I wish to share how I experienced [the incident in the training workshop]. It was like the group was trying to absolve itself and the tutor for making a mistake. It felt reminiscent of when I was a child in the queue in a chip shop and an Indian person would walk in and people in the queue would talk about Indian takeaway food.

I spent the next ten minutes in an angry frightened daze and missed the first part of the exercise – I don't know why I was so dysregulated by what I had witnessed. Thinking about it now, perhaps it is because I witnessed a very bad wrongness and I felt angry on your behalf and then frightened of my rage and of what I imagine might be your outrage. I spent lunch time wondering what to say to you and how to let you know that I saw something that wasn't okay, but I didn't know where to start. 'So, Neelam, how are you with the unconscious racism in the room?' is not a conversation I knew how to have. I faltered and decided to do nothing. My usual strategy. Sorry. I should have spoken up in the group and I did not.

The question that I want to ask in the group and have been too scared to, is why we are not talking about the experience of being marginalised, from the standpoint of being British Asian and female. Why are we not talking about the experience of racism when someone is in a minority race, in a group, and someone/everyone doesn't see that and yet says that they do? Why are we not talking about the powerful experience of holding our identity in our names and our skins and faces? How is that different when we are in a minority ethnic group and when we are not? Why are we not trying to find out how, for a Brown person, the experience of being invisible in a group of white people informs racial identity and how that plays out? Why are we not talking about how to have these conversations safely in the group? I think because it is an issue that is so core to identity and so emotive and built on aeons of racial injustice.

There is also so much I don't understand about my own felt response that confuses and frightens me, but I need to find a way to speak out against a wrongness when I see it in front of me and help my co-workers. I need to stop hiding from a conversation about things that confuse me, to risk discovering something I may not like in myself and the outrage of someone else if I unwittingly make hurt. I need to change to look after my colleagues. Otherwise, I am complicit in racism, and I must stop doing that.

In this moment I don't know if what I am saying is helpful or problematic for you. I would be interested to know. If you wish to challenge or question me, please do. Please phone, email or ignore me as you need.

We did speak after this email, and it was a healing experience.

Tools for anti-oppressive practice

I would like you to take a moment to reflect on how you are feeling after reading this chapter. I invite you to reflect on and write down what comes up for you when you read the following questions and take them to personal therapy, supervision or a support group to explore them further and process.

For people of colour:

- What is the history to your name? What significance does it hold?
- How do you feel about your name?
- Have you had your name forgotten, mispronounced, anglicised, or have you been called by another person of colour's name? Perhaps you have had a different experience with your name that hasn't been written about in this chapter. If so, what parts of you get activated when reading about my experience? Where are you holding this in your body? Allow yourself to sit with this feeling for a minute or so. What feelings come up?

What can you do?

- When someone mispronounces your name, forgets it or misidentifies you, correct them, and continue with the task at hand. Do not apologise, but thank them if this feels right for you.
- Later, take the impact of this to a safe place to explore further with other people of colour.

For white people:

- How does reading this chapter make you feel? Where are you feeling it in your body? What happens when you sit with it?
- What significance do names have for you?
- Do you remember a time when you forgot someone of colour's name or mispronounced it? What was that like for you?

- Have you called a person of colour by another person of colour's name? How did that make you feel?

What can you do?

- If you forget someone's name, just ask them what it is rather than use it for an opportunity to interpret or analyse.
- Apologise for getting their name wrong; notice how this feels. Apologising is really important as it will contribute to the person of colour's healing process.
- Ask how someone's name should be pronounced, if you are unsure.
- Sit with the feeling when you forget someone's name or have mispronounced it. Name the feeling and make a note of what comes up for you. Then take this to supervision to explore further.

To white therapists who take some of these reflections to supervision or other reflective spaces to explore further, I ask that you be mindful of supervisors and peers of colour in these spaces. The exploration of your whiteness may impact therapists of colour in ways you are unaware of and may trigger their racial trauma. In such cases, it is important to be open to the relational dynamic that emerges as conversations around race take place; talk about how these reflections impact your supervisors and peers of colour; talk about the racial dynamic between you; this is where the learning and healing takes place. Reflective spaces should not be a place where there is an expectation that the supervisor/peer of colour will tell you what to do and give you a list of books to read; they may offer this to you and might be able to signpost you, but be aware of the 'demands' you make of them. Alternatively, you may choose to explore your reflections with a white supervisor/colleagues/peer who is actively anti-racist and is in the process of 'doing the work' themselves.

For therapists of colour, be mindful of where you take your reflections. Does it feel safe to explore with a white supervisor some of the questions I have asked in this chapter? Or with a group of white peers? If not, find a supervisor of colour or a peer group of colour. Meet with these people regularly if you are able. Once you have found your safe space, give yourself permission to name some of those experiences that you previously felt were 'making a fuss' – no microaggression is too small. Importantly, remember how microaggressions can feel like a 'death by 10,000 cuts' (Turner, 2021, p.81) and that it is okay to want your experiences to be validated and heard. Explore the long-term impact of any repeated microaggressions, whether that is someone getting your name wrong or anything else that falls under this category.

Conclusion

Writing this chapter has helped me heal. I no longer believe that *my name* is the reason for white people getting my name wrong. Mispronouncing my name or forgetting it is not *my* fault or problem; it is a white people's problem within a white supremacist society in which English names are seen as the norm. Yes, we live in England, and of course to a degree English names are the norm. However, this does not justify the othering of names from other cultures, and their mutilation and destruction.

And, as explored in this chapter, forgetting or mispronouncing the name of a person of colour, or re-labelling them, is not a benign experience – it is not harmless. Further still, if it happens in the context of an educational organisation, it reflects a systemic disrespect for the student's identity, cultural heritage and history. Educational organisations and trainers need to make a commitment to working through their own racism and unconscious bias so that they are able to identify and navigate issues of difference and diversity in their training rooms. Not doing this reinforces and maintains white supremacy and protects white privilege. It is also the responsibility of each and every practitioner and trainee to address their own feelings of racism, privilege, internalised oppression, powerlessness, cultural shame and identity formation within personal therapy, supervision and by attending relevant CPD. Only then can racism within the counselling profession be truly excavated and addressed so that practitioners of colour and clients do not continue to be harmed, under-represented and under-served.

References

Allport, G.W. (1937). *Personality: A psychological interpretation*. Holt.

Archer, L. (2008). The impossibility of minority ethnic educational 'success': An examination of the discourses of teachers and pupils in British secondary schools. *European Educational Research Journal*, 7(1), 89–107.

Cousins, S. & Diamond, B. (2021). *Making sense of microaggressions*. Open Voices.

DiAngelo, R. (2019). *White fragility: Why it's so hard for white people to talk about racism*. Penguin.

Ellis, E. (2021). *The race conversation: An essential guide to creating life-changing dialogue*. Confer Books.

Gaspar, A. (2023). Call me by my name. In N. Zahid & R. Cooke (Eds.), *Therapists challenging racism and oppression: The unheard voices* (pp.77–89). PCCS Books.

Hirsch, A. (2018). *BRIT(ish): On race, identity and belonging*. Random House.

Hofstede, G.J., Pedersen, P.B. & Hofstede, G. (2002). *Exploring culture*. Intercultural Press.

Irons, P. (2002). *Jim Crow's children: The broken promise of the Brown decision*. Viking Penguin.

Kaur, J. (2022). *Brown girl like me: The essential guidebook and manifesto for south Asian girls and women*. Bluebird/Pan Macmillan.

Kohli, R. & Solorzano, D.G. (2012). Teachers, please learn our names! Racial microaggressions and the K-12 classroom. *Race, Ethnicity and Education, 15*(4), 441–462.

Menakem, R. (2017). *My grandmother's hands: Racialized trauma and the pathway to mending our hearts and bodies*. Central Recovery Press.

Michael, A. (2015). *Getting names right*. [Blog]. www.teachingwhilewhite.org/blog/2017/10/2/getting-names-right

Nadal, K.L., Griffin, K.E., Wong, Y., Davidoff, K.C. & Davis, L.S. (2017). The injurious relationship between racial microaggressions and physical health: Implications for social work. *Journal of Ethnic & Cultural Diversity in Social Work, 26*(1–2), 6–17.

Nadal, K.L., Griffin, K.E., Wong, Y., Hamit, S. & Rasmus, M. (2014). The impact of racial microaggressions on mental health: Counseling implications for clients of color. *Journal of Counseling and Development, 92*(1), 57–66.

O'Keefe, V.M., Wingate, L.R., Cole, A.B., Hollingsworth, D.W. & Tucker, R.P. (2015). Seemingly harmless racial communications are not so harmless: Racial microaggressions lead to suicidal ideation by way of depression symptoms. *Suicide and Life-Threatening Behavior, 45*(5), 567–576.

Palsson, G. (2014). Personal names: Embodiment, differentiation, exclusion, and belonging. *Science, Technology, & Human Values, 39*(4), 618–630.

Pierce, C., Carew, J., Pierce-Gonzalez, D. & Willis, D. (1978). An experiment in racism: TV commercials. In C. Pierce (Ed.), *Television and education* (pp.62–88). Sage.

Sears, W. & Sears, M. (2003). *The baby book: Everything you need to know about your baby from birth to age two*. Little Brown & Company.

Sue, D.W., Capodilupo, C.M., Torino, G.C., Bucceri, J.M., Holder, A.M.B., Nadal, K.L. & Esquilin, M. (2007). Racial microaggressions in everyday life: Implications for clinical practice. *American Psychologist, 62*(4), 271–286.

Turner, D. (2021). *Intersections of privilege and otherness in counselling and psychotherapy: Mockingbird*. Routledge.

Walton, W.E. (1937). The effective value of first names. *Journal of Applied Psychology, 14*, 396–409.

Wykes, E.J. (2017). 'What would it be reasonable for the kid to be called?'– Negotiating the racialised essentialism of names. *Identities, 24*(2), 198–215.

Zitkala-sa. (1921). *American Indian stories*. Hayworth Publishing House.

2. Cultivating intersectional nuance within the dissociative confines of capitalism

Rachel Cooke

I believe we're being told destructive lies about mental health.

We are living, it's declared through various channels, through a 'mental health crisis'. Mental health services in the UK cannot handle the public demand: between one and two million people are on NHS waiting lists, while another eight million don't meet the thresholds for access to mental health services and are being left without care (Thomas, 2022).

Our society's mainstream understanding of mental health issues locates the problem inside the individual, specifically within the brain/mind, and ignores the politics of suffering. This doesn't seem to be working well for most of us, unsurprisingly: we exist in a traumatising and traumatised world; we're living through an ecological emergency, through a worldwide economic meltdown, burdened with grief, fear and illness in the wake of a global pandemic. Many of us are more isolated than ever, while revelations about the government, police and institutions obliterate our trust in those meant to protect us.

I imagine that you have already witnessed and recognised that suffering emerges within our experiences (and histories) of trauma and oppression. I believe we cannot continue to isolate 'mental health problems' from our broader societal structures, in the therapy room, or anywhere else. Perhaps you're already engaging with this reality deeply in your life and practice; maybe the meaning of this is very new to you, or you're somewhere between the two, with growing awareness but without much clarity or a path of action.

I'm deeply motivated by the process, the practice, of deciphering how to be a useful therapist in the context and contradiction of connection, meaning, joy and hope, alongside the intolerable disconnection, injustice, violence and atrocities that constitute the architecture of so many of the systems we live under: imperialism, White supremacy, patriarchy, colonialism, classism, transphobia, queerphobia, ableism, ageism, cis-heteronormativity, neoliberalism, consumer capitalism… to name but a handful. How do you make sense of this? What can be done? Where do we go from here as therapists?

The contact

A lot of what informs how I think and practise currently can be traced back to a therapeutic relationship I had with two people, a couple,[1] and more specifically to one of our early sessions, where I made several mistakes.

It's uncomfortable and enlivening for me to share some of what happened with you. I do so in the hopes of it being poignant and instrumental for you, in your practice and your life. The revelations from and deep impact of this relationship initiated paradigm shifts in my beliefs and understanding. This couple taught me more about social justice and social theory, maybe even about therapy, than the sum of what I'd learnt before I met them. It took time to unravel and dig into what they sparked in me, and it is an ongoing process – they set in motion an appetite that changed my values, my sense of self and my course of action.

For more than five years previous to this encounter, I had practised integratively, with a focus on person-centred therapy but drawing on psychodynamic, CBT, Gestalt and existential approaches, as well as psychoneuroendocrineimmunology (PNEI), which is the study of the intimate, bidirectional relationship between psychological processes, physical health and the immune, endocrine and nervous systems. This suited my curiosity and capacity for (what I believed to be) diverse perspectives, but incorporated little recognition of social context, which I now find tragic.

I was very fortunate to work with these two people as part of a relationship therapy training I was undertaking. They were referred by an acquaintance on the course and knew little to nothing about me before we began. We contracted to have eight sessions together, for which they paid me a nominal fee because of the training context. Because of this, we were able to have an especially candid relationship, albeit an often poor reflection of my knowledge and skill as a therapist. I have condensed our sessions in order to give readers as much as possible to mull over, and perhaps pursue further, in this short chapter.

I sensed in this couple a disappointment and fatigue that I couldn't yet place from the moment they saw me for the first time and we greeted each

---

1. The people described here are composites based on clients I have worked with and are not identifiable to any one person or relationship, to protect client confidentiality.

other in the therapy space. They spent substantial time sharing their identities, significant life experiences and current realities with me, and how they seemed to possess almost every marginalised identity possible between them. 'We've been very fortunate in our education, and are a societally acceptable age, I guess. Besides that, it's infinite jeopardy,' said X, ruefully. I was pleased to be able to recognise that she was referencing the term 'multiple jeopardy', which pre-dates the theory of intersectionality and is founded on the idea that each form of discrimination is multiplicative rather than additive (Settles & Buchanan, 2014).[2]

'You're going to have your work cut out for you,' Y remarked, with what I sensed was resignation and a smidgen of pity for me. In my ignorance (and arrogance), I thought this unlikely: I'd worked with a wide array of 'complex' people by that stage, from cult and war survivors to people living with dissociative 'disorders', to psychiatrists, politicians and activists. (I don't use the term 'disorder'; I prefer the word 'adaptation' to diminish the pathologisation and stigma of what I have come to view as people's patterned responses to trauma, rather than 'dysfunction' (Brüne, 2016; Del Giudice, 2018).)

I learnt that X (they/she) was a black genderqueer therapist working for the NHS, in their mid 30s. Their parents had roots in Nigeria and Jamaica. They identified as demisexual, used a wheelchair, were agnostic, had fibromyalgia, and were brought up middle class in Singapore. Her first language was Malay. She was a survivor of childhood sexual abuse. They were very active in Extinction Rebellion, on the fence about having children, and polyamorous but in a relationship only with Y at the time. In addition to fibromyalgia, she had been diagnosed as having bipolar disorder, borderline/emotionally unstable personality disorder (BPD/EUPD), dyslexia, and complex post-traumatic stress disorder (CPTSD), by different psychiatrists. She had most recently been diagnosed with premenstrual dysphoric disorder (PMDD). Of those diagnoses, they agreed only with CPTSD and PMDD only.

Y (she/her) was a working class, mixed-heritage trans woman in her early 40s. She was a working class social worker, and had been diagnosed with ADHD, chronic fatigue syndrome (CFS) and epilepsy. She had Irish traveller

---

2. Multiple jeopardy is the theory that the various factors of a person's identity that lead to discrimination or oppression, such as gender, class or race, have a multiplicative effect on the discrimination that they experience. The model proposes that membership of multiple marginalised groups places individuals at risk for negative experiences and reduced wellbeing. Dr Deborah K. King (1988) coined the term in 1988 to account for the limitations of the double or triple jeopardy models of discrimination, which assert that every unique prejudice has an individual effect on a person's status, and that the discrimination one experiences is the additive result of these prejudices. 'Multiple' in the term 'multiple jeopardy' refers not only to the various forms of prejudices that factor into discrimination, but also to the relationship between these prejudices (King, 1988).

and Japanese ancestry and was brought up Catholic in England by adoptive parents. She was atheist, wanted to have kids, and was monogamous but curious about exploring non-monogamy. She also defined as fat and a fat activist, and shared that she was a sex worker in the past, as she felt it was relevant to some of what she wanted to bring to sessions. She was now also a carer for her father.

The couple had been together for half a decade, both were in significant financial difficulty and had worked with many therapists, both individually and as a couple.

I felt energised by the potential for very rich, stimulating and dynamic therapeutic work together. There was so much for me to consider and hold in mind. It didn't occur to me that I might not be able to support them adequately with my relatively scant knowledge and experience of some aspects of their lived experience and identities, I considered myself well versed in working with marginalised people. This conflation and dilution of issues and human beings was problematic from the outset.

'It's a lot to take in and maybe take on, but we're also exhausted from feeling like we're a lot, being told we're a lot, and having that constantly reinforced and penalised by society,' X said. 'To be transparent, and no disrespect, we wouldn't normally work with someone from your demographic.'

I felt myself brace slightly around my diaphragm and ribs in response to a fleeting discomfort with being judged as inadequate. At the same time, I leaned forward in my seat to come closer to them, in a desire to understand and reassure these people. I realised later that there was also a will to, and confidence that I could, prove myself to them (which was outside of my conscious awareness at the time): 'I can feel the weight of your fatigue and want to understand and support you. Would you be willing to share which parts of my identity you're referring to?'

'Sure – racialised as white, I'm guessing cis, potentially straight, probably middle class, neurotypical and able-bodied. I recognise I'm making assumptions there, a lot of them, and it's crass to reduce you to these categories, but we need to have filters to conserve our energy, as people with complex identities, and particularly as spoonies.[3] Are you familiar with that term?'

I felt capable and self-assured. I recognised and respected this question as another filter, a test of whether they could trust me to understand and hold them.

---

3. The spoon theory is a creative metaphor used to describe the experience of chronic illness and its limitations on energy levels and ability to engage in everyday activities. Coined by Christine Miserandino (2003), it uses spoons to represent units of human energy. Healthy people have more spoons (of energy) than people with an illness that causes chronic fatigue, who therefore need to plan and make more conscious decisions about how they 'spend' their spoons of energy in a day. The term is used with reference to other conditions such as ME, CFS, fibromyalgia, Ehlers Danlos syndromes and various 'mental health' conditions.

'I am, and I've worked with many people with disabilities and chronic health conditions. I can really understand your wariness and I hope you can feel safe with and confident enough in me for our relationship to serve you. Would you like to know more about my identity?'

'Yes, thank you,' came the tentative response, 'that might be helpful.'

I had long dispensed with any adherence to the notion of presenting as a 'blank slate' as a therapist, but it was fairly new territory for me to self-disclose so early and specifically. I sensed it was important, if not crucial, for me to be transparent with them so they might feel secure enough for us to work together. I also felt confident from reading research that supported this approach (Farber, 2006; Audet, 2011; Gibson, 2012; and more recently Johnsen & Ding, 2023). Jolley (2019) also found that self-disclosure appeared to enable more equitable power relationships in therapy and supportively normalised clients' experiences and distress.

I shared that I'm queer, white Irish and have synaesthesia, which comes under the umbrella of neurodiversity.[4] Also that I grew up middle class, although the class system in Ireland is somewhat different to England.

They looked at me with what I received as caution and a new smattering of optimism.

'What is it that you'd like to look at in your relationship with each other and yourselves here?' I asked.

This was, in summary, their shared response: 'We really struggle with energy and maintaining hope in relation to our day-to-day work, which is mixed up with social justice work and our shared and separate activism, and how to support each other in that. Then there's dealing with our health stuff, our sex life, not feeling very connected to community, managing trauma triggers and just generally finding, creating and allowing ourselves to experience joy in a world that's brimming with injustice. We're also trying to decide if we want to have children, and if we do, how and when is the best time to get moving on that, considering our health, access to services and a plethora of reservations about having and raising kids in this precarious world. So… nothing too tricky.'

I found myself invigorated by their raw honesty and self-awareness and what struck me as deep intentionality and investment in their lives: 'A breeze

---

4. The term neurodiversity was introduced more than 20 years ago by autism advocate Judy Singer, an Australian social scientist who is on the autism spectrum. It is defined as the range of human mental or psychological neurological structures or behaviours, seen as not necessarily problematic but as alternative, acceptable forms of human biology (Armstrong, 2010). Synaesthesia is a name given to a neurological trait or condition that results in a merging of senses that aren't usually connected. Dyslexia, dyscalculia and 'cognitive interference' from synaesthetic experiences have been reported by some synaesthetes (Asher et al., 2006).

then,' I responded to their wry humour. 'How's your mental and physical health currently?'

Y took a moment to squeeze X's hand before X responded, 'I'd appreciate us using different expressions to "mental health" and "mental illness". Can we do that?'

I had no idea what was coming next, but didn't yet feel fazed.

'Of course, let me know what terms you use and if you're willing, would you bring me up to speed on their meaning for you?'

'Yeah, I've had enough of my pain being called "mental illness" throughout my life, it's dehumanising and inaccurate,' X said. 'My distress is about poverty. It's about being racially abused. About being sexually harassed on an almost daily basis and the looming climate crisis. I work for the NHS, so I'm exposed, day in, day out, to these terms and diagnoses reinforcing the current biomedical framework, which says that suffering and what we call "mental illness" are caused by faulty brain chemistry and genetics, or good old "personal failing", rather than looking at our social contexts. I prefer the expression "psychosocial or socioemotional wellbeing and distress", to acknowledge the relational and contextual dimensions to our experience. Doesn't quite roll off the tongue, but it's a substantial shift in perspective.'

I was aware of being deeply impacted by what she'd just said and struggled to manage the ripple effects through my body. It was as though she was speaking to me while underwater, or in a language I vaguely recognised but couldn't make sense of. I felt like I'd been hit by a ton of bricks. That I'd been duped but didn't quite know in what way or by whom. I was embarrassed not to understand more about what X was saying. I felt unexpectedly young and incompetent. I also noticed a current of grief pulsing around my body in the form of a heaviness in my arms, constriction in my throat, and a clawing sensation down my midline from neck to tailbone. I wondered, 'How much of this is mine, how much theirs, how much is coming from way, way outside the room?' as I attempted to rapidly account for the vastness of their, and my own, historical and social contexts.

I was in disequilibrium. I also recognised feeling shame that I'd been so easily thrown. I did what I could to stabilise myself by gently stroking and squeezing my own arms, and took some longer, fuller breaths. Within a few moments, I was able to detect an emerging sense of deep curiosity, a recognition of being on the edge of something very significant. I wanted to share this with them: 'Okay, this is hitting me hard and I can feel how important this is to you. I have some reading to do, but I believe I grasp what you're saying. I hope that I, and these sessions, can support your relationship and your work on your psychosocial wellbeing.'

'Thanks. I'm glad to be here with Y, I really am,' X said. 'I feel privileged to be able to take the time to do this and support our relationship. I'm also so tired of therapy, either getting six sessions with a worn-out NHS therapist like me, or paying through the nose to see someone privately, committing to CBT or ACT homework, emotional regulation skills, trauma management, self-care practices, doing "the work". It's never ending, and it's demoralising when so many people are out there abusing their power, hoarding money and resources, damaging the environment without a second thought, never mind the destruction caused by billionaires and corporations. I want and need to rest, but when I do, I berate myself for being lazy and unproductive.'

I was lost for words and felt the deep hollowness of living under late-stage capitalism that X was speaking about carved into my chest cavity. Growing up, meritocracy had been modelled to me as a solid worldview: if you kept your head down and worked hard, you would be successful, healthy and happy in life. Working in 'business' and entrepreneurship were things to aspire to. When I left school, I began to glimpse the flaws in our economic system, but its impact and shadow remained half-formed for me. While training as a therapist, I came to wholeheartedly believe that counselling and psychotherapy were all about supporting individuals (or couples and small groups, at most) to understand themselves better, process their experiences and emotions and learn new skills and resources in order to thrive in life. I had worked with dozens of people in severe financial difficulty and poverty over the years but had not properly questioned the relationship of their suffering to living under capitalism.

I felt a dawning dread. I also wondered how I might be congruent with what was going on for me here, without deflecting, intellectualising or disappearing into a hole of shame and placing a burden of responsibility on these two people for holding or educating me in my destabilised state.

Before I could gather myself to respond, X went on: 'I know I'm going off on one and I'll come into my body more in a moment, but right now I'm fucking angry about living on the breadline, even with the privilege and supposed opportunity of higher education. Many people don't see classism as a legitimate form of violence because they believe being poor is indicative of people's character, of their laziness, rather than systemic oppression. They don't see that poverty is traumatic. I don't know if you own your own home, but by the time Y and I retire, if we can ever afford to on our salaries while supporting our communities, we'll have bought multiple houses for landlords because the banks say we can't afford our own. How can I ever have a decent baseline felt sense of safety under these conditions?'

She wasn't finished. 'Then there's how so much of mainstream feminism's blueprint for empowerment is just about women participating in capitalism the way cis men historically have, rather than working towards a world where everyone's basic needs are met. We're banging on about intersectional feminism now, but it's not yet playing out. It's depressing how much feminists, particularly feminists racialised as 'black', were talking and writing about all of this mid-last century, yet we've barely budged from there. Do you know what I'm on about? Have you read black feminist discourse?'

I hadn't. Until I was asked directly by X, I believed I had an adequate amount of knowledge about Black feminism. On reflection, I knew the names of some well-known activists; I'd read quotes here and there and some articles I couldn't immediately call to mind; I'd made a couple of rudimentary points in social media discussions. In short, I didn't even have the basics. I was embarrassed to recognise how White-focused my feminism had been up to this point.

'I haven't and I'm going to make it a priority. There's a lot in what you're sharing, X. I'm aware of your frustration, your fatigue and what sounds like anguish. I feel some of the enormous weight of that in my body right now. I'm reminded of what you said earlier about me being "racialised as white" and how that might impact, or already be impacting, my relationship with you both.'

I was attempting to be relational, to bring our conversation back to what was going on in the room, between us. X and Y glanced at each other.

'I'm impressed you picked up on that, but this is likely to be arduous for all of us,' X replied, sounding resigned again. I assumed that it was just too uncomfortable for them to talk about race, or that they assumed I wouldn't be able to discuss it without dismissing them or collapsing into White guilt.

'I'm not going to push you if you really don't want to go there, but I also want you to know that I'm here for it. I'm also sorry, I should have brought race up between us sooner,' I said.

'Why?'

'Because I'm in contact with our difference.'

I sensed them both bristle and Y cut in, protecting X in that moment I think; her voice was slightly strained: 'Sure, but there's lots of difference between us besides simply what's called race. I personally don't want or need you to single out one aspect of our perceived – by you – identities and then define us by that. This is already quite different to working with an English therapist for us, considering the history of Ireland and also its connection with X's Jamaican heritage.'

I sat up straighter and frowned. I didn't know anything about Ireland's connection with Jamaica; I was more concerned with showing off a particular kind of cultural competence: 'I wouldn't be so arrogant, and I think racist, as to draw parallels between being white Irish and being a person of colour,' I replied.

I was activated. In attempting to be (and certainly seem) humble, sensitive and aware, I had not actually been attuned to the people in front of me. I could feel their dismay and withdrawal from the tinges of white saviourism and self-righteousness in my words and demeanour, which I wasn't able to acknowledge. I knew I'd damaged the ground between us. We lapsed into a tense (for me, at least) silence. X and Y winced at me, or for me, or maybe both, and the three of us took some moments to steady ourselves.

'This must be difficult for you,' Y came in, kindly. I could see X was less enthusiastic about excusing me: 'We've been here with a lot of therapists and different professionals already, you know? I'm struggling to maintain enough optimism that you can hold us, for us to be able to really delve into mine and Y's relationship, and that's a pity.'

My face warmed intensely, the skin on my chest and shoulders began to prickle and I had an impulse to shrink back in my seat and to drop my gaze. I felt threatened. I was struggling with experiencing myself as a disappointment, maybe even inept and probably having been racist. Again, I took a few moments to stay with my own discomfort so that I could remain available to these people, my clients, and root myself back into my role in our relationship.

Then I asked: 'Can I check if there's anything that might be supportive in working with me? And, more importantly, are there any adjustments or accommodations I can hopefully make to give this relationship the best chance of being useful to you?'

I tracked some settling and relief in their postures and facial expressions: 'Thank you for asking. You seem quite open and invested in us. That might be enough if you are willing to do some reading and critical thinking. You'd be surprised how much more that is than we have gotten from a lot of therapists,' Y said, softly. I felt flattered but dejected for the field of therapy.

'You also seem to understand that impact is more important than intent, though intent also has validity, and my sense of your warmth and care for us helps me to feel safe enough here, considering the doubtless differences in our current realities and lived experience. Can you keep listening to comprehend and respond, instead of listening to react and defend?'

'I will do all I can.'

'Great.'

With a raise of an eyebrow, X sought a more concrete commitment from me: 'Would you do some reading on the history of race, intersectionality, conventional medicine and therapy under capitalism before we meet again?'

This may translate to some readers as presumption on their part about my level of knowledge; as too great an expectation of a therapist; or perhaps that I was obviously operating outside of my professional competency and should have immediately stopped working with them or referred them on; or maybe even that this should all have been 'grist for the mill', in popular therapy parlance. But they were onto something. I had read (I believed) fairly widely on feminism and racism, as well as, to a degree, challenges to psychiatry, the pharmaceutical industry and therapy. I wasn't, however, up on intersectionality and Ireland's history, beyond broad brushstrokes; nor did I have much environmental awareness, language around classism, capitalism, imperialism, colonialism, non-monogamy, sex work or fat activism, among others, nor any therapy training that had engaged with these subjects.

There were more epiphanies to come. Soon after, Y brought a personal recent experience of racism to a session and shared how hypervigilant she was feeling.

'It sounds like you're struggling with self-regulation and experiencing some faulty neuroception[5] due to the trauma you've experienced, Y. I wonder if it would be helpful for us to talk about and experiment with some nervous system regulation practices and exercises?' I wasn't just throwing jargon at her; I knew from what she'd shared with me already that she'd understand these ideas and terms from trauma therapy and polyvagal theory. I hoped she'd feel seen and comforted by my directness and my offer to build skills together.

'This is all very... white,' Y responded, with a deflated shrug.

'I'm sorry, do you have the energy to say more? I'm stumped on this one.'

'I don't want to suggest that the nervous system stuff isn't useful, it's just a pretty blinkered framework.'

At the time I could barely glimpse the broader context, particularly since discovering polyvagal theory and nervous system-focused therapy had been revelatory for me. I now understand that a lot of trauma theory and healing speaks about 'self-regulation', which can be very useful, as Y recognised, but highly problematic if there isn't an acknowledgement of the wider systemic context of fundamentally damaging structural oppression (Fannen, 2021). What does 'faulty neuroception' mean when many of the wounding, traumatising conditions in a person's life persist indefinitely, from 'brutal transphobia, to relentless racialised aggressions, to the violence of everyday life under a profit-driven, dehumanising economic system' (Fannen, 2021, p.171)?

This interaction with X and Y, on top of our many others relating to narrow and restricted therapeutic lenses, concepts and frameworks, led me to consider how the majority of our current, major therapy modalities were developed in the last century, almost all by middle-class, older, White, cis men, in North

---

5. Neuroception is the word that Stephen Porges created for the concept of our brains unconsciously detecting cues of safety or danger from the external (and internal) environment and shifting into defensive or safety autonomic states, with faulty neuroception being when the person detects danger where there is none (Porges & Furman, 2011).

America and Europe. How could these approaches possibly encompass and accommodate the experiences of people from diverse cultures, societies, identities and environments?

In the same session, X shared how exhausted she was of finding herself crying, enraged and on the verge of a panic attack in particular situations where she became triggered, which she had recently come to recognise were more pronounced in the week before she menstruated. I responded to her with: 'It seems your body's keeping the score,' knowing they'd recognise my reference to Bessel van der Kolk's bestselling book on trauma (2014), and hoping it would be a validating comment, as well as inviting her to explore her trauma responses with me.

'Well, van der Kolk's viewpoint on bodies anyhow,' she retorted. Cue another pause as we realised I couldn't fathom what she meant. 'You know about Freud's hysteria though, right?' X asked encouragingly.

'That one I do.'

'It's no different to the current misogynistic borderline bullshit, which I was diagnosed with before I finally found someone who recognised PMDD. I don't want that Western label either, but at least it's less stigmatised and abhorred by therapists and society than BPD.'

I knew of the misogynistic history behind Freud and hysteria: that, on encountering symptoms in women patients of what was then known as hysteria (hallucinations, insomnia, anxiety, amnesia, intense emotion, partial paralysis and others), Freud initially saw the causes as rooted in childhood sexual abuse (CSA) (Masson, 1988). He abandoned this theory when it was rejected by colleagues, seemingly out of fear of being discredited and losing his status. Many now see this initial connection with CSA as highly accurate (Connell & Wilson, 1974; Herman, 2015).

Borderline personality disorder, more presently known as emotionally unstable personality disorder (EUPD), is a notoriously controversial diagnosis, widely criticised by those who challenge the whole system of psychiatric diagnosis. It's difficult to diagnose due to overlapping symptoms with a number of other conditions (PTSD, complex trauma, bipolar, ADHD, autism, anxiety, psychosis, PMDD), and around 75% of people diagnosed with BPD are women (Wirth-Cauchon, 2001; Johnson, 2021). I had very recently read the theory that BPD is the contemporary version of a hysteria diagnosis (and that hysteria evolved from women being accused of witchcraft, and being tried, tortured and murdered for it in past centuries) (Tasca et al., 2012).

'Based on the amount of trauma and neglect I experienced as a child, combined with relentless racism, sexual harassment and assault, by mostly cis men, on top of the constant, oppressive challenges of day-to-day living under capitalism and patriarchy and so on, I think it's more than understandable that I'd have these emotional and bodily responses.'

Too right. I validated X's suffering and her framing of her current experiences as responses to trauma. I asked them if they knew that people of colour are diagnosed with personality 'disorders' at a higher rate than white people in England, and that the diagnosis rate is higher among Black and mixed-ethnicity women than among men of the same ethnicities (gov.uk, 2017).

'That's validating and depressing,' X said quietly, before continuing: 'Seriously, haven't I done enough healing yet? We talk and read so much about healing, about being your "authentic self", about being a whole or integrated person. Is there truly a fully healed place to arrive at, or is it just another neoliberal concept designed to keep us in the machine of consumerism, hyperproductivity and never-enoughness? Another workshop, another course, another therapy modality. How can there be an "authentic self" when we're perpetually bombarded and shaped by the messages and manifestations of patriarchy, what we call white supremacy, classism, neoliberalism and the rest from birth and beyond?'

But of course. We don't live in a vacuum. Van der Kolk's 'view on bodies' suddenly landed with me, with his powerful emphasis on *individual* recovery, though he does acknowledge the contexts in which trauma occurs. In the sea of trauma books and resources existing at the time, a White, Global-Northern, cis man putting the weight of 'science' behind his message fit with the most dominant cultural norms and made it more likely to gain more public attention and traction (Fannen, 2021). I was reminded that I had a lot of work ahead of me.

Before I could decide what to do with this, X changed course. 'Rachel, thank you, it means a lot that you reflect and really try to view and experience the world from my perspective. It doesn't change the chaos and oppression in the world, but I do feel a little less alone and a little more hopeful. Maybe now would be a good time to talk about race. I don't expect this to sink in right away with you. Sorry if that sounds condescending. Basically, I'm not interested in using the terms "race", "white", "black" or "mixed race", because they serve to reinforce the notion of racial essentialism, of biological differences, that simply don't exist.'

Once again, I was floored. What X said made so much sense and was also bewildering. The next month saw me devouring books and research papers while I continued working with them. The fierce desire to understand in more nuanced ways and from diverse perspectives has continued since. I felt compelled to know what else I might be ignorant, misinformed, myopic and just plain wrong about – for my clients, for myself, and for society, and as a lifelong endeavour.

We completed our sessions with these two people having had some difficult and constructive conversations, not only with me but with each other. They expressed appreciation again for the effort I put into understanding and supporting them in their suffering and their empowerment. They shared that it had been an enriching and restorative experience in some ways, and I hope this effect was enduring. The time we had together was unfortunately short and we didn't have time to substantially develop or find conclusion to many of the challenges they detailed when we met. I remain very grateful to them for their patience and willingness to allow me into some of their world.

Inquiry

In *Capitalist Realism: Is there no alternative?*, political and cultural theorist Mark Fisher (2009) talks about how the pandemic of personal anguish that afflicts our time cannot be properly understood, or healed, if it is viewed as a private problem afflicting damaged individuals. I'm curious whether it yet strikes you, the reader, as imperative that therapy serves as a space in which the politics of historical context, systemic harm and ongoing oppression are deeply acknowledged; a space where the focus isn't simply on reducing or eliminating distress but on seeing a huge proportion of human suffering as survival responses to an oppressive world.

These two people I worked with were tolerant and gracious towards me. I would have understood, even then when I had much less understanding and awareness, if either of them had exploded in frustration, withdrawn and ended our sessions. My good intentions and openness to understand them, as well as to learn more, went a substantial way, but could have easily been insufficient. To be frank, the relationship may have caused either or both of these people significant harm, for all I know, as much as I hope that was not the case, considering the plethora of gaps in my knowledge and how much they needed to ask of me for me to have a chance to support them meaningfully.

I wasn't used to being challenged by clients on the meaning and process of therapy or my knowledge of social justice issues. It was fortunate for all of us that I felt engaged by Y and X and wasn't too activated into defensiveness, deflection or shutdown. I recognise now that many of my previous clients had the odds stacked against them in terms of feeling safe enough to call me out or even simply let me know if they felt missed, dropped or even slighted by me. If they were accessing free or low-cost support through the NHS, a charity or a training scenario, they may have been afraid to lose the (potential for) support if they expressed their hurt or questioned me. They might have believed that this was how therapy was 'supposed to be'. They simply might not have felt empowered enough, within the hierarchy of power between us, considering my role and intersections of privilege, perhaps most significantly in relation to race. I couldn't grasp this because I was rather rigidly fixed in seeing myself as sensitive, compassionate, professionally experienced and culturally competent, while hiding behind being 'relational'.

There is so much to be said for more relational approaches to therapy rooted in the here-and-now process of the therapeutic relationship, but they can't replace the indispensable relevance of context of both the therapist and client(s). There is substantial material on the intersection between politics and psychotherapy that explores the ways in which the particular content of political ideologies influences different therapeutic models (Totton, 2000; Tweedy, 2016). More recent attention to the relational aspects of therapy has emphasised how the content of therapy is influenced by the political stance of the therapist (Loewenthal & Samuels, 2014), whether acknowledged or not.

My experience with this couple led me to seriously consider how I respond to a client revealing to me that I have made a blunder in relation to their identity or lived experience. On one hand, a client shouldn't *have* to educate a white therapist on what it means to live as a person of colour; a queer trans client shouldn't *need* to educate a cis therapist about transphobia and cis heteronormativity, and yet there must be a place of recognition that no therapist, no person, is going to completely understand the subjectivity of another. I believe the learning here is in immersing ourselves in the world of our clients as best we can, with keen awareness of context. Can we engage with and invest in people with marginalised aspects to their identity or lived experience without assuming that all clients of colour, all disabled people, all trans people (or all White people) are going to have the same needs, or the same perspectives on race, gender or otherness, for example?

I accept that it's not possible for individual therapists to have all the knowledge or all the answers. It's also not generally seen as our role as therapists to attempt to provide 'solutions' to the challenges faced by the people we work with. Nor do I believe that we usually need to have the same or very similar identities and lived experience as our clients for it to be a helpful relationship. However, the therapist's role does involve acquiring particular areas of knowledge and skills so as to be able to support the client meaningfully, safely and ethically. In my experience, we also need to be far more humble about, and cognisant of, when it's becoming apparent or likely that we are not well placed to support a client, and to have the means to refer them to someone more suitable. Even if we do believe ourselves to be knowledgeable and experienced, I have found that *assuming* that we know the correct way to meet a client on these issues is highly likely to lead us away from meaningful contact.

I would usually spend more time exploring with clients what was important to them about their questions to me and the meaning held by my potential, and actual, responses to them. The relative brevity described here was partly because of X and Y's jobs, their level of experience of therapy and their frankness with me, along with the simultaneous fragility and resilience of their particularly marginalised experiences. This also led me to sometimes respond more cognitively or intellectually to them than I generally find most helpful for clients, and which I believe was supportive to them in this instance. I want to give more consideration to the oppressive and racist aspects of my process and behaviour in the interactions I've detailed here, to own that fully, and I'm also mindful of the constraints of space considering how interactive and intersectional so much of what happened between us was, which brings me back to context.

The C word in a sick society

There is currently a gaping hole in mainstream therapy training and discourse that positions individuals as entrepreneurial agents whose suffering is attributable to personal or biological failures, rather than to harm caused by oppressive systems. What I was exposed to, and came to recognise during therapy with this couple, led me into shocking, murky, troubled waters in terms of my knowledge/ignorance, my self-image, and more moral and existential issues. I felt itchy and uncomfortable about what our conversations had opened up, like a snake waiting to shed old skin that hadn't yet found a suitable surface to rub against to slough off my hoary scales. Having begun to engage with the glaring, and more insidious, aspect of the field of therapy having been overwhelmingly developed and dominated by Eurocentric (mostly European and North American) white, middle-class and middle-aged, cis het men, I knew I needed to more deeply investigate the criticisms of therapy. Buckle up.

One of the recurring criticisms of our field is that it is, or at least supports, a capitalist endeavour that patches people up to churn them back into the workforce; that its goal has been to help people *adapt* to oppression and simply cope with the ongoing trauma of colonial, capitalist, patriarchal (and so on) systems. Some sources assert that the function of therapy under capitalism is to inculcate conformity to capitalist requirements *while maintaining the illusion of individual freedom* (Radical Therapist Collective, 1974; Tweedy, 2016; Davies, 2021; Lichtman, 2001). In *Against Therapy*, Masson makes the case that psychotherapy is coercive, immoral and ineffective (Masson, 1988). In *On Mental Health and Psychotherapy in Late Capitalism*, Lichtman (2001, p.66) describes therapy as a 'mode of conformity to the prevailing system of corporate and state domination'.

Even if you find some of those assertions extreme, I imagine you can recognise that the goal of much therapy revolves around the client's functional and productive life within current society. Psychotherapist Sue Gerhardt has written compellingly about how, in modern societies, we often confuse material wellbeing with psychological wellbeing (Gerhardt, 2010). She discusses how successfully and relentlessly consumer capitalism reshapes our brains and reworks our nervous systems in its own image. Dabiri (2021) writes of how, when your employer says work-life balance is important, what they're saying is that, at work, you're not living; it's work or life, work versus life. At work, you're not seen or treated as a living being but as a machine, to perform, or simply as any old object to be used.

Black feminist activists, as my client X lamented, were discussing capitalism and class mid-last century – Angela Davis, bell hooks, Audre Lorde, Alice Walker in the US; in the UK, Amy Ashwood Garvey, Claudia Jones, Gerlin Bean, among many others. I find it inspiring and, as X experienced it, demoralising that so long ago people were writing about how therapy makes us 'sick people who need "treatment" rather than oppressed people who must be liberated' (Radical Therapist Collective, 1974, p.8) and how we need to change the basic social institutions that give rise to the need for therapy (1974, p.105).

How sensible is it to measure 'good' mental health by how well a person adjusts to living in late-stage capitalist society that roils with oppression and injustice? Many of us are living in a dystopian nightmare, within an economic system built on presumed scarcity, wealth hoarding and insurmountable greed. To me, it's abundantly obvious that the 'mental health crisis' is a symptom and the underlying 'disease' is an economic system that exploits, divides and alienates.

As psychologist David Smail was saying from the 1970s until his death in 2014:

> What caused people distress was not so much their own mistakes, inadequacies and illnesses as the powers and influences that bore down upon them from the world beyond their skin. (Smail, 1996, p.10)

Y and X shared the interminable fatigue and misery of living in financial hardship, despite having 'respectable' professions, which is not the case for the majority of people. As I write, the top 1% of households own close to 50% of the total personal wealth in the world, while the bottom 50% hold only 1%. And within the top 1% are 175,000 ultra-wealthy people, each with more than $50 million in net wealth – that's less than 0.1% of the world's population owning 25% of global wealth (Credit Suisse, 2020, 2021).

Capitalism as a dissociative state

As this couple so powerfully pointed out, the language of polyvagal and trauma theory – 'regulation' and 'safety', as well as 'resilience' – is problematic. I think we need to radically question who determines what a 'regulated baseline' is in a rapid, restrictive, alienating and dissociating culture (Fannen, 2021). What might understanding be of 'regulation' across different cultures? We might appear to be 'regulated' in the context of another day at the office, even though we might be bodily contracted, disconnected from sensation and feelings, in discomfort or pain, breathing poorly, with terrible posture. 'In this sense, many of our environments and given norms are themselves dysregulated and dysregulating, which we are then being asked to self-regulate in' (Fannen, 2021, p.157). With this in mind, the notion of 'self-regulation' begins to look very like self-control in the service of fitting the requirements of productivity-obsessed capitalism (Fannen, 2021).

And the issues aren't only with regulation and staying in our 'window of tolerance'. Behavioural neuroscientist Stephen Porges proposed his polyvagal theory in the 1990s, and it has become a cornerstone of contemporary thinking around trauma in the Global North (Porges et al., 1994; Fannen, 2021). He talks about the cues we give each other through tone of voice, smiling and eye contact, particularly highlighting what is called prosody (the expressiveness of speech – intonation, rhythm, pauses, melody of language). But these elements aren't universally experienced in a single way worldwide. Individual people and different cultures have substantially different cultural norms around these cues (Fannen, 2021). Invisible initially, it can suddenly seem very obvious when pointed out.

The language of 'the science of safety' presents similar complexity: who gets to define what safety is? Who gets to decide on behalf of someone else what that is, when they may not have much, or any, contextual information? Safety is of course experienced in different ways by different people. We must keep a firm grip on the reality that many people's lives are constantly under threat – people of colour living under structural racism, people in prison, trans people, those living in poverty and many more (Fannen, 2021).

Of course, these psychological and therapeutic theories and models seek to serve connectivity, community and healing, but it is also true that they are reductive, generalising and can be inappropriate to the point of potentially leading to misinterpretation and grave harm.

Club (bio)med

X and Y were very invested in interrogating and dismantling the less than helpful aspects of conventional (Global Northern) medicine. This approach to medical treatment has progressed at an astonishing rate over the past 40 years. A child who developed leukaemia in the late 1970s had a 20% chance of survival; today it is 80% (Davies, 2021). Amazing improvements can be found in almost every area of medicine, with one exception: what we call mental health. Not only have clinical outcomes broadly flatlined but, according to some measures, they've worsened (Davies, 2021). This is despite tens of billions of pounds having been spent on psychiatric and psychological research in the past two decades; £18 billion spent on mental health services annually in the NHS and, astonishingly, nearly a quarter of the entire UK adult population now being prescribed at least one psychiatric drug each year (Davies, 2021).

I recognised, in almost one fell swoop in one of the sessions with X and Y, that I had unconsciously adopted an exclusively biomedical lens, despite my avid interest in 'alternative' medicine. Fannen (2021) details how biomedicine offers us narratives as if they are objective truths. It usually splits the mind from the body as if they are separate entities, and splits the mindbody from other people, from social contexts, animals, ancestors, the earth, the cosmos, the soul, as if we aren't deeply interconnected (Fannen, 2021). Biomedicine is increasingly recognising that systems do interrelate, heralding 'new' disciplines such as psychoendoneuroimmunology. However, this can be seen to replicate a familiar colonial pattern by claiming that science has made these 'discoveries', when many indigenous traditions have recognised and honoured such interrelationships all along (Fannen, 2021).

This system screens, assesses and diagnoses 'mental illnesses' and 'disorders' based on clusters of symptoms on which opinion frequently shifts over time and can be quite arbitrary. These 'disorders' are then treated with medication that is, at best, palliative, and talking therapies that instruct the person how to correct the negative thinking that is deemed to have led to distress in the first place, or seek to place the root of their suffering in their family and childhood experiences. Such an approach ignores the social, cultural and environmental factors at play in every person's life and masks the need to address systemic causes of understandable human distress.

Eurocentric power structures tend to make this single perspective the most definitive way of understanding human emotional distress. This has the effect of marginalising other perspectives and knowledge frameworks that are deemed inferior, particularly those rooted in non-European cultural traditions, which often challenge Global Northern assumptions and don't tend to lend themselves to the contemporary obsession with quantitative research to measure outcomes and promote 'evidence-based' practice. Categorical diagnoses are not the only way to view what we call mental illness. Throughout history, there have been myriad ways of understanding psychosocial suffering that incorporate the lived experience of the person. Lived-experience narratives represent and respect culture, trauma histories, identity and context (Fannen, 2021[6]). Is much, some or any of this familiar to you? Can you recognise its importance and make it a priority to explore?

Use your words, use 'em wisely

I was very struck by these clients' attention to language in our sessions. It was clear to me that this couple actively wanted to challenge the biomedical framework without abandoning its constructive aspects, without becoming pedantic or dogmatic, while also holding the societal, cultural, personal subjectivity of language with respect. So much meaning and misunderstanding can be held in our words and there is much contemporary debate about how useful diagnostic, and generally labelling, language is.

Language is of course important. In some situations, the language used is a matter of life or death for the people involved. I'm not interested in turning how articulate one is into another form of competition and hierarchy (living under capitalism is quite enough, thanks), or expecting people to be able (or need) to verbalise every aspect of our experience. I *am* interested in us collectively becoming aware and *specific enough* for us to minimise time spent debating, arguing, justifying and splitting hairs over ideas or experiences that we haven't defined or agreed upon. We need to be on the same page, not fighting over semantics that aren't even shared. We need to continue to develop our skills in communicating meaning without erasing, homogenising or diminishing. Definitions need to be expansive, fluid and precise at once. X and Y taught me so much of this in the short time we spent together, and it was clear how much stability, nourishment, conservation of energy and resilience this brought to them individually, as well as in their relationship with each other and their broader lives.

Might you reconsider your approach to using words and terms that cleave body from mind/brain, that medicalise, pathologise and unhelpfully intellectualise, such as mental health, mental illness, disorders and various diagnoses, along with the utilitarian and productivity-focused language of capitalism? I don't suggest that you impose this approach on clients, particularly if identity labels and diagnoses are supportive and valuable to them, but you

---

6. Lisa Fannen's book *Warp & Weft* (2021) cites more than 250 very pertinent books, articles and online references in the bibliography. So much of what I would want to expand upon here, and more, has been artfully compiled and carefully, tenderly, clearly elucidated in this book. Fannen writes at depth about the complex influences of moral, social, political and spiritual frameworks, and reminds us that tools and healing practices can be helpful, but 'need to sit within wider practices of collective care, social change and systemic transformation to have meaning and efficacy' (p.133). She has made the book available free online at https://threadsbook.org/warp-weft-online-2

might bring up the topics with them and experiment with some of this in different parts of your life. For instance, clients and people who see spirituality or religion as a salient aspect of their life may prefer the term 'psychospiritual' health/wellness as an alternative to 'psychosocial' or mental health/illness – roll it around on your tongue and see how it feels (Fannen, 2021).

I'm reminded of Ibram Kendi, who has renounced the term 'microaggression'. He says:

> I detest its component parts – 'micro' and 'aggression'. A persistent daily low hum of racist abuse is not minor. I use the term 'abuse' because aggression is not as exacting a term. Abuse accurately describes the action and its effects on people: distress, anger, worry, depression, anxiety, pain, fatigue, and suicide. (Kendi, 2019, p.46)

I've seen a common trend in how many terms develop and often outgrow their usefulness and precision, as illustrated by the connection between witchcraft and hysteria, BPD and potentially PMDD, or the deluge of ADHD and autism diagnoses (clinical and self-diagnosed) and the sweeping labelling of 'trauma' and attachment styles in the last five to 10 years. Some of these terms are/were potentially very helpful in articulating patterns of symptoms, experiences and behaviour, in offering greater granularity of awareness and in providing validation and a sense of clarity and hope, before they begin to somewhat or seriously limit that. I'm thinking of Resmaa Menakem, who teaches somatic abolitionism and chose to shift the term person (or body) of colour, to disrupt the norm, as he explains in this interview with Krista Tippett (2020/2021):

> Menakem: I don't say 'bodies of color' anymore, because what I'm trying to do is, I'm trying to reclaim the idea that I'm actually a human.
>
> Tippett: So you're saying that you're formed by the culture, physically –
>
> Menakem: Bodies of culture. That's right.

This appears to have occurred with aspects of identity in parts of the world as well, where we have exploding quantities of terms for gender and sexuality, for example, but can sometimes end up in knots attempting to define ourselves in particular aspects of our experience. Dabiri (2021) talks about how rigid identities need to soften. She says:

> 'Difference' produces new subjects of inquiry, that then *infinitely multiply exclusion in order to promote inclusion*. Difference now precedes and

defines identity. It relies on the subject X; insert race/gender/sexuality/class/disability. This atomizes the limitless variety of subjectivity into lists of 'knowable' categories that 'reduce' in order to acknowledge, flattening the complexity of being into neatly bounded classifications that produce a subject defined by their difference who can be governed and appealed to, not to mention targeted for advertising, accordingly. (Dabiri, 2021, p.141, original italics)

What is so often a desire for belonging and sense-making in defining ourselves can result in increasingly atomised, inflexible and disconnecting categorisation. How might you acknowledge and discuss this in your life, with clients, with students, with colleagues, with supervisees, with people in power?

Know your (own and others') history

I find that we talk incessantly about educating ourselves, about continuing professional development (particularly as therapists), without having much of a plan for exactly what, how and why we're going to learn.

The couple in this chapter astonished me with the breadth and depth of their knowledge, along with their capacity for critical thinking. There is a lot of opportunity to investigate and transform how we do things with supportive information and networks of people. Dystopian times have the potential to inspire utopian conversations (and actions) around how we actually want to spend our lives, find pleasure, sleep, lay out our cities, give birth to and raise children, grow food, have sex and cohabit with the other-than-human world. Can we tap into some current priorities?

> ... there is a huge deficit in knowledge about the consequences of colonialism, an understanding of the ways in which the imperial conquest redesigned the world according to its logic. (Dabiri, 2021, p.137)

It's knowledge, not information, that holds power. If information is individual bits of data, knowledge can be viewed as the application of that information, synthesised through some form of processing or critical thinking. Even more importantly, applying knowledge and sharing it is where the real power is. With so much data, information and insights coming at us all the time, a critical skill is our ability to make sense of things. This is, of course, not only achieved through cognitive or brain-based activity (hello capitalism and White supremacy culture), there are many kinds of knowledge and knowing that can be very embodied processes, but that learning often involves at least some reading and discussion to gather information, and I would say a commitment to cultivating critical analysis. How do you choose what to read? How conscientious are you about having a diversity of sources and evaluating how much of the material you retain and apply?

Do you know much about the relationship between racism, colonialism and capitalism relating to your own history, ancestry and where you live now? I expect many of you know more than you did a few years ago, considering the proliferation of material since the resurgence of the Black Lives Matter movement after George Floyd's murder.

How do you hold the impact of that relationship in your mindbody? How might you even begin to consider and answer that? What about the impact of the climate crisis and its ongoing impact on our sense of safety in the world? Where and how do you hold that awareness and tension?

On a connected note, I'm reminded of Greta Thunberg, who recently called for a system-wide transformation when she said we won't ever be returning to normal, because 'normal' is already a crisis. What we refer to as normal is built on the exploitation of people and the planet. She recognises that the climate crisis 'has its roots in racist, oppressive extractivism that is exploiting both people and the planet to maximise short-term profits for a few' (Thunberg, 2022).

I'm not only talking about engaging with heritage history here. The awe this couple inspired in me did compel me to further explore Ireland's history of being colonised and ruled for more than 700 years by Britain, which I'd believed myself to be reasonably clued up on from my childhood history classes and the persistent chip I retained on my shoulder about England and English people, even after living in London for a decade. This investigation led me to discover Ireland's overlooked history as an active coloniser in the empires of Britain and other European powers, which was shocking, confronting and fascinating (Morgan, 1994; Foley & O'Connor, 2006). I also unearthed that a substantial percentage of the Jamaican population claim Irish ancestry and Irish people are the second largest ethnic group in Jamaica after Jamaicans of African ancestry. I hadn't known this, even though I lived in Jamaica for half a year in my mid-20s. This expanded to learning about the black Irish of Montserrat in the Caribbean, as well as the white Irish 'Redlegs' of Barbados. It has added a richness and depth to my understanding of my own heritage and identity that is precious and grounding. I invite you to consider some areas of your own and others' histories that this book has touched upon and immerse yourself in them.

The fundamental fabric(ation) of race

Saad writes: 'You cannot dismantle what you cannot see. You cannot challenge what you do not understand' (2020, p.36).

It's now widely accepted that race is a social construct (Allen, 2012; Coates, 2015; Kendi, 2019; Fryer, 1984; Rutherford, 2020; Eddo-Lodge, 2017; Dabiri, 2021). For many people, even therapists who have completed anti-oppressive and cultural competence training, this still doesn't mean much, or is confusing. How can it be that race doesn't exist when we talk about it all the time and see the devastating impacts of discrimination and oppression? Racism is real because people enact it, based on the human-invented classification system of race. However we seem to forget that the number of races in the world has never been agreed upon, and nor is there agreement on what the essential features of each race might be (Fryer, 1984; Dabiri, 2021). The emergence of the approach to human taxonomy that relies on physical traits, including skin colour, coincided with European empire-building, in an era of exploration, exploitation and plunder (Fryer, 1984; Dabiri, 2021).

I came to *What White People Can Do Next: From allyship to coalition*, by Emma Dabiri, in late 2022.[7]

Dabiri sees a momentous opportunity for us to 'reconfigure attitudes and reignite imaginations' that she sees as currently 'being squandered by an "anti-racist" narrative that inadvertently reinforces much of what it claims to want to overcome' (Dabiri, 2021, p.3). She packs a punch with the pronouncement that the concept of allyship doesn't engage effectively with the fact that people can continue to perceive people of colour as inferior alongside being committed to their 'protection' (Dabiri, 2021, p.3).

We've seen the world through the lens of race for close to 500 years now. While the notion of racial difference originated in the English colonies in the 1660s, it was in the 19th century that this evolved into 'scientific racism' (Dabiri, 2021, p.45). The concept of a 'white' race was invented to create a narrative and to enshrine in law the rights, superiority and access to resources for people racialised as white, as well as the right to subjugate black people. When we are talking about and being anti-racist, it's really key that we don't reinforce the truth status of a system that was invented to create racism (Rutherford, 2020; Dabiri, 2021):

> It's crucial to connect the dots between the origins of global capitalism, colonialism and the invention of race. Doing so highlights the fictitious nature of race, as well as revealing the motivations and incentives behind its creation and upkeep. (Dabiri, 2021, p.78)

---

7. Like *Warp & Weft* (Fannen, 2021), Dabiri's book synthesises and deftly articulates with zest, exactitude and wisdom a great number of fragmented ideas that had been percolating for me. Dabiri wrote her PhD thesis on the construction of racial categories, before publishing the bestselling *Don't Touch My Hair* (2020).

I think most of us recognise that there is no singular 'Black', 'White', 'Brown' or indigenous experience. The clients I introduced in this chapter illustrate this plainly. We know that genetically there is more difference within groups than between them, so that the DNA of a black British person with Jamaican parents is likely to be closer to that of an Irish person than to the DNA of a Nigerian. Equally, 'blackness' is an invention. Africans don't consider themselves 'black'. On the African continent, they are Yoruba, Akan, Dahomey; they only become Black in Europe or North America (Dabiri, 2021; Fryer, 1984). Dabiri says that making blanket statements about the behaviours, beliefs, actions and desires of diverse groups of people who have been grouped under fictive and generic 'races' actually highlights how many of us still apparently believe that race exists as a *natural biological reality* (Dabiri, 2021 p.14). She frequently places inverted commas around 'black', 'white' and 'mixed race', intentionally disrupting the status quo of the terminology because of how it can perpetuate the notion of race as a biological reality (Dabiri, 2021, p.3).

Political scientist Adolph Reed is another fascinating, lesser-known voice whose writing on race you might be interested to explore. He is convinced that we're too focused on race in Global Northern society and not enough on class. He asks whether race is the primary problem today, or the outgrowth of a system that oppresses all people. He speaks and writes about the deep structural roots of the racial wealth gap in the US (which certainly has some relevance in the UK) and what he calls 'race reductionism', which he says consists of two elements. The first is a presumption that race as a category can explain social phenomena. The second is the idea that every grievance or injustice that affects a person of colour, *or* a person of non-colour, can be reduced to race (or can be reduced causally to race or to racism) (Reed, 2000, 2022). In no way does he suggest that the effects of racism aren't real; he implores us to develop discernment and critical thinking skills in relation to what we ascribe to racism.

Many pieces of this jigsaw slotted into place for me in relation to the couple I presented in this chapter and what they shared with me about their (similar and divergent) views about race when I read Dabiri. I invite readers to view Whiteness as a knowledge system, rather than as a racial identity; to realise that anyone can adopt it and be conditioned to see the world through its lens. The statement, 'You do not have to be "white" to have internalized the white gaze' (Dabiri, 2021, p.143) brought this together for me. It did this not so neatly or reductively that I feel at all sure of how to speak and write about racial identity or ethnicity (my own, and certainly not for other people), but enough to divest from these archaic, corrupted, obsolete terms where possible and appropriate. I continue to reflect on this and discuss it sensitively and respectfully with others. I hope you will too.

What would be truly radical would be to sound the death knell for the fiction that white people constitute a *race* and that this race is imbued with any 'natural' abilities unavailable to others. (Dabiri, 2021, p.61)

On the horizon

I see intersectionality to be the acknowledgement that each of us has our unique experiences of discrimination, privilege and oppression, and that we must consider and account for all we can that marginalises a person, particularly as therapists. I believe that what we need going forward is not more intersectionality of *identities*, rather intersectionality of our *issues*: our shared struggles, needs and desires for a better society (Dabiri, 2021).

Converging our struggles, and our understanding of them, is the work of *coalition-building*, where people can come together and work towards change. It is here that 'we can start to tell new stories, rather than fall back along fault lines that were designed to divide us in order to better exploit us' (Dabiri, 2021, p.26). I find it compelling to consider how a multitude of oppressions and forms of disadvantage might have a common origin, which can help us identify ways of coalition-building that concentrate on the source of the problem, 'while remaining mindful of the different textures of our varied but interconnected struggles' (2021, p. 41).

Do you have spaces to engage in coalition work? If not, how might you join or create them? Does this angle and invitation resonate with you and invigorate you? Does it make you want to withdraw into familiar ways of thinking and feeling about social change? At this point you might be feeling despondent, stirred, shaken, seen, or any number of things. I imagine that you would like to have a stronger sense of direction in your desire to understand and support diverse identities and lived experiences, as well as to cultivate wider change. I believe passionately that those of us who support people in distress have a key role in social transformation. Instead of trying to improve 'mindsets', change 'thought patterns' or teach 'emotional regulation', or even 'nervous system regulation', in therapy, we need to change race- and class-based hierarchies, the housing and economic systems and so much more that governs our daily existences. Our institutions and our government policies need to be transformed.

The best suggestions I have found from reading, researching, sitting with, observing and talking to people are quite simple and as follows: *learn, discuss, take action, organise and build coalitions*. In terms of our work as therapists, this can also look like validating, broadening, normalising, disclosing and contextualising with our clients.

How do we organise around the constraints of living under these pernicious systems? It can feel overwhelming to be up against these behemoths and seem as though the field and practice of therapy are defunct. We must not distort our desire to soothe people's distress and be helpful or let it blur the path towards societal transformation. Focusing solely on relieving individual suffering gets in the way of our capacity to hold onto the imperative for social change. It obstructs our ability to keep the need for anger, for movement, for greater consciousness, for networks, for destruction as a positive force in clear sight.

I'm interested in how we can simultaneously draw from and critique ideas, frameworks and conceptualisations. I want us to engage in social justice topics not only when they impact us personally and/or those close to us, but also those beyond the most personally visible and impactful. I hope that we fight and care for each other, that we commit to the struggle, because of the suffering we *all* experience under oppressive systems, and that we do this, not because we share similar experiences, but because we all deserve to live with dignity, safety and in community.

When I asked practitioners for ideas and suggestions for anti-oppressive practice, I was struck by how reluctant many were to respond. Wouldn't therapists be clamouring to add to the literature? Many people spoke about not wanting to be prescriptive, some about how anxious they felt about sharing what they had to say in case they were judged; some didn't see the value in another book on anti-oppressive practice when there are already so many; some believed they didn't have anything useful to add. This echoed my research and discussions about my own reticence to devote a lot of space to discussing how individual therapists might practise anti-oppressively. This is not because particular interventions and practices, suggestions for further learning and ideas for practitioners' self-care aren't immensely important, but because we already know this. I can offer a smattering of suggestions that may build on what you've been encountering here and elsewhere.

There is so much that I would like to include and explore, but there isn't the space here. I hope you will research these fields further: eco-anxiety and the challenges for (environmental and otherwise) activists; sex work and the current gradual societal shift from sex negativity to being more sex positive, and now increasingly 'sex critical';[8] the childfree movement and call to abolish the nuclear family; fat phobia and fat activism; conditions and 'disorders' that have been found to impact people of colour more than those racialised as 'white'; different forms of intersecting oppression besides (and including) misogynoir; critical disability studies, queer studies, crip theory, and more. However, here are some routes that I think are fundamental.

---

8. See http://sexcritical.co.uk/2012/07/27/what-is-sex-critical-and-why-should-we-care-about-it and https://www.rewriting-the-rules.com/sex/sex-critical

Resources

Psychologists for Social Change[9] is a network of applied psychologists, academics, therapists, psychology graduates and others who are interested in applying psychology to policy and political action. They believe that social, political and material contexts are central to people's experiences as individuals. Do consider getting involved.

We need social change that invests in young people and more community-led services such as Healing Justice London[10] and 4front.[11] These organisations work to heal trauma in marginalised communities through building social connectedness, social action and creativity towards equitable futures of community-centred health free from violence and oppression.

Joining the Psychotherapy and Counselling Union (PCU)[12] will likely be eye-opening and give you access to a wider network of community and socially oriented therapists. They (and I) believe that neither therapists nor clients are well protected by 'regulatory' or membership bodies in our statutorily unregulated profession.

The Radical Therapist Network[13] is a collective of international therapists dedicated to anti-oppressive praxis. Through transformative justice and intersectional frameworks, they put community healing and education at the heart of their work to dismantle white supremacy, systems of violence within the world of therapy, and society at large. RTN aims to work sustainably to offer community-based learning and support spaces to unlearn and heal from colonial and white supremacist culture.

The modalities of therapy I have encountered that embrace and explore social context include liberation psychology, some forms of somatic therapy, relational cultural theory, narrative therapy, trauma-informed therapy, (intersectional) feminist therapy, ecotherapy, radical therapy, queer and GSRD therapy. There are many gripping texts and resources a couple of clicks or a library visit away.

Decolonisation

Many therapists are taught that there are distinct differences between the mainstream types of therapy practised: behavioural, humanistic or psychodynamic. Some big names cross over these divides and come up

---

9. www.psychchange.org
10. https://healingjusticeldn.org
11. www.4frontproject.org
12. www.psychotherapyandcounsellingunion.co.uk and also www.ppstrust.org, which supports both psychologists and therapists.
13. www.radicaltherapistnetwork.com

repeatedly, including Freud, Jung, Rogers and Yalom. Their theories on 'mental illness', human behaviour and causes of suffering have had deep and widespread influence. They almost certainly powerfully shape your practice. The homogeneity of these pioneers is stark; they existed in a context that privileged and was predominantly White, male, heterosexual, cisgender, Eurocentric and colonial.

As we've discussed here, traditional forms of therapy often feed into ideas of neoliberalism that disregard the context in which communities of colour face racism and systemic discrimination. Decolonising therapy involves looking at how what could now be termed the 'mental health industrial complex' continues to inflict harm on people by remaining apolitical. Decolonising is picking up a lot of traction at the moment and is part of a wider move towards understanding and dismantling the oppressive systems we have operated under. Decolonised approaches centre community, spirituality, social justice and the innate wisdom of each of us over the analysis or diagnosis of experts.

Practically speaking, this usually means working in groups or sharing circles. While I continue to believe in the healing potential of individual therapy and the space it creates for deep exploration, I have found that group-based community healing practices offer something unique that cannot be achieved in the traditional therapy room. Meaningful structural transformation won't happen overnight, though the pandemic has taught us that substantial changes can happen much more quickly than many previously thought.

Anti-oppressive practice

Anti-oppressive practice (AOP) is a theory and approach that recognises the oppression that exists in our society/space. It aims to mitigate its effects and eventually equalise the power imbalances that exist between people. It also recognises that all forms of oppression are interconnected in some form (Aqil et al., 2021). When defined as an approach to social issues, it focuses on how larger systems create and protect the unearned privilege and power that some groups have, while at the same time creating, maintaining and upholding difficult and unequitable conditions for other groups of people (Baines, 2017).

AOP has been an influential clinical approach in social work practice in many countries since the millennium (Curry-Stevens, 2016), but is still unfamiliar to many therapists beyond understanding the vague connotations of the name. It draws on several disciplines to deepen our understanding of the world and enable us to think more critically, including anti-racism, decolonisation theory, feminism, queer theory and disability justice, among others. Anti-oppressive practice strives to use these disciplines to give people the tools needed to better understand how power and privilege work within society at all levels (Aqil et al., 2021). It also supports the development and facilitation of programmes and practices that can shift our societal dynamics in ways that decrease and eliminate oppression. Anti-oppressive practice also aims to improve skills in critical consciousness, which is the combination of critical action and reflection. It requires that we step back and think about our practices or policies, ask probing questions about how they impact those around us and those we work with, and then act on the conclusions in tangible ways. A grounding in anti-oppression equips practitioners with tools to recognise the impact of present and historical contexts, cultivate critical self-reflection and address systems of oppression.

Liberation psychology

Rather than a specific approach, liberation psychology is a framework for taking account of how people and communities are shaped by their experience and history of oppression. It challenges the idea that psychology is a value-neutral science and instead argues that psychology (and therapy) has often supported, whether intentionally or not, the status quo and thus helped maintain an unjust and unequal society (Martín-Baró, 1996). Liberation psychology was developed by the Spanish/Salvadoran social psychologist Ignacio Martín-Baró and flourished in Latin America. It has begun to expand into the US and very recently the UK.

Liberation psychology explores the effects of dominant power and its structures on the oppressed, together with the lived impacts of poverty, social injustice, censorship, repression and violence. Liberation psychologists aim to hear, amplify and incorporate in their theory and practice the voices and knowledge of those 'others' most affected by the types of oppression identified above. This framework sees people not as patients but as potential social change makers in the project of freedom, valuing their own heritages, creativity and experience, rather than being shoehorned into a White, Eurocentric and individualistic idea of therapy. It directly challenges the social, cultural and political causes of distress through collective social action (Comas-Díaz & Torres Rivera, 2020). The philosophy of liberation psychology stresses the interconnectedness and co-creation of culture, psyche, self and community. It says they must be viewed as interconnected and evolving multiplicities of perspectives.

Final thoughts

It might feel very difficult to hold onto the value of the field and practice of therapy under these conditions, and I leave it to you to decide what to do with this information. I'm hoping that it stimulates movement and change, rather than decimates your passion and livelihood. Like strike action, this chapter, this book, is designed to disrupt and unsettle. One of our potent and very valuable skills as therapists is to be able to stay with discomfort, work through it and glean what might be most needed or helpful. Let's get cracking.

References

Allen, T.W. (2012). *The invention of the white race* (2nd ed.). Verso.

Aqil, A.R., Malik, M., Jacques, K.A., Lee, K., Parker, L.J., Kennedy, C.E., Mooney, G. & German, D. (2021). Engaging in anti-oppressive public health teaching: Challenges and recommendations. *Pedagogy in Health Promotion, 7*(4), 344–353. https://doi.org/10.1177/23733799211045407

Armstrong, T. (2010). *Neurodiversity: Discovering the extraordinary gifts of autism, ADHD, dyslexia and other brain differences*. ASCD publications.

Asher, J.E., Aitken, M.R.F., Farooqi, N., Kurmani, S. & Baron-Cohen, S. (2006). Diagnosing and phenotyping visual synaesthesia: a preliminary evaluation of the revised test of genuineness (TOG-R). *Cortex, 42,* 137–146.

Audet, C.T. (2011). Client perspectives of therapist self-disclosure: Violating boundaries or removing barriers? *Counselling Psychology Quarterly, 24*(2), 85–100. https://doi.org/10.1080/09515070.2011.589602

Baines, D. (2017). *Doing anti-oppressive practice: Social justice social work*. Fernwood Publishing.

Brüne, M. (2016). Borderline personality disorder: Why 'fast and furious'? *Evolution, Medicine, and Public Health 1,* 52–66. doi: 10.1093/emph/eow002

Coates, T.-N. (2015). *Between the world and me*. Spiegel & Grau.

Comas-Díaz, L. & Torres Rivera, E. (Eds.). (2020). *Liberation psychology: Theory, method, practice, and social justice*. American Psychological Association.

Connell, N. & Wilson, C. (Eds.). (1974). *Rape: The first sourcebook for women by New York radical feminists*. New American Library.

Credit Suisse. (2020). *The global wealth report 2020*. Credit Suisse. www.credit-suisse.com/about-us/en/reports-research/global-wealth-report.html

Credit Suisse (2021). *The global wealth report 2021*. Credit Suisse. www.credit-suisse.com/about-us/en/reports-research/global-wealth-report.html

Curry-Stevens, A. (2016). Anti-oppressive practice. *Oxford Bibliographies Online Datasets*. https://doi.org/10.1093/obo/9780195389678-0203

Dabiri, E. (2020). *Don't touch my hair*. Penguin Books.

Dabiri, E. (2021). *What white people can do next: From allyship to coalition*. Penguin Books.

Davies, J. (2021). *Sedated: How modern capitalism created our mental health crisis*. Atlantic Books.

Del Giudice, M. (2018). *Evolutionary psychopathology: A unified approach*. Oxford University Press.

Eddo-Lodge, R. (2017). *Why I'm no longer talking to white people about race*. Bloomsbury Publishing.

Fannen, L. (2021). *Warp & weft*. Active Distribution. https://threadsbook.org/warp-weft-online-2

Farber, B.A. (2006). *Self-disclosure in psychotherapy*. Guilford Press.

Fisher, M. (2009). *Capitalist realism: Is there no alternative?* Zero Books.

Foley, T. & O'Connor, M. (Eds.). (2006). *Ireland and India: Colonies, culture and empire*. Irish Academic Press.

Fryer, P. (1984). *Staying power: The history of black people in Britain*. Pluto Press.

Gerhardt, S. (2010). *The selfish society: How we all forgot to love one another and made money instead*. Simon & Schuster.

Gibson, M.F. (2012). Opening up: Therapist self-disclosure in theory, research and practice. *Clinical Social Work Journal, 40*(3), 287–296.

Gov.uk. (2017, updated 2021). *Personality disorders*. www.ethnicity-facts-figures.service.gov.uk/health/mental-health/prevalence-of-personality-disorder-in-adults/latest

Herman, J. (2015). *Trauma and recovery: The aftermath of violence – From domestic abuse to political terror*. Basic Books.

Johnsen C. & Ding, H.T. (2023). Therapist self-disclosure of sexual orientation revisited: Considerations with a case example. *Journal of Gay & Lesbian Mental Health, 27*(1), 46–58. doi: 10.1080/19359705.2022.2030898

Johnson, M. (2021). Neuroqueer feminism: Turning with tenderness toward borderline personality disorder. *Signs: Journal of Women in Culture and Society, 46*(3), 635–662.

Jolley, K.H. (2019). I'm human too: Person-centred counsellors' lived experiences of therapist self-disclosure. *European Journal for Qualitative Research in Psychotherapy, 9*, 12–26.

Kendi, I.X. (2019). *How to be an antiracist*. Random House.

King, D.K. (1988). Multiple jeopardy, multiple consciousness: The context of a black feminist ideology. *Signs: Journal of Women in Culture and Society, 14*(1), 432–472. doi:10.1086/494491

Lichtman, R. (2001). On mental health and psychotherapy in late capitalism. *Capitalism Nature Socialism, 12*(1), 57–86. doi: 10.1080/104557501101244820

Loewenthal, D. & Samuels, A. (Eds.). (2014). *Relational psychotherapy, psychoanalysis and counselling: Appraisals and reappraisals*. Routledge.

Martín-Baró, I. (1996). *Writings for a liberation psychology*. Harvard University Press.

Masson, J.M. (1988). *Against therapy: Emotional tyranny and the myth of psychological healing*. Atheneum Publishers.

Miserandino, C. (2003). *The spoon theory*. www.butyoudontlooksick.com

Morgan, H. (1994). An unwelcome heritage: Ireland's role in British empire-building. *History of European Ideas, 19*(4–6), 619–625. doi: 10.1016/0191-6599(94)90043-4

Porges, S.W., Doussard-Roosevelt, J.A. & Maiti, A.K. (1994). Vagal tone and the physiological regulation of emotion. *Monographs of the Society for Research in Child Development, 59*(2/3), 167–186. https://doi.org/10.2307/1166144

Porges, S.W. & Furman, S.A. (2011). The early development of the autonomic nervous system provides a neural platform for social behaviour: A polyvagal perspective. *Infant & Child Development, 20*, 106–118. doi: 10.1002/icd.688.

Radical Therapist Collective. (1974). *The radical therapist: Therapy means change not adjustment.* Pelican.

Reed, A. (2000). *Class notes: Posing as politics and other thoughts on the American scene.* New Press.

Reed, A. (2022). *The south: Jim Crow and its afterlives.* Verso Books.

Rutherford, A. (2020). *How to argue with a racist.* Weidenfeld & Nicolson.

Saad, L. (2020). *Me and white supremacy: How to recognise your privilege, combat racism and change the world.* Quercus.

Settles, I.H. & Buchanan, N.T. (2014). Multiple groups, multiple identities and intersectionality. In V. Benet-Martínez & Y.-Y. Hong (Eds.), *The Oxford handbook of multicultural identity* (pp.160–180). Oxford University Press.

Smail, D. (1996). *How to survive without psychotherapy.* Routledge.

Tasca, C., Rapetti, M., Carta, M.G. & Fadda, B. (2012). Women and hysteria in the history of mental health. *Clinical Practice & Epidemiology in Mental Health, 8*, 110–119. doi: 10.2174/1745017901208010110

Thomas, R. (2022, August 23). NHS fails on mental health care targets as waiting list rises to 1.2 million. *The Independent.* www.independent.co.uk/news/health/nhs-mental-health-waiting-list-b2145432.html

Thunberg, G. (2022, October 30). *Greta Thunberg: The Climate Event.* London Literature Festival.

Tippet, K. (2020, June 4/2021, April 15). *Resmaa Menakem: Notice the rage; notice the silence* [Podcast]. On being with Krista Tippett. https://onbeing.org/programs/resmaa-menakem-notice-the-rage-notice-the-silence

Totton, N. (2000). *Psychotherapy and politics.* Sage.

Tweedy, R. (Ed.). (2016). *The political self: Understanding the social context for mental illness.* Karnac.

Van der Kolk, B. (2014). *The body keeps the score.* Allen Lane.

Wirth-Cauchon, J. (2001). *Women and borderline personality disorder: Symptoms and stories.* Rutgers University Press.

3. Attending to self, attending to others: the impact on the Black therapist of client presentations of racial trauma

Ohemaa Nkansa-Dwamena

This chapter will explore the dual process of being a therapist of colour and human of colour. I will describe and delve into my own experience, as a qualified therapist, of navigating the impact of racial trauma while holding the therapeutic space for my clients' presentations of racial trauma.

In recent years, with the advent of the Covid-19 pandemic and the amplification of the Black Lives Matter movement, access to therapeutic support has become more pronounced among people of colour. There appears to be an increased need for a safe space to heal from both historical and present trauma, and a desire among clients for therapists of colour to support their journey (Race Equality Foundation, 2020). Therapists of colour have historically held these spaces, and continue to do so, often while experiencing repeated instances of trauma in a professional context and in their personal lives. The combination of this race-based traumatic stress (or racial trauma), increased caseloads and pressure on availability, in addition to engaging with individuals with similar experiences, can lead to secondary trauma and burnout for therapists of colour (Lipscomb & Ashley, 2020). Our understanding of racial trauma as experienced by clients and therapists of colour can contribute to continued learning, advocacy and therapeutic development in the areas of race and inclusion.

Racism and racial trauma

The impact of racism and discrimination has received increased attention in clinical and academic literature. Recently, calls for the recognition of racial trauma and its long-term, far-reaching impact on people of colour have also increased (Comas-Díaz et al., 2019; Odafe et al., 2017). In addition, researchers and practitioners have appealed for racism in its many forms to be declared a public health crisis, due to its complex impact on functioning, social inequities and advancement for people of colour (Andrews, 2021; Fenton et al., 2020; Devakumar et al., 2020).

Research has shown that chronic exposure to racism can have detrimental behavioural outcomes and is linked to autoimmune disease activation (Thames et al., 2019). It can also trigger mental health presentations, including depression and anxiety (Paradies et al., 2015). The negative effects of exposure on stress-related diseases have also been highlighted in research, as well as the impact on self-esteem and sense of self (Bhui et al., 2018). It is argued that racism endangers wellbeing through its ability to minimise or weaken coping mechanisms, due to the cumulative effect of its impact (Bhui et al., 2018). It can contribute to intergenerational trauma, when the effects of the experience of racial trauma and discrimination are passed down unintentionally in families of colour (Degruy-Leary, 2017).

People of colour who live with both an awareness and the experience of racism may exist in a perpetual state of vigilance and have to find ways to assimilate into their various environments in order to protect themselves from recurrent racial discrimination, including microaggressions, minimisation and tokenism. This might include overcompensation or, conversely, a protective approach of blending in. However, this manner of existing can become challenging when events or situations activate a sense of vulnerability, a re-living of a traumatic experience, or exposure to suppressed memories related to incidents of oppression and discrimination (Carter, 2007).

Shell and colleagues (2021) speak to the race-related stress and secondary traumatic stress that therapists of colour may experience, especially in this line of work at this time. In their paper, they surveyed 250 therapists to determine the link between race-related stress and therapist functionality, wellbeing and mental health. Their results showed a direct correlation between race-related stress (in this case measured by three subscales: individual, cultural and institutional racism) and likelihood/risk of burnout and stress in Black therapists.

The effects and experiences of racism have been present, and grappled with, long before the amplified events of the last few years, including the Covid-19 pandemic, the persistent violence towards people of colour (Raghavan & Jones-Nielsen, 2021) and the resurgence of the Black Lives Matter movement. For some people of colour, the therapeutic space has been a place for validation and empowerment in trying to navigate these experiences. Research also speaks to the desire some people of colour have to engage with a therapist who is also of colour, due to the potential for shared experience and understanding in the relationship. However, it could be suggested that this kind of therapeutic dyad has added complexity, since both client and therapist may be triggered by similar racial and intersectional stressors. A therapeutic hermeneutic process (Smith, 2007) may occur where therapists of colour are helping clients of colour to make sense of their world while they themselves are also noticing and making sense of their own processes in relation to the shared phenomena. This will be illustrated and explored in the next part of this chapter.

A therapist's lived experience

> The very serious function of racism is distraction. It keeps you from doing your work. It keeps you explaining, over and over again, your reason for being. Somebody says you have no language and so you spend 20 years proving that you do. Somebody says your head isn't shaped properly so you have scientists working on the fact that it is. Somebody says that you have no art so you dredge that up. Somebody says that you have no kingdoms and so you dredge that up. None of that is necessary. (Morrison, 1975)

This quote by Toni Morrison has always resonated with me personally and professionally. As a Black African female counselling psychologist working in the mental health field, I have always been acutely aware of my 'otherness' and have centred race, intersectionality and difference in my practice. I strive to adopt a holistic and inclusive approach with clients, elevating their uniqueness and sense of self, in defiance of the notion that race, culture and intersectional identities have no place or relevance in the therapy room or in our training. I have noted in my personal and professional experiences that racism can be wielded as a tool to minimise and keep people of colour in a 'lesser' position. Sometimes this has taken the form of microaggressive comments, which have caused me to question and doubt my abilities, leading to over-compensatory behaviours to disprove the rhetoric that I am not capable. Partially due to lived experience, I became very conscious about doing some necessary work, in the form of writing, clinical work, teaching, collaborating and supervising, to bring issues pertaining to race, identity and inclusion to the forefront. It is also very possible that, in doing this, I additionally found ways to exist in spaces and cope where inclusive practice may not have been high on the agenda and where I have often been the only person of colour. I have been acutely aware of the impact of repeated exposure to racism and how questioning, doubting and grappling with this can have a deeper impact that is sometimes suppressed in order to navigate different environments and continue to do work that feels so important.

As such, my commitment (alongside that of many of my esteemed colleagues) to reframing our curriculum, training and practice has been longstanding. In the beginning of 2020, with the genesis of the Covid-19 pandemic, the disproportionate impact on communities of colour highlighted the structural issues and inequities that have long been present, including health disparities, economic inequalities and access to culturally sensitive support (Raghavan & Jones-Nielsen, 2021). Engaging with people in therapy and working through their grief, loss and trauma was a layered experience for me. There were shared moments of reward, empowerment and validation. I also experienced moments of heaviness, anger and fatigue, as I was concurrently weighed down by my own losses and experience of the pandemic.

Then a series of race-related deaths and attacks happened in plain sight, recounted and recorded. That these occurred in the US did not take away from the pain they caused me. I thought that some of the coping mechanisms that I had been using, such as taking care of myself, leaning into my personal and professional support systems and giving myself intentional space to process my feelings, had given me some grounding and the tools to manage the uncertainties of those months. However, what I witnessed re-opened old wounds regarding my identity and my Blackness. Memories of discriminatory experiences I had as a child and as a young adult rose again, clearly and painfully, to the surface: memories of the name calling, the deliberate exclusion from groups, feeling othered. The ways in which race discrimination and racism had permeated the lives and wellbeing of the people I knew and loved also re-emerged. In the days, weeks and months following the death of George Floyd, I oscillated between numbness, confusion, anger, sadness and rage. I recall periods of feeling utterly drained and sullen, then finding spouts of energy before lapsing into exhaustion again.

Much of my own experience was reflected and shared in the therapy room. Many of the clients of colour I saw during this period wanted to talk about their pain, their frustration and their disbelief about what was happening. For some, the combined impact of the Covid-19 pandemic and the witnessed acts of violence against Black bodies had brought them to therapy for the first time. I sought my own personal therapy, and felt it important to access support from a group of other therapists of colour to check in with where and how we all were at this time. I felt seen and held in these spaces. I also didn't feel I had to explain what I was experiencing, as there was a shared understanding and knowing.

I marched with thousands of people during the Black Lives Matters protests, feeling the combined hope and sadness while reliving the trauma of the previous few months. I was straddling the positions of speaking up for the needs of people of colour and feeling myself to be in a privileged position to do this (I am alive and I have a voice), while also experiencing my own trauma responses, as well as vicarious trauma through my work with clients, both past and present. It was not easy to differentiate between my own and vicarious trauma and as they often seemed to overlap. I frequently experienced feelings of numbness, irritability and withdrawal and had vivid dreams during this time. I resonated with clients' expression of immense fatigue and anticipatory grief about what would happen when the social media posts died down, when the dialogue around these issues quietened, and when the realisation hit that the work was ongoing, often slow, sometimes painful, sometimes frustrating, and that, as individuals of colour, we had no opportunity to opt out of the awareness of the realities of what had been taking place throughout our whole lives, in sometimes subtle and at other times very overt ways.

I also had candid conversations with my family at this time. In particular, my exchanges with my father helped me to make further sense of my responses, as well as those of my clients. As a Black man working in healthcare during the 1980s and 1990s, my father's experiences of racism contributed to his decision to seek work opportunities outside of the UK in order to support his family and advance his career. We had never previously had deep conversations about his experiences before this, or about the impact his decision had on my identity development. It had been important to him that he prioritise and protect me. He affirmed me and instilled a sense of racial and cultural pride.

However, this troubled time of Covid-19 and the aftermath of George Floyd's killing prompted us to share and reflect as adults at a depth we hadn't been able to when I was younger. I believe we both had the words to describe things in a way we hadn't before. My father named the disappointment he felt at continuously being passed over for promotion, despite being highly qualified. He spoke about the repeated instances of disbelief on people's faces when he was identified as the attending health professional. My father is not a verbose person, but I heard in his words and saw in his face the tiredness that came with having to endure repeated slights, yet still show up as his most competent self. He was reflecting a common narrative that I saw in my work with clients and my exchanges with colleagues and friends – that, despite the traumatic impact of these experiences, you still have to show up and be present and competent in harmful spaces.

I started to reflect intensely on the dialogues and experiences I was having at this time. My journal was the repository for my reflections. It felt important to capture this journey as a tool for my healing, but also to build a narrative around experiences that seemed to hold so many emotions and meanings. I felt it important to observe and learn from the dual personal and professional positioning I continued to find myself in, as it had implications for my professional practice and personal growth. How I might differently engage with my work? What I might be more cognisant of in relation to working with race in the therapy room? These implications might also serve as learning for other professionals. I wanted to continue to be present in my work, but also be mindful of the need to take care of myself.

I am sharing excerpts of these entries here in the hope that they convey the manifestations of this process and contribute to continued learning about the themes pertaining to racial trauma and duality in this chapter.[1]

8 June, 2020
5.00am

I could barely sleep last night. I am returning to work today and I feel unsettled. My eyes opened much before my alarm went off. It is light outside but feels so dark in this room. I feel like there is a huge foot on my chest. I tell myself to breathe... in a few moments the feeling will subside. It does, but not fully, and I have to will myself to get out of bed and move through it. In every space I have existed for the last week, there has been a conversation about race. Different conversations, necessary conversations, but I notice I haven't taken as much space to pause and reflect. The weight of the foot continues to lessen as I write this, although I notice that I am still feeling unsettled.

Yesterday, I had a session with H, a Black client. We have many moments of silence in our sessions – they have felt safe and contained. Yesterday the silences felt heavy with grief. H described feeling anxious and in shock. How viscerally triggering the video of George Floyd was. They talked about how this has been exacerbated by intense and focused discussions in most areas of their lives, and in places where these dialogues had never previously taken place. They speak to how much more acute it feels to be the only person of colour in their professional space and how lonely they feel within it. I too have often been the only person of colour. Why is this different now? I previously normalised this. So has my client. I came to expect it. H states they are surprised when they see another person of colour in the same vicinity as them. Maybe this is how we have coped.

As H reflected, I noticed my body temperature rising. My face felt hot, and internally I felt I was filling up with ounces and ounces of liquid. I was afraid I would spill over. I checked in with H and asked what they were experiencing

---

1. Identifiable details of clients and other individuals and settings have been changed to protect privacy and identity.

in their body and in the room as they reflected on their journey. They described feeling like they were treading water, that the feeling of their feet on the ground felt inaccessible. This resonated for both of us. We closed our eyes, and we inhaled. It felt important to feel jointly anchored. We exhaled. We could breathe. It was not lost on us that we were here and able to do this.

And I am wondering what this means for me now? How do I continue to have these dialogues in these professional spaces when I am grappling with my own feelings? I know this is why I am slow to leave the confines of my bed. I want to freeze time, if only for a little bit. I want to feel some relief. I want to stay in that moment with my client where, for a significant few minutes, we felt light and held.

24 June, 2020
7.00am

Yesterday was a long, exhausting day. This is an all-too-common feeling lately. I have a feeling that this may take some time. I have a feeling that my prose might seem cold and emotionless. I know that I am probably finding a way to reflect on this, but I need to pace myself. I know this too is a part of my process.

I attended a supervisory group. We are two months into this pandemic, so meetings are predominantly taking place online. At this point, Zoom feels like an embedded part of my environment. Yesterday our exploration focused on ways in which we could support clients of colour in the therapeutic space. Questions arose – how do we find the appropriate language? How do we meaningfully engage? Valid and important questions, and yet I feel that these questions are being directed at me – I am the only clinician of colour in this group. The Zoom screen holds pictorial squares of white practitioners. And my Black face stands out, because how could it not? I don't want to look at myself. I don't want to look at the screen. I feel like there is a huge spotlight on me and I cannot get away. In that moment I crave the physical presence of others who look like me. My peers are talking about the therapeutic work, but they are also, inadvertently, talking about my lived experiences. I wonder, can they see me? Can they see my Blackness? My thoughts are interrupted by a long silence in the room. One of my peers enquires about my wellbeing. My throat feels tight. 'I'm fine,' I respond. But, 'Please don't ask me anything else,' I whisper internally; 'I feel like gallons of water are about to erupt from my tear ducts, and I don't want to do that here, in this room where I am the only one.' The conversation continues. I am oscillating between relief and a desire for things to speed up. I want this session to be over. My chair feels too small. My chest feels too full.

The session is coming to an end. One of my peers looks at me through the screen and reflects that they did not feel that, as a group, they fully engaged with how I might be feeling at this time. Something in the way they phrase this causes me to come undone. A valve is turned on and the tears flow. I cannot stop them.

They feel imbued with the traumatic dialogues I have had with clients over the last few months. They hold unexpressed pain. A series of memories flash before my eyes – being called derogatory names in school; being questioned about my intellectual ability; feeling like I do not belong. My tears feel hot with anger at the unfairness. The injustice. The loss of lives. I have to switch off the video and step away from the screen. I feel exposed. Processes that my clients of colour have described taking place in their settings, in spaces in their lives, I am also experiencing in that moment. I close my eyes and, again, I breathe. I allow myself to cry for as long as I need to. I don't try to avoid this or put on a composed version of myself. I let it be.

Eventually I return to the meeting, noting that I feel a little more centred. However, the feeling of vulnerability is still present. I am nervous about exploring what has just occurred in the space, but also aware that this conversation is necessary. I recall the words of an impactful supervisor: have the necessary dialogues, but take your time, take care of yourself and do not hold responsibility for others' processes. I hold this in mind as I turn my video back on.

Analysis of excerpts

The combined narratives in the previous section speak to several issues and themes that pertain to the experiences of therapists of colour and their duality of professional and personal identities, in addition to the impact of racial trauma and race-related stress for both clients and therapists. I will attempt to unpick this in the following sections, highlighting the most salient points as avenues for reflection and learning. This will be followed by suggestions for anti-oppressive/anti-racist practice that may go some way to addressing some of the themes discussed.

Both excerpts describe incidents of racial trauma and briefly speak to how these can be experienced by therapists of colour through engagement with their clients and in their own lived experience. In their paper on the experiences of therapists of colour during the Covid-19 pandemic, Miu and Moore (2021) recount their personal stories of working with clients of colour while navigating their own fears and vulnerabilities regarding systemic, structural and individual racism. Much of what they describe chimes with what I have outlined above: that, for therapists of colour, what has felt intensely apparent is that the privilege our profession affords us does not protect us from racism, and how this is highly likely to be relived to some degree when working with clients. Miu and Moore stress:

> professionals of colour are exposed to all forms of race-based stress, ranging from direct racism in society, patients' discrimination, or vicarious exposure from news and patients' accounts. (2021)

Often in therapeutic practice, our understanding of and engagement with issues pertaining to race, culture and diversity are drawn from our experiences in the clinical work and the journeys of our clients. The expressions of my client in the first journal entry may cause some pause for the reader as you reflect and digest what it meant for my client to feel unanchored but also to find grounding in a therapeutic space where the gravity of their experience and the exploration of their identity were seen and engaged with. This could be an example of what we mean by 'culturally sensitive practice'. The experiences I detailed may also offer some insight into how we might both practise and collaborate in an anti-racist manner. This might include how we can better relate to one another in the field when engaging with dialogue around race and also support other strands of the professional journey, such as anti-racist supervisory engagement. We can also work in collaboration outside therapy through peer dialogue, advocacy and allyship.

Self-care and racial trauma

Descriptions of feelings of heaviness, fatigue and groundlessness are recurrent in the journal excerpts, and they consistently feature in the narratives of clients I have worked and work with. A focus in therapy, and in my own process, has been the importance of self-care and, within this, practising connecting to and being grounded within my body, allowing me to feel anchored. It has also been about taking intentional rest. This has sometimes taken the form of meditation. Also important has been validating engagement with colleagues, friends and family. In my work with clients, meditation, mindfulness and actions that support self and community empowerment have also been meaningful. Examples have included individuals speaking up for changes in their contexts in ways they had never felt able to before, and others being clear and boundaried about how they contribute in terms of social justice, such as relinquishing sole responsibility for facilitating change. Such acts of self-care reflect aspects of clinical models that have been developed as a way to foster healing and transformation and enhance safety in response to racial trauma (Bryant-Davis & Ocampo, 2006; Comas-Díaz, 2016; Dunbar, 2001).

For clients and therapists of colour, engaging in acts of self-care is an important aspect of processing the impact of vicarious and racial trauma present in our work and personal lives (Comas-Díaz, 2016). Self-care and rest can therefore help in some way to liberate, as the centring of self becomes paramount (Giordano et al., 2021), in contrast to feeling overly exposed or weighed down.

Straddling positions of privilege and oppression

To be a qualified psychologist or therapist suggests that, on some level, we are in a position of privilege. When we consider the intersecting identities (Crenshaw,

2014) we hold as individuals, our positions of privilege and oppression shift according to our contexts, experiences and where we are in our life journey. It is a strange position to straddle when it is apparent that this status does not protect us from the devastating effects of discrimination we may experience related to our own race, gender, sexuality, religious beliefs and so forth. Talking about race and racism and finding ways to collaboratively dismantle systems while simultaneously recounting and working through one's own experiences in the therapy room, continuously, in meetings and in other spaces, can be tiring. It can trigger a mixture of feelings and states. This can include validation, if a person feels heard and seen. However, vulnerability or re-traumatisation may occur if there is a sense of feeling exposed, misunderstood or unsupported.

In their paper, Crowell and colleagues (2017) speak about the importance of counselling psychologists taking up the mantle of social justice. They highlight that therapists of colour have always been involved in justice for Black lives. This resonates with the experiences I previously described. This journey can be marked with feelings of disappointment, as oppressive structures and approaches are slow to shift. In addition, consistent engagement professionally and personally with traumatic material may take a toll, emphasising that professional privilege does not protect practitioners from the impact of discrimination. It also speaks to the importance of a collective approach to anti-racist practice, where everyone takes an active role in dismantling discriminatory practice and systems. This is necessary to lessen the focus or responsibility that may be placed on therapists of colour and clients, as the load may exacerbate experiences of race-related stress or trauma.

In an article exploring the current state of Black therapists' mental health, Stallings (2020) interviewed practitioners about the increased expectation to deliver training and workshops, to share their experiences and to hold space for individuals because of their race. One therapist queried her ability to facilitate a therapeutic group with people of colour, to educate her colleagues about race and racial sensitivity and also consciously to attend to her own mental health and wellbeing. She reflected on the struggle to balance these demands. As described in my journal excerpt earlier in this chapter, even with the best intentions, conversations around race and culture are mainly initiated and led or facilitated by therapists of colour (Crowell et al., 2017).

This may also be experienced in the therapy space, where clients of colour may find themselves educating their therapists about the blind spots in their practice or experience being unseen in the therapeutic relationship because their therapist is unable to consider experiences through an intersectional lens or acknowledge cultural, structural and systemic impacts on people of colour. Navigating the positions of lived experience and educator can be sapping of energy, and therapists of colour may need explicit support and space to step back when needed. Clients require therapists who can be open, respectfully curious and culturally and racially aware, and who have the capacity to provide a space where the person can feel safe enough to be their whole self.

Anti-racist practice

Learning from professional and personal narratives

To combat racism, racial trauma and the disproportionate impact on therapists and clients of colour, several approaches can be adopted by mental health professionals in different settings and contexts.

My journal entries demonstrate that there is a tangible risk that therapists of colour face in relation to race-related stress and trauma. Earlier, I raised the importance of shared responsibility in engaging with anti-racism as a route to support both clients and therapists of colour in the field of therapy.

Decolonising therapy

One of the ways in which the areas identified above can be attended to is through engaging in a consistent process of decolonising therapy and therapeutic spaces. This means taking up actions, approaches and ideas that unlearn/relearn/learn to transform colonial impacts in the therapeutic realm. This lends itself to liberatory practice in which the lenses that can shape practice, the development of services and continued professional development are widened. This can make our therapeutic spaces and delivery more accessible and better able to meet the needs of our clients. Mullan (n.d.) captures this process in her reflections about decolonising therapy:

> To decolonize therapy is to reconnect to the humanisation of therapy and our practices, to reclaim spaces, to include systems and oppression into our practice and analysis and to rehumanize therapists, as well as to centre the person and their cultural and political identities back into the work.

It behoves all therapists, at the very least, to begin from this position to provide support that is more attuned to understanding the experiences of individuals of colour. A limited approach is misaligned with what is supposed to be at the core of our ethical values as therapists: to do no harm, treat all individuals with dignity and respect, and situate diversity within practice (BPS, 2021; BACP, 2018). There are ways to approach this, including developing awareness of the impact of historical trauma on therapists of colour in their work and identity as practitioners by reading relevant material in this area, researching stories and engaging with film, music and so on, as other sources of knowledge (Charura & Lago, 2021). Such trauma may manifest as fear and anxiety, disconnection from feelings, and identity threat, as described in the presented journal excerpts. This awareness might better help professional peers and colleagues to understand how an individual of colour might exist in the world, how they might cope, how they might see themselves, and how they might relate to their environments and to other people in their immediate and wider contexts. My own experience of this is captured in my descriptions about my navigation of predominantly white spaces.

I recall my own early training as a counselling psychologist where my learning was principally informed by a Eurocentric lens, with very limited space given to cross-cultural issues or the adoption of an intersectional lens. Consideration of where we draw our learning from and expanding the sources of our practice to account for different voices and perspectives are also crucial. This means moving beyond traditional modes of learning and expanding engagement with voices from across the spectrum. Knowledge and resources are available in the stories of those with lived experiences, through different media, beyond journal articles and books.

Additionally, sensitive engagement in necessary dialogues about race and intersectionality can also support learning. As in my journal excerpt, it is important to consider how we conduct these dialogues, particularly in less diverse teams and settings. Openness, respect and permission to get things wrong could be some of the starting points for these conversations. Interrogating our own attitudes, defences and blind spots can also feature in this process. Adoption of a culturally sensitive and holistic approach (Kareem & Littlewood, 1999) is also necessary to engage with the impact of the weathering – the physiological effect of chronic racial stress, disparities and discrimination (Geronimus, 1992). In addition to this, it is essential that therapists and clients are seen as their whole selves in their contexts. This means dropping assumptions, checking biases and adopting a non-pathologising approach so that they are not only seen through a single lens.

Beyond the therapeutic space

Attending to and addressing racial trauma is not just located within the therapeutic space. As explored in the beginning of this chapter, race and racial issues exist at a structural and institutional level and have far-reaching impact on people of colour. They include inequality in mental health systems and inappropriate, unattuned therapeutic engagement. Bhui and colleagues (2018) expand on this further in their report on the effect of racism on mental health:

> For those who require treatment, the ability to access appropriate therapy at a time they need it is potentially limited if services are seen as unwelcoming or negative, and are stigmatising; if people's personal experience and fears of racism are not taken seriously or denied – not least if they have experienced racism – the fear may be of not being believed, or of having to make accommodations and tolerate indignities, or their experiences may be more indirectly or subtly denied. The experience of not being heard, or being mistrusted, or being treated with hostility, are commonly expressed by services users, and reveal implicit power dynamics that act as a context for inequalities. (p.9)

Alongside individual and community approaches, changes in the structural and institutional sphere are necessary for other shifts to take root (Olusoga, 2022). Specifically, in regard to mental health and racial trauma, it is important that services are both equitable and accessible in their delivery and approach, offer culturally relevant psychotherapy, and consciously create teams with diverse perspectives by actively recruiting individuals with differing backgrounds and intersectional identities. Such an approach eases the disproportionate responsibility that is often placed on the shoulders of therapists of colour, and indeed on clients, to both navigate and address racial issues (Rathod et al., 2020).

Within and external to institutional settings, addressing and mitigating racial disparities in mental health and the ongoing impact of racial trauma will have wider impact when this responsibility is shared. A persistent impact of racial trauma is the re-exposure that individuals and therapists of colour must endure regarding race-based stressed and trauma (both direct and indirect), and if an expectation is placed on them to address, solve, understand, minimise or 'cope' with racial issues, this perpetuates harm and the systems of oppression and privilege (Jenkins, 2016).

Conclusion

Recently, a colleague and I examined the ways in which discussions and reflections regarding race and racism have expanded, with much-needed dialogue and increased awareness about the grief, trauma and history impacting individuals of colour. We were also struck by how, in some spaces, exploration and actions have diminished, even as racism continues to adversely impact communities and individuals. Meanwhile, the impact of racial trauma continues. There is no quick and easy fix.

Our continued engagement with the issues, exploring them from different perspectives, taking a trauma-informed approach, hearing and recording the different experiences and challenging ourselves to continue learning, actioning and instituting changes are just some of the ways in which we continue to collectively dismantle oppressive systems and structures. At the very least, it will contribute to minimising the re-exposure and reliving that perpetuates racial trauma and stress.

References

Andrews, K. (2021). Racism is the public health crisis. *The Lancet, 397*(10282), 1342–1343.

BACP. (2018). Ethical framework for the counselling professions. BACP.

Bhui, K., Halvorsrud, K. & Nazroo, J. (2018). Making a difference: Ethnic inequality and severe mental illness. *British Journal of Psychiatry, 213*(4), 574–578.

British Psychological Society (BPS). (2021). Code of ethics and conduct. BPS.

Bryant-Davis, T. & Ocampo, C. (2006). A therapeutic approach to the treatment of racist-incident-based trauma. *Journal of Emotional Abuse, 6*(4), 1–22.

Carter, R.T. (2007). Racism and psychological and emotional injury: Recognizing and assessing race-based traumatic stress. *The Counseling Psychologist, 35*(1), 13–105.

Charura, D. & Lago, C. (2021). *Black identities + white therapies: Race, respect + diversity*. PCCS Books.

Comas-Díaz, L. (2016). Racial trauma recovery: A race-informed therapeutic approach to racial wounds. In A.N. Alvarez, C.T.H. Liang, & H.A. Neville (Eds.), *The cost of racism for people of color: Contextualizing experiences of discrimination* (pp.249–272). American Psychological Association.

Comas-Díaz, L., Hall, G.N. & Neville, H.A. (2019). Racial trauma: Theory, research, and healing: Introduction to the special issue. *American Psychologist, 74*(1), 1–5.

Crenshaw, K.W. (2014). The structural and political dimensions of intersectional oppression. In P.R. Grzanka (Ed.), *Intersectionality: A foundations and frontiers reader* (pp.17–22). Westview Press.

Crowell, C., Mosley, D., Falconer, J., Faloughi, R., Singh, A., Stevens-Watkins, D. & Cokley, K. (2017). Black lives matter: A call to action for counseling psychology leaders. *Counseling Psychology, 45*(6), 873–901.

Degruy-Leary, J. (2017). *Post-traumatic slave syndrome: America's legacy of enduring injury*. Joy DeGruy Publications Inc.

Devakumar, D., Shannon, G., Bhopal, S.S. & Abubakar, I. (2020). Racism and discrimination in COVID-19 responses. *The Lancet, 395*(10231), 1194.

Dunbar, E. (2001). Counseling practices to ameliorate the effects of discrimination and hate events: Toward a systematic approach to assessment and intervention. *The Counseling Psychologist, 29*(2), 281–310.

Fenton, K., Pawson, E. & de Souza-Thomas, L. (2020). *Beyond the data: Understanding the impact of COVID-19 on BAME communities*. Public Health England.

Geronimus, A.T. (1992). The weathering hypothesis and the health of African-American women and infants: evidence and speculations. *Ethnicity & Disease, 2*(3), 207–221.

Giordano, A.L., Gorritz, F.B., Kilpatrick, E.P., Scoffone, C.M., & Lundeen, L.A. (2021). Examining secondary trauma as a result of clients' reports of discrimination. *International Journal for the Advancement of Counselling, 43*(1), 19–30.

Jenkins, J. (2016). #Blacklivesmatter in psychotherapy. *Psychotherapy Bulletin, 51*(3), 49–52.

Kareem, J. & Littlewood, R. (Eds.). (1999). *Intercultural therapy: Themes, interpretations and practice.* Blackwell Publishing.

Lipscomb, A.E. & Ashley, W. (2020). Surviving being Black and a clinician during a dual pandemic: Personal and professional challenges in a disease and racial crisis. *Smith College Studies in Social Work, 90*(4), 221–236.

Miu, A.S., & Moore, J.R. (2021). Behind the masks: Experiences of mental health practitioners of color during the COVID-19 pandemic. *Academic Psychiatry, 45*(5), 539–544.

Morrison, T. (1975, May 30). A humanist view. In Portland State University; Morrison, T., St. John, P., Callahan, J., Callahan, S. & Baker, L. *Black Studies Center public dialogue, part 2.* [Audio recording.] Special collections: Oregon public speakers. http://archives.pdx.edu/ds/psu/11309

Mullan, J. (n.d.). *What is decolonising therapy?* [Blog.] https://www.decolonizingtherapy.com/what-is-dt

Odafe, M.O., Salami, T.K. & Walker, R.L. (2017). Race-related stress and hopelessness in community-based African American adults: Moderating role of social support. *Cultural Diversity and Ethnic Minority Psychology, 23*(4), 561–569.

Olusoga, D. (2022, February 20). Much as we love the NHS, we can no longer ignore the ethnic inequalities that beset it. *The Observer.* www.theguardian.com/commentisfree/2022/feb/20/much-as-we-love-nhs-no-longer-ignore-racial-inequalities-that-beset-it

Paradies, Y., Ben, J., Denson, N., Elias, A., Priest, N., Pieterse, A., Gupta, A., Kelaher, M. & Gee, G. (2015). Racism as a determinant of health: A systematic review and meta-analysis. *PloS One, 10*(9), e0138511.

Race Equality Foundation. (2020). *Black and minority ethnic voluntary sector organisation are coping and adapting to the coronavirus pandemic for now, but their future is unsure.* [Blog.] https://raceequalityfoundation.org.uk/health-care/black-and-minority-ethnic-voluntary-sector-organisation-are-coping-and-adapting-to-the-coronavirus-pandemic-for-now-but-their-future-is-unsure/

Raghavan, R. & Jones-Nielsen, J.D. (2021). *Mental health and wellbeing briefing paper.* Race Equality Foundation.

Rathod, S., Persaud, A., Naeem, F., Pinninti, N., Tribe, R., Eylem, O. & Irfan, M. (2020). Culturally adapted interventions in mental health: Global position statement. *World Cultural Psychiatry Research Review, 14*(1–2), 21–29.

Shell, E.M., Teodorescu, D. & Williams, L.D. (2021). Investigating race-related stress, burnout, and secondary traumatic stress for Black mental health therapists. *Journal of Black Psychology, 47*(8), 669–694.

Smith, J.A. (2007). Hermeneutics, human sciences and health: Linking theory and practice. *International Journal of Qualitative Studies on Health and Well Being, 2,* 3–11.

Stallings, E. (2020, July 16). *How are black therapists doing right now?* [Blog.] Medium. https://elemental.medium.com/how-are-black-therapists-doing-right-now-c834287edbb6

Thames, A.D., Irwin, M.R., Breen, E.C. & Cole, S.W. (2019). Experienced discrimination and racial differences in leukocyte gene expression. *Psychoneuroendocrinology, 106,* 277–283.

4. Call me by my name

Anita Gaspar

If we are going to create spaces that are more inclusive, respectful and collaborative, we must understand and address these interactions. (Jana & Baran, 2020, p.1)

Comparing myself to the legend that is Samuel L. Jackson is not something that I do with any frequency, but I can relate to something that happened to him when he was being interviewed live on American television in 2014. The White interviewer asks him what the response has been to an advertisement he was in that had aired during the recent Superbowl. Jackson initially looks confused but then quickly realises that the interviewer is referring to a commercial featuring fellow black actor Laurence Fishburne.[1] The interviewer, to his credit, admits his mistake and says it is his fault; he also laughs and jokes as Jackson, who is visibly affected, says, 'We might be all black and famous but we all don't look alike.' 'You're the entertainment reporter and you don't know the difference between me and Laurence Fishburne?' he scolds.

It seems that being an A-list celebrity at the top of the box office ladder does not protect you from being mistaken for another person of a similar skin colour and/or ethnicity.

This is one of two chapters in this book about names. Neelam Zahid's opening chapter movingly explains the importance of names and the richness of their meaning in her South Asian culture (Zahid, 2023). There seems to be a range of ways in which the names of those who are regarded as 'different' or 'diverse' can become a source of difficulty for those who appear to sit comfortably in the mainstream (although it is important to note that the mainstream is

---

1. www.bbc.co.uk/news/entertainment-arts-26134784

maintained by these microaggressions). This difficulty manifests in various ways, including mispronunciation, forgetfulness (sometimes repeated), a peculiar emphasis on the name as it is said, as if the speaker is trying hard to get it right, and what I have chosen to write about here: misidentification.

Misidentification as a phenomenon

Alleyne writes: 'What ceases to be a coincidence must be a phenomenon' (Alleyne, 2022, p.115), and a phenomenon needs a name. The nature of microaggressions means that they occur in a casual, offhand way, and may be differentiated from outright acts of racism, although this by no means signifies that their impact is minimal. Perhaps it is for this reason that there is a tendency among those on the receiving end to brush them off and not give them much time or attention. There is also the fact that it may not feel possible or safe to do so in the moment. But when we reframe something that keeps happening to us and see that thing as a phenomenon, we can situate it within a wider context, and it becomes much more than an annoying thing that keeps happening to us. It also means that we can identify it more quickly and recognise it for what it is when it occurs again, and this may give us different options as to how we respond in the future.

The idea to write about the phenomenon of misidentification arose from the fact that it has happened to me so often in the world of psychotherapy. I am also aware from conversations with colleagues of colour (some of whom I have, of course, been mistaken for) that I am not alone in experiencing this and that it can be a source of distress. Misidentification has shown up in different ways: for example, directly being called by the name of another woman of colour; being asked questions or receiving emails that have nothing to do with me and subsequently clarifying with a peer or colleague that they were intended for her, and, astonishingly, being called by the name of another woman of colour on Zoom calls — astonishing because my name was clearly readable on the screen.

I also see it happening frequently in the media and, as already mentioned, fame and a public profile do not make a difference. Even occupying the second highest office of state in the country (and being the subject of frequent political commentary and debate at the time) did not ensure that Kwasi Kwarteng's photograph, rather than that of another black man, Bernard Mensah, President of International for Bank of America, was published in an article about him in a national tabloid.[2] When American Muslim journalist and activist Noor Tagouri spotted the issue of *Vogue* that featured her on a news stand, she asked her companion to film this momentous event. You can watch the footage[3] and

---

2. www.bbc.co.uk/news/uk-63100715
3. www.youtube.com/watch?v=viTq1ag44lk

see her palpable excitement as she looks at the full-page photograph of herself turning to dismay/anger as she believes her name has been spelt incorrectly, before the realisation sets in that her image has been captioned with the name of Pakistani actress Noor Bukhari. When comedian and actor Lenny Henry was knighted, ITV used footage of the black chef Ainsley Harriott to illustrate their news feature about the event.[4] It is ironic that, in the last two examples, misidentification occurred during what were moments of recognition for the individuals concerned.

A note on microaggressions

I use the term 'microaggression' as defined by Sue and colleagues (2007, p.273):

> Brief and commonplace daily verbal, behavioral, or environmental indignities, whether intentional or unintentional, that communicate hostile, derogatory, or negative racial slights and insults toward people of color.

Microaggression, with its suggestion of smallness or 'microscopic', may also contribute to the fact that these slights and invalidations are not taken seriously; as Turner says: 'I don't really like the word "microaggressions" because I think it minimises the experience, and these events are really very insidious' (quoted in Jackson, 2021, p.25). Others have also written about how the term is not fit for purpose (Kendi, 2019; Tulshyan, 2022), and Jana and Baran (2020) replace it with 'subtle acts of exclusion'.

Perhaps what is most important to remember if there is any doubt about the enormity of microaggressions is that they are a form of racism, and racism causes trauma. And it is microaggressions that are experienced on a daily basis by many people of colour, far more than overt acts of racism, although the latter do, devastatingly, happen all too often. Turner describes microaggressions as 'a form of psychological death' (2021, p.81), and Sue believes that 'this contemporary form of racism is many times over more problematic, damaging, and injurious to persons of color than overt racist acts', citing research by Pierce that 'the cumulative effects of racial microaggressions may theoretically result in "diminished mortality, augmented morbidity and flattened confidence"' (Sue, 2003, p.48).

An example of misidentification

There was one instance of misidentification that affected me profoundly and

---

4. www.theguardian.com/media/2015/dec/04/itv-ainsley-harriott-lenny-henry-knighthood

made me aware, in a way that I had not been previously, of the impact and implications of the phenomenon. In order to preserve confidentiality, I have changed many identifying details in my description of this event, including the names of the other people involved and the circumstances in which the exchange occurred. However, my description of the nature of the interaction and my response is authentic.

A year or two after I qualified as a counsellor, I attended an in-person continuing professional development (CPD) event. It was a day-long conference with different workshops and seminars and a number of people were there whom I had come across through my training and work. In between sessions, I was delighted to bump into Alex, a white peer from a counselling skills course we had undertaken some years previously and with whom I had felt a connection. We agreed to catch up over lunch.

In the years since we first met there had been big changes in Alex's life, resulting from a tragic event. They told me about this and the impact on them in an open, emotional and moving way. I felt very involved in the conversation and understood implicitly that they would not have shared such a personal story in such detail without also feeling a level of trust and closeness. From a therapeutic perspective, I understand this to have been a meeting at relational depth (Mearns & Cooper, 2005) and felt very good about myself in the moment. I remembered how I had felt that Alex and I might have become friends before losing touch, and that this chance meeting was happily providing the opportunity for us to reconnect.

About 20 minutes before the end of the lunch break, Alex's recounting came to a natural end. There was a pause as they looked at me, then said, 'So what's been happening in the world of Leila?' and I realised that they had used the name of another woman of colour from the counselling skills course. This interrupted my relaxed state and previous feeling of attunement with them. The shift was a shock and had a physical impact on me. I looked at Alex in confusion and felt a sensation in my eyes that I can best describe as 'dry tearfulness', which I now understand as an impulse to cry while simultaneously feeling that I had to protect myself from crying. I frowned and said, stuttering, 'I – I'm Anita.' Alex looked down and then at me and said, 'Yeah, yeah, I know, so how are you?' I felt the heat of blood rushing to my face and heard my voice change as my throat became dry. I didn't know what to say but started to talk in a superficial way about my private practice. I found myself faltering as I became aware in that moment that I genuinely did not know if Alex knew who I was and whether they had simply mistaken my name or my entire identity. As the conversation continued at a banal level, nothing that they subsequently said enabled me to confirm either way and I found it too excruciating to ask and clarify. After about five minutes, Alex said they had spotted someone they needed to talk to and moved away. I remained where I was, trying to take in what had happened and compose myself before joining another workshop.

Analysis

As I said, the reason that I have chosen this example of being misidentified is because it highlights the pain and actuality of not being correctly identified perhaps more than any other that I have experienced. It was what preceded it – namely the feeling of connectedness– that meant that it had a more jarring effect than misidentification usually does. As a consequence, this has enabled me to understand the phenomenon at a more profound level. But Alex's reaction, in my experience of misidentification, *is* typical and falls within a familiar range. Other classic responses include silence, a change of subject, an indignant 'Yes, I know', or a difficult-to-read facial expression. On one occasion at work, a white colleague entered the room and, standing at the door, asked me a question that I immediately understood was intended for a colleague of colour, rather than me. I said, 'I think you must have me mixed up with someone else,' and they simply left the room. It is important to understand that these responses, which we may understand as defences such as denial or disavowal, are part of the phenomenon and are notable in their lack of attention to what has just occurred.

Homogenisation

It is possible that, if Alex *had* attended to the mistake, it would have exposed the fact that they did not know which female of colour from the counselling skills course I was, and this, in turn, may have revealed the underlying ugly truth that they had not been able to see Leila and me as separate people: we were simply two interchangeable females of colour. The examples of famous people are important to remember here, because this supports the idea that there is a barrier to seeing people of colour as individuals, even when those individuals are household names on the receiving end of such globally recognised signifiers of excellence and achievement as Oscars and knighthoods. This barrier results in seeing people of a similar ethnicity as a homogeneous group. Alleyne (2022) writes:

> Homogenization is the opposite of the interconnected nature of intersectionality, and leads to marginalization – reacting against this requires an effort that involves explaining, justifying and defending one's entitlement to a full existence. (p.178)

Who would want to do this while just going about their daily life? When understood in this way, brushing off and minimising microaggressions (when you are on the receiving end) makes a lot of sense.

When I first started to ponder this as a phenomenon a few years ago, it did not have a name. I searched 'racial misidentification' and 'ethnic misidentification' online and shuddered as I read the results. They related to the identification of bodies in the context of forensic examination: that is, when a body has been found in suspicious circumstances and a pathologist is trying to identify them and establish their ethnicity and other vital information. I shut my laptop and decided that this could not possibly be used as a way of describing this experience that I had had so often. Shuddering is an involuntary shaking response to disgust or unpleasant feelings, and it makes sense when I think about it in the light of the experience with Alex. I have to reluctantly admit that there is a deeply unpleasant parallel – namely, being seen simply as a female body of colour, lifeless, with no identifying features other than the colour of my skin. This speaks to the sense, when we are on the receiving end of misidentification, that our identity and uniqueness are obliterated.

A lack of relationality

Zahid has written here about the 'puzzle of racism' (2023, p.13), which means that, as people of colour, we may have to try to make sense of what is happening to us without input from the white other, or at least without what could be regarded as constructive relational input.

Alex's 'Yeah, yeah, so how are you?' had the impact of making it difficult for me to talk coherently and caused confusing physical sensations: wanting to cry but not feeling safe to do so, and blood rushing to my face, which I interpret as part of a fight or flight response (van der Kolk, 2014), when a previously relaxing and secure environment became something completely different. The lack of any visible or deliberate attention to what had happened on Alex's part, and their seemingly normal and conversational question that immediately followed, contrasted with my reaction and left me doubting what had occurred. Even while writing this chapter, I have at times wondered if I am blowing this incident and subject out of proportion, but 'Knowing *what* we feel is the first step to knowing *why* we feel that way' (van der Kolk, 2014, p.95, original italics): if we pay attention to our physical sensations and responses, we can understand our experiential reality, even if the other denies it. The phenomenon of gaslighting has entered the public lexicon in recent years, specifically in relation to coercive control, and it often plays a part in microaggressions:

Gaslighting describes the act of manipulating others to doubt themselves or question their own sanity; people confronted for committing microaggressions deny the existence of their biases, often convincing the targets of microaggressions to question their own perceptions. (Johnson et al., 2021)

By not acknowledging their mistake when it was pointed out to them ('I'm Anita'), and responding 'Yeah, yeah', Alex implied that they knew my name, leading me to question my lived experience.

It is worth repeating – responses that do not attend to the mistake or hurt, or simply do not acknowledge what has happened in any way, are part of the phenomenon and suggest that there are feelings in the white other that shut down what I would regard as a reasonable response. In the exchange with Alex, a reasonable response in the moment might have been, 'I am so sorry, I realise I have forgotten your name,' or 'I feel really embarrassed to ask but can you remind me of your name?' and their tone and non-verbal communication would have formed part of the response.

Non-verbal communication might have taken the form of closing their eyes and shaking their head; it might have involved blushing or a kind of grimace. It might have involved both hands or one hand placed on the forehead or face, a gesture known as a facepalm. The facepalm has a page on Wikipedia (it also has its own emoji) on which it is stated:

> The gesture is found in many cultures as a display of frustration, disappointment, exasperation, embarrassment, horror, shock, surprise, exhaustion, sarcasm, shame, or incredulous disbelief.

It is the embarrassment and shame that I am interested in here, as these are emotions known for being difficult to express or acknowledge. Shame is 'a physiological, all-encompassing body experience' (Ellis, 2021, p.79) that can give rise to excruciating sensations. It makes sense that anyone would try to avoid feeling this way and understandable why bypassing it is preferable. I believe it is this omission that creates a hiatus in the relational field and means that a hurt is not attended to with a simple apology in the moment. Ellis writes: 'Shame has destructive implications for interpersonal relationships' (2021, p.77), and this helps me understand what happened with Alex, where a previously warm and attuned connection was effectively destroyed. Alleyne further helps me understand the rupture when she writes that it is:

> the energy that is utilized in keeping the shame covers on, and the investment built up in holding on to the shallowness of pride, that

prevent humility and grace from being let in to repair and heal. (2022, p.100)

Self-care and tools for anti-oppressive practice

I have written this from my lived experience as a woman of colour, but whoever you are, whatever your ethnicity and skin colour, there will be feelings that arise as you read this chapter. Perhaps the most important point to take is that misidentification is a microaggression, and that microaggressions cause harm and give rise to feelings that need to be acknowledged and understood, on both sides. What follows may aid the process of understanding, and it is important to note that this will be different, depending on which side of the dynamic you sit. A space that will enable you to engage honestly needs to feel safe and facilitative, and this may mean, at least initially, a racial affinity group.[5] In line with this, I have addressed some of what follows to those on the receiving end of misidentification and other microaggressions, and some to those who perpetrate them.

The loss of identity

I have spent many hours exploring the phenomenon of misidentification on the internet and see how the Jackson–Fishburne mix-up has become something of a joke, with both actors talking about it on chat shows, eliciting laughs and, in the case of Jackson, even wearing a t-shirt stating: I'M NOT LAURENCE FISHBURNE. This does not change the fact that, when I watch the interview clip, I see his expression and tone change and detect hurt and anger in them; I see how he does not collude with the laughter of the interviewer or let him move away from his mistake, and I feel moved by the honesty and what I understand as the risk involved in that. Likewise, the clip featuring Tagouri is a useful example to focus on because we see her reaction in real time, as she goes through a process of what I understand (and can relate to) as disbelief, shock and anger as she realises that she has not been correctly identified. It is surely not a coincidence that these are all emotional states commonly associated with grief (Bates, 2021), and I believe that there is a significant loss that is experienced when we are misidentified: the loss of our identity and unique selves.

In the process of researching for and writing this chapter, I have been struck by how often death is mentioned in relation to microaggressions (see 'A note on microaggressions' and 'Homogenisation' above). Alleyne writes of microaggressions that, 'They are largely experienced as hostile, marginalizing

---

5. Racial affinity groups provide separate spaces for people who share a racial identity.

and erasing' (2022, p.260), and Ellis states: 'There is a profound sense of loss experienced when people of colour become fully aware of how race has influenced their lives' (2021, p.232). Metaphorical death as a one-off event is one thing but 'the death by 10,000 cuts' of which Turner writes (2021, p.81), and which was coined by Sue (Sue & Sue, 1999), speaks to the everyday nature of microaggressions that, in certain environments, may be experienced as a never-ending assault on the self.

This means that, for people of colour, self-care needs to be an ongoing practice, and there will be an element of tending to grief in this. The nature of microaggressions means that there is rarely an acknowledgement of the harm they cause and, as already mentioned, we ourselves may not be in a position to draw attention to them. Our physical sensations and responses are a source of information that can help us understand how we feel, and these need to be processed with a safe and compassionate other. This could be a therapist, peer or friend, and finding a community where experiences can be shared and a sense of connectedness felt is incredibly healing. And, just as our bodily responses tell us what does not feel safe, they also help us understand what regulates and soothes us. Often this comes in the form of art, nature and movement, but it may not be obvious and so it is important to identify – by, for example, observing when you are able to breathe deeply or the tension in your muscles relaxes.

Part of self-care is also knowing when we are carrying trauma that needs attention in a safe and contained space, with the help of a trained professional who can help us work within our window of tolerance (Siegel, 1999). This involves feeling safe enough to explore the feelings and sensations that are part of the trauma response, but within a 'window' where we are not so activated that we become retraumatised (Ellis, 2021).

Engaging with whiteness

DiAngelo writes:

> The simplistic idea that racism is limited to individual intentional acts committed by unkind people is at the root of virtually all white defensiveness on this topic. (2018, p.73)

As long as you, as a white person, believe that racism is something that is an act committed only by bad people, you will not be able to tend to the hurt that you cause. Here too there may be a sense of loss as you let go of a long-held notion that you do not associate yourself with racism, but if you do not let go, your defensiveness will continue to cause harm to people of colour.

Menakem (2017) makes the distinction between clean pain and dirty pain: 'Avoidance, blame, and denial are paved with dirty pain' (p.166). I recognise all of these in the responses to misidentification that I have experienced. He also writes:

> It often means facing what you don't want to face – what you have been reflexively avoiding or fleeing. By walking into that pain, experiencing it fully, and moving through it, you metabolize it and put an end to it. In the process, you also grow, create more room in your nervous system for flow and coherence, and build your capacity for further growth. (p.165)

Once again, it is attention to bodily sensations that send a message that needs to be listened to. This might be a 'facepalm moment' or a forceful desire to flee. Whatever it is, recognising how defences manifest in your body will help you identify that a hurt has been caused. It is important to note that these can be extremely challenging feelings to tolerate (hence the impulse to avoid them), and they will most likely need to be processed in a safe and contained space where you can explore your relationship to your whiteness. But, in the moment, an apology can at least provide an acknowledgement of what has just happened and, importantly, prevent confusion for the person of colour.

Some questions and areas that may facilitate the process of exploration are:

- Are you aware of an instance in which you called a person of an ethnic minority by the name of another? Really engage with this memory and try to recall how you felt and what you did in the moment. Try to identify the feelings and what they mean to you. Ponder what you may have been avoiding through the way that you responded in the moment.

- What relationships have you had with people of ethnic minority in the past? How might this relate to your misidentifying them in the present?

- Is there a difference between what you do when you make a mistake normally and what you do when you misidentify someone? What do you make of any discrepancy?

- Mistakes and slips happen; by understanding these as microaggressions, you are acknowledging the harm they cause. Rather than trying to eliminate these altogether, which you are unlikely to achieve if you have not engaged with race at a meaningful level, focus on how you can recognise and tend to mistakes when they occur. Nothing will change if they are minimised or disregarded, and the cycle will continue.

Engaging in this kind of enquiry is what is known as 'doing the work' and it is an ongoing endeavour – ongoing because, as DiAngelo (2021, p.173) writes: 'No one arrives at a racism-free state.'

Resource yourself

Throughout this chapter, I have made reference to authors who have written extensively on the subject of race and racism. Turning to this source material will provide you with a vast richness of words of wisdom and insights into the trauma of racism. These words are a generous gift, born out of the pain that writing on this subject necessitates. But if books and reading are not how you inform yourself, find the medium that works for you and seek what you need in the way that you would if you wanted to learn about anything. Type a phrase into a search engine, follow people on social media who are speaking intelligently about race, ask your colleagues and peers what has helped them, what podcasts they are listening to or documentaries they have seen. You will be able to find what you need without asking the people of colour around you; remember that their experience is very different from yours.

Healing experiences

My psychotherapy training involved attending an experiential group on a weekly basis. During one of these sessions,[6] an incidence of misidentification occurred when a white peer used my name as they addressed another student of colour in the group. I took the risk of bringing this to their attention and they apologised and thanked me for letting them know. As the hurt was acknowledged and addressed through their apology, the focus shifted from me, and I was able to relax in my body. The white peer spoke about their experience and the pain that they were experiencing in the realisation of the misidentification and I spoke about mine, but without obligation. I was met with compassion from the group and my peer acknowledged the value to them in being able to attend to a rupture.

Sue writes in relation to racism that the greatest challenge society and the mental health professions face is 'making the "invisible" visible'. That can only be accomplished when people are willing to openly and honestly engage in a dialogue about race and racism' (2004) Writing this chapter has helped me understand how what seems invisible is actually felt at a profound level on both sides, because we are relational beings. This knowledge has validated and clarified the feelings I have experienced so many times in these exchanges.

---

6. I have received permission from the individuals concerned to represent this incident as it occurred and to disclose the information given.

It has highlighted the deep need for engagement and attention and made me aware of what may shut down the possibility of these. Ellis says:

> It needs to also again be emphasised that we cannot really hope to do this work by ourselves. We need to join with others of like mind and, when we do so, much is possible. (2021, p.268)

I have experienced this, in therapeutic spaces with peers and colleagues of colour, and I also experienced it in the experiential group with my white peer. I imagine and do not underestimate the work my peer has done (and continues to do) in understanding their relationship to Whiteness and race and, more than 10 years later, I consider them a dear colleague and friend, someone in whose company I feel safe and comfortable when discussing difference and race.

References

Alleyne, A. (2022). *The burden of heritage*. Karnac Books.

Bates, S. (2021). *Languages of loss*. Yellow Kite.

DiAngelo, R. (2018). *White fragility: Why it's so hard for white people to talk about racism*. Penguin.

DiAngelo, R. (2021). *Nice racism: How progressive white people perpetuate racial harm*. Penguin.

Ellis, E. (2021). *The race conversation*. Confer Books.

Jackson, C. (2021). The big interview: Dwight Turner. *Therapy Today, 32*(4), 24–29.

Jana, T. & Baran, M. (2020). *Subtle acts of exclusion: How to understand, identity and stop microaggressions*. Berrett-Koehler Publishers, Inc.

Johnson, V. E., Nadal K.L., Sissoko, D.R.G. & King, R. (2021). 'It's not in your head': Gaslighting, 'splaining, victim blaming, and other harmful reactions to microaggressions. *Perspectives on Psychological Science, 16*(5), https://doi.org/10.1177/17456916211011963

Kendi, I.X. (2019.) *How to be an antiracist*. Bodley Head.

Mearns, D. & Cooper, M. (2005). *Working at relational depth in counselling and psychotherapy*. Sage.

Menakem, R. (2017). *My grandmother's hand: Racialized trauma and the pathway to mending our hearts and bodies*. Central Recovery Press.

Siegel, D.J. (1999). *The developing mind: Toward a neurobiology of interpersonal experience*. Guilford Press.

Sue, D.W. (2003). *Overcoming our racism: The journey to liberation.* Jossey-Bass.

Sue, D. W. (2004). Whiteness and ethnocentric monoculturalism: Making the 'invisible' visible. *American Psychologist, 59*(8), 759–769.

Sue, D.W. & Sue, D. (1999). *Counseling the culturally different: Theory and practice* (3rd ed.). John Wiley & Sons. Tulshyan, R. (2022). *Inclusion on purpose: An intersectional approach to creating a culture of belonging at work.* MIT Press. Sue, D.W., Capodilupo, G.C., Torino, G.C., Bucceri, J.M., Holder, A.M.B., Nadal, K.L. & Esquilin, M. (2007). Racial microaggressions in everyday life: Implications for clinical practice. *American Psychologist, 62*(4), 271–286.

Turner, D. (2021). *Intersections of privilege and otherness in counselling and psychotherapy: Mockingbird.* Routledge.

Van der Kolk, B. (2014). *The body keeps the score.* Penguin.

Zahid, N. (2023). What's in a name? Why names matter for people of colour. In N. Zahid & R. Cooke (Eds.). *Therapists challenging racism and oppression: The unheard voices* (pp.11–29). PCCS Books.

5. A need for deep learning – not training

Joanna Traynor

I grew up in the 1960s and 1970s on a council estate in north-west England. I was the only Black kid for miles around. When I was nine years old, I successfully argued the case that the Middle Eastern mother of Jesus was probably not blonde and that I should therefore play the part of Mary in the school nativity play. Not one boy would volunteer to play Joseph alongside me, so it was a lone-parent Black Mary who challenged the orthodoxy that Christmas, and I did well. I had everyone in stitches. Not long after I discovered that, like Jesus, I too had been born out of wedlock, but of course my mother could not claim to be a virgin to get herself out of that one. She put me in a home. I spent the rest of my childhood in care, moving between children's homes and foster families.

Beginnings

My mother abandoned me to a Catholic children's rescue society run by a man everyone called 'the Canon'.[1] He believed education to be the gateway out of poverty and crime, as well as the cure for low aspirations. He knew I was a clever kid – when I bothered to apply myself – but my schoolteachers didn't think I was the right kind of clever to warrant consideration for a scholarship to a well-respected private convent school. My schoolteachers didn't know that being called names like *nig-nog, wog* and *sambo* every day was hurtful – or they didn't care. My response to these daily humiliations was always immediate and usually physical, so I found myself in trouble quite a lot. This probably explains why these same teachers selected 12 girls they believed to have more promise

---

1. I have disguised the identities of all the people mentioned in this chapter and changed significant details. 'The Canon' (now long dead) might have recognised himself and, I hope, been glad to know how he influenced my life.

than me to be put forward for the Catholic scholarship. But they hadn't counted on the Canon, my child rescuer in chief, who campaigned strongly to get me added to that list as girl number 13. Only three girls were successful; I was one of them. Consequently, I avoided having to attend the local comp, which served as a feeder school to the local borstal. Instead of using fists, kicks and headbutts to get by, I would now have to use all my wits to defend myself. That was much harder to do in a school full of rich kids and posh teachers who all believed I would never amount to very much.

My childhood experience of school certainly convinced me that education was not for me, so when I left school and care, the Canon reluctantly dispatched me to a hospital, to live in and train as a nurse. Here patients could and did refuse to be cared for by 'blacks', and some of the staff were openly racist, refusing to allow Black colleagues to even sit in the staff room with them during breaks. I found the work demanding and often demeaning, so reneged on my promise to myself that there'd be no more education. With a couple of poor A levels up my sleeve, I decided to embark on a psychology degree, hoping to discover the point of it all, I suppose – the point of the never-ending cycle of life and death; the painful, often tragic consequences of human ignorance and fate; the humdrum finality of so many people's epic but ultimately unsuccessful battles to stay alive – battles I had been forced to watch play out, day in, day out, up close. Why?

In truth, I didn't learn much. I spent the entire three years of my degree in bed, in love or at parties, surrendering just a few weeks of each academic year to prepare for exams and to turn in essays. One of two Black people in a cohort of 100-plus student psychologists, I learned very little about why I attracted so much negative attention from the adults who passed through my life: the landlords who refused to rent their rooms to me, the lecturers who marked my papers significantly lower than my peers, the shopkeepers who threw change at me, the taxis who drove straight past me, and sometimes directly at me. Studying psychology could not provide a route through to that kind of wisdom. Back then, the psychology academics were still trying to prove they were engaged in bona fide scientific enquiry, and spent all their time and effort generating statistical analysis and evidence to prove anything and everything, rendering the whole subject so dull and unpalatable that I gave up on it. I failed to engage and left the course with an honour's degree, but no wiser than when I'd joined it.

The search for answers

That desire to understand the dissonance of my experience – the shocked feelings that erupted after I'd ticked all the boxes, come up with the goods, delivered exactly to someone else's expectations, only to discover I was still just not good enough – that feeling had been repeated time and again, so I came to suspect, and then to know, that something else was at play – something beyond my control. I'd wanted to understand the relationship dynamic that produces layer upon layer of dissonance: the shopkeeper who won't meet your eyes; the White boyfriend's mother who won't even meet you; the employer's refusal to promote you; the customer's rancour and rudeness; the people who choose to stand rather than have to sit next to you – the friction, the frisson, the judder that erupts in any relationship where racism, unspoken but felt, hovers like a ghost from a past in which I had not been present. Over the years, I've normalised a lot of racism – I find it viscerally shocking when I sit and reflect on just how much.

Education could not enlighten me and my lack of respect for it meant a proverbial herd of wild horses could not have dragged me back to it, ever again. However, my hunger for learning about the human condition went unabated. It was born of the mental ill health I succumbed to, unable to make sense of the racist vibrations I was having to adjust to on becoming a Black female care leaver in a White world. There was no access to therapy back then – only psychiatrists writing up prescriptions on psychiatry wards full of women too depressed to care for their children. I wanted to know more, learn more, find ways to come to terms with my situation, yes; but I also wanted to help others who, through no fault of their own, were unable to get on with their lives and be happy.

I volunteered for the Samaritans and learned a lot, and this was good preparation for working on a Rape Crisis hotline for a couple of years. Here, the value and power of therapeutic intervention revealed itself to me in all its magnificence and reignited the dream I'd nurtured – to become someone who could 'help' people in distress, someone who could deliver hope. But I knew that to be a professional therapist would mean going back to school – again.

My first 'Introduction to Counselling' course blew me away. It was the first and most enlightening, deeply felt educational experience I'd ever had. Carl Rogers rocks. I was given a new, more powerful lens through which to see the world and all the people in it. I was given a way to understand people differently – their experiences and back stories, their limited line of sight, their defence systems, their trials and tribulations. I was given permission to take down the walls of my own defences and to give the guards at the gates to my own feelings one day off a week. My peers – all White – were accepting of me. The White male tutor fielded my questions and challenges with ease, respect and curiosity. I felt like I belonged there – the first time I felt like I belonged anywhere. This 'belonging' feeling is rare – I've only ever experienced it on one occasion since with the same level of surprise, intensity and relief. It was when I stood alone, in Broad Street, in the centre of Lagos, in Nigeria. Huge numbers of Black people pushed and rushed past me, not seeing me, not shying away from me, just moving around me, swarming, humming, carrying themselves on a sea of such colour – accepting me. I felt free there, in public. I belonged.

Welcome to my world

By 2017, I'd been a qualified counsellor in private practice for just over five years. Business wasn't great back then, so to widen my opportunities, and to deepen my own understanding of my practice, I decided to upgrade my qualification by applying for accreditation with my professional association.[2] I saw that I could meet most of the criteria, but there was just this pesky matter of producing some written assignments totalling more than 6,000 words.

I wrote them up on holiday, on a beach in Thailand. I enjoy writing when I can focus on it, with no distractions. Laptop on my lounger, waves crashing at my feet, emerald-green sea as far as the eye could see – I wrote from the heart, with enthusiasm, curiosity and with a critical eye on my own vulnerabilities, blind spots and gaps in my learning. When I'd finished, the sound of those waves crashing onto the shore felt like a round of applause from the Gods. I felt like I'd made it – achieved something of true value for myself. When I got back to England, I sent off my completed application, and then waited. And waited. Six months later, the association informed me that I'd failed my application for accreditation due to not fulfilling one of the 15 criteria. I was told:

> To meet criteria x.x, you will need to explain in the case material the issues of difference and equality between you and your client and how you addressed these during the counselling process.

I was stunned. I was that kid back in school again, with the teacher who didn't see me, or didn't care to. I'd managed everything else fine – I'd logged and evidenced more than 500 hours of supervised therapy in three different placements over three years. I'd logged five years of continued professional development. I'd written three other essays and met the other 14 criteria to that proverbial T. But I'd failed the whole thing because I hadn't explained the difference between me and the client I chose for my case study – a wealthy, educated White woman living in a rural part of the country, where I didn't and would never belong, with a big family and an even bigger reputation. Here is an extract from the assignments that I sent in support of my application:

---

[2]. I won't name it, but it would be impossible to disguise its identity.

As a black woman, I'm acutely aware of the damage caused by discrimination, conscious and unconscious. I work with many privileged clients with huge resources (human and financial), but emotionally, they can suffer just as keenly as the most impoverished. Early in my practice, I felt fear of discrimination by clients towards me, but as my confidence grew, my courage was rewarded – with healing for clients and learnings for me. Certainly, I believe the client-therapist relationship to be an equal one. The clients teach me as much as I help them – if not more so.

I'd worked with this woman in a job as an itinerant counsellor. Like a vet on call, I zipped around the countryside, travelling from one GP practice to another to see their patients. The client was dealing with a bereavement issue – a loss of great significance. This is how I described her in the case study I wrote as part of my accreditation submission:[3]

> Linzi was 47 years old, of English/White heritage, married with 2 daughters and a severely disabled son. Rich and resourceful as she was, she'd been laid quite low by an unusual turn of events... Having trained and worked in areas of high deprivation, this woman reminded me that we're all equal under the cloak of misery and no matter how rich or well-resourced we are, we will still need help if we're suddenly plunged into darkness.

The client had exhausted the number of NHS-funded sessions she was able to have with me, but was still in need of further specialist counselling support. As it happened, back then I also volunteered as a counsellor and supervisor for a specialist trauma-focused bereavement charity. I suggested to the client that she get her GP to refer her to the charity, so she could continue her therapy with me.

I wanted to explain in my written case study how I'd felt some discomfort with this arrangement at the time – after all, she could easily have paid for private therapy – because I wanted to demonstrate how difference and equality were impacting on the client–counsellor relationship. I wrote as follows:

> I think it was only then that I realised what had troubled me about suggesting Linzi be referred to the [charity name]. She would be jumping the queue for a service that was run on donations. And so I asked Linzi to contribute towards the cost of her bereavement therapy to help improve equality of access for all.

---

3. I have of course changed the details here, to protect her identity.

When I appealed to the professional body against the rejection, I was told:

> While your submission describes the actions you took, both the differences between yourself and your client (we cannot assume that you are not rich, for example) and the impact of your actions on the therapeutic relationship are implied rather than stated. Because of this it is not possible to change the decision.

I felt not seen, not heard, not valid. I've learned to live with failure, with being deemed not good enough; I've had a lifetime of that. It wasn't about that. And I value genuine opportunities to learn something new. But I felt this wasn't what was going on here.

In counselling, I thought I'd found a world where I belonged – a profession I could genuinely develop in. But this tick-box diversity agenda threw me – it threw me away and put some distance between me and what I loved and valued as authentic, meaningful and viscerally nurturing. In doing so, the professional body had created a vibration of mistrust that interrupted my flow, destabilised me, and I recognised the feeling immediately – it was racism.

I am of mixed race, half African, half Irish/English. I often feel not Black enough, because the world I grew up in was so White. I had no Black family or friends, nor even any idea where my colour came from until I was in my late 20s. Perhaps the assessor of my application didn't think I was Black enough either?

This was Eric Berne's Gotcha game (originally known as the 'Now I've Got You, You Son of a Bitch' game, which was considered misogynistic) (Berne, 1973). It was being played out in plain sight through this process of accreditation. Maybe it still is. So why play the Gotcha game? And what is the prize for winning it? Berne developed and named transactional analysis (TA) as a more intellectually accessible, financially affordable and readily applicable form of psychotherapy that could give clients more bang for their bucks than the slow, intense and intrusive methods of the School of Psychoanalysis. After years of study, Berne applied to qualify as a psychoanalyst, but he was judged inadequate by the San Francisco Psychoanalytic Institute, and he used this rejection to galvanise his efforts to bring something new to the field of therapy (Steiner, 1974).

In his breathtakingly robust effort to share his TA approach with clinicians, in *What Do You Say After You Say Hello?*, Berne (1974/2018) used a description of the dream of a wartime code-breaker (Berne worked with World War II veterans) to illustrate his views on the value of psychoanalysis. The code-breaker's dream saw him carrying an excruciatingly heavy bag of pebbles along a pebbled beach. As a metaphor for the meticulously detailed work needed to break the code of the Japanese, the code-breaker could only relieve himself of a pebble from his load if he could find a matching one on the beach. Berne used the metaphor to argue that psychoanalysts were setting their clients the same challenge as the one faced by the code-breaker in his dream. The transactional analyst would and should just help the man put his bag down so he could go on his way (Berne, 1974/2018). Berne believed the use of a powerful TA intervention could cure a longstanding psychological issue in just one session, and he urged practitioners of TA to aim to do just that.

The Critical (interchangeably Controlling) Parent ego state, in TA terms, like all ego states, manifests in voice, posture and behaviour. The Critical Parent, when benign, will stop a child running in front of an oncoming bus or report a colleague for stealing. The ego state brings out one's need to protect, to stay within boundaries of contract and to uphold values and rules that serve the community and, closer to home, the family. The Critical/Controlling Parent ego state is not as effective or benign when it is used to enforce an activity or world view that only serves to tranquilise the anxieties of our inner Child, or Child ego state.

The Controlling/Critical Parent is not derived from Freud's superego (Berne, 1961/2021), although the mindset shares some of its functional features. The difference is that 'reality' for Berne's ego states represents the 'real people' we become when we're exhibiting these postures, tones of voice and behaviours.

My professional body had taken a formalised Critical Parent role in the transaction we were engaged in. I received their criticism and judgement in my Child ego state – a regressive mindset (Berne, 1973) governed by stored archaic feelings and routines from the past. The professional body had delivered what was for me a hammer blow; it was blindly critical and aggressively destructive of *all* my efforts because my articulation of difference didn't fit with its worldview. My adapted Child ego state (the mindset that adapts to the Parent by complying or rebelling, whichever option is most likely to get its needs met) had been so heavily bruised by so many previous educational experiences that this further blow felt particularly damaging. It was my own fault, of course. I'd voluntarily invited a Critical Parent into my life, so perhaps I should have been better prepared for their somewhat predictable (in retrospect) transactional reaction to my academic offering.

The professional body in question was unconsciously operating a Gotcha game, with its Controlling/Critical Parent ego state ostensibly 'playing by the rules' but seemingly forgetting the core purpose of its organisational endeavour – to support professionals, its members, in the helping industry, working at the psychological coal face of mental ill health. The game is to be right, to keep on being right, to insist that you are right, and to enjoy the power that comes with being right. All this happens at the expense of the very real need to be mindful of the emotional terrain being excavated when race and power are in the spotlight. In its bid to 'protect' its self-defined standards, the professional body exposed one of its own members to what *'felt like'* a racist attack. Its rejection of both the application and the subsequent appeal did not serve to educate or enlighten; rather, it dismissed and invalidated the complexities of racial discourse on the page and in the therapy room, and what might be going on inside a Black counsellor's head when their 'racism antennae' have been alerted.

If the process of accreditation seeks to determine if a therapist is sensitive to the impact of difference on a client relationship, perhaps the provision of an instrument more focused on the therapist's blind spots rather than their awareness might be more fruitful. In this instance, the professional body must have assumed that all its members were from the dominant White culture because the ask – to explain how my awareness of difference impacts on the client–counsellor relationship – was cognitively loaded; it presupposed I had an anchored sense of safety, and came without a trigger warning, which as a Black therapist, if I was to answer that question with full authenticity, I would undoubtedly need. If the professional body itself had been able to see outside of its rigid framework to recognise that difference impacts on the relationship at the transferential and, most interesting of all, the transpersonal level (Clarkson, 1995), it would also have appreciated and recognised that a description of how such a difference impacts cannot be crystallised into a soundbite to fulfil the criteria of section x.x.

The professional body had taken a Critical Parental role when a Nurturing Parent would have been far more likely to generate richer and more fully embodied evidence of good practice. The Gotcha game is played unconsciously and gives the Parent a sense of power and superiority, which it needs because unconsciously it doesn't feel fully confident in its ability to deliver on its vision or fantasy. Additionally, such Critical Parent behaviour only invites the Child to rebel – and I did. I rebelled. I appealed. I kicked up a fuss. I'm still scarred – here I am, still bloody going on about it. I am one big Child. It's the one ego state I find difficult to dial down because, all my life, the cultural Critical Parent of the White Patriarchy has kept me in Child, doing to me, denying me, discounting me, deceiving me.

In retrospect, I think I can now say that the assessors of my application probably made the right call. I probably wasn't explicit enough about my Blackness and what I felt the impact of it might have had on the client and our therapeutic relationship. Nor was I explicit enough about the discrimination that wealthy people often experience from the stiff upper lip brigade who still occupy an influential space in Western culture. I'd failed to properly detail the dysregulation I feel as a Black woman confronted by a rich, White, middle-class woman who, in our first session, looked like she'd rather throw up than speak to me. I'd alluded to my fear of discrimination from clients, but I didn't get much further than that. But should I really have to? White counsellors don't have to describe the pain and shame of being the target of racist clients, so why should I? And yet, to fulfil the criteria of the assignment as instructed, that is exactly what I was asked to do.

I'd failed, then. I'd failed to write about the unwanted but instinctive pain and shame I felt at not being the White counsellor the client would have preferred me to be. I'd failed to put the dissection of that pain and shame in writing in order to please some faceless, and very probably White, assessor. I'd failed to explain that the disquiet I felt on meeting this client was not unusual (Dhillon-Stevens, 2011) for me. I also failed to explain that I still feel nervous and vulnerable every time I know I'm going to meet a new White client who's been referred to me; that I have to put my chin up and shoulders back and hope that, if they *are* fazed by my colour, they'll see past it, or I can at least help them to. I failed to mention that it takes courage to do this work if you're Black in a largely White environment. I failed to describe how magnified the risks of therapy are for White clients who have to work with someone like me, taking them further outside of their window of tolerance than they'd bargained for. I'd failed to describe how much more is going on in that first session when I am working with a White person, compared with my first sessions with Black people. I failed to include in my case study the fact that, on this occasion, I was able to use my well-crafted presentation skills to mirror the client's posture, to speak in a confident tone and to fall fully into the busy-ness of creating a working relationship with her (Clarkson, 1995). These real-world relationship distractions helped me to overcome my fear of the client's racism in the transferential relationship and dial down her fears and distress, in order to clear a hygienic space for both of us to meet in an emotional and psychological place of equality (Dhillon-Stevens, 2011). So they were right; I failed. I failed big. But just not for the reasons they gave me.

My father at the White man's table

Fast-forward a few years, I am now poacher-turned-gamekeeper. I am working in London as a lecturer, teaching integrative counselling skills to university students. There's a whole module devoted to diversity and inclusion, and I relish the opportunity to give my students an opportunity to learn about the embodied nature of difference and diversity in the therapeutic relationship. The goal, as I see it and teach it, is to enjoy the shifting rhythms of alterity

(Smith, 2015), to feel the difference between communion and solitude, togetherness and separateness, curiosity and opaqueness, familiarity and strangeness. But to do this well, we need to find out how much we *don't know* about the impact of *our own* cultural heritage before we can begin to fully open our hearts and minds to the client's cultural baggage. These can be examined using genograms (Hardy & Laszloffy, 1995). We need to be able to re-imagine our past with a cultural lens that focuses on the inheritance of norms that may obstruct our ability to generate a visceral I-Thou phenomenon (Buber, 1958) in the therapy room. I had prepared myself for these teachings; I'd taken my lesson plans to supervision to review my rationale and objectives and test whether my material and approach would be sufficiently robust to deliver them. However, I hadn't properly prepared myself for what might come up on the training days when, during triad work, I had to listen to the students' own experiences.

Part of the counselling lecturer's work is to sit and listen to student counsellors in role play.[4] On this one afternoon, I joined a session just as the 'client' began to share her own story of racism in her family with her 'counsellor'. The 'client' described her father as a controlling, critical parent. I'd already heard quite a lot about this student's father in other role-play sessions I'd sat in on in previous weeks. Her family was wealthy, her father an international lawyer. He expected his daughter to excel at everything. She was White, with very fair skin and strong red hair. Well-spoken. Well-educated. She was a confident, compassionate trainee therapist, and a good learner. She always delivered intellectually muscular essays that felt to me somewhat at odds with her much softer voice in the classroom. It was as though her father – her inner Parent – wrote the essays for her. Now, though, she was being a 'client' giving her fellow student some material to work with.

'My father often had African men round for dinner.'

'Really?' says the 'counsellor', as surprised as I was.

'Well, yes. He went to Nigeria a lot, quite frequently. That's where he made his money.'

'Doing what?'

'He worked as a lawyer, in the oil business, and so when the Nigerians came to the UK, he'd have them over for dinner. I used to like that. Only one day, when I was a teenager, they came to dinner and after they'd left, I said to my dad how lovely I thought they were, one of them in particular. He turned to me and growled. He told me I was never to bring a Black man home to his house, or he'd disown me.'

---

4. Here again, I have significantly changed all identifying details.

'And how did you feel about that?' the student 'counsellor' asked.

'Well, I suppose it was just him being Dad. I've never really thought about it until now. I would never say anything like that to my own children. Things are different now, aren't they?'

This all hit me like a punch to the stomach. My own father is Nigerian. I found him on the internet in my late 30s. I felt sick, sickened. I felt very alone. I needed air. The scene she'd described was replaying in my head. I imagined it was my own father sat at her father's table. I could hear the friendly chat round the table. I could see my own father sitting there, enjoying the food, being polite, making jokes, feeling accepted. He would have talked geo-politics but made jokes to keep it light. He would have admired the house. He would have been interested in the family, the children, their education and ambitions. He would have been the perfect guest.

I could hardly look at the two students. Neither of them looked at me – it was just another 'triad' exercise for them. I felt weak. My centre of gravity had gone. As soon as I could, I left them and went out, to compose myself. I was angry that they didn't see me, care about me, care about my dad. They only cared about their counselling practice. I had to carry on teaching, but I didn't know what to do with those feelings. I felt I was no longer the teacher. I was the Child, hiding my pain and shame behind a whiteboard. I had not yet understood that I, the therapist, was still holding onto trauma in my body, or 'dirty pain', as Resmaa Menakem beautifully describes it in his book, *My Grandmother's Hands* (Menakem, 2021). I could not stay present and notice the sensations without reacting to them. I was in them. They were in me. I could not leave my father at the table without taking care of him.

The yawning gap

To pass the module, the students had to write a set essay on 'Diversity and Multiculturalism in Practice'. The guidance was for students to reflect on their own cultural upbringing and how that might hinder or assist with their practice. My student with the racist father spent a lot of time and space in her essay talking about how being female might limit her understanding of the male psyche. She failed to mention the fact she'd been raised by a racist. Her omission of this felt like another slap on the face.

Now it was my turn to be the assessor. Now I had the chance to help a student to truly understand how important it is to be aware of the damage she could inflict, not just on a client but on colleagues, peers and, dare I say it, lecturers too. I really needed to point out to her the potential she had to inflict violence, not on my body as physical damage but, as Aileen Alleyne puts it, 'to the soul' (Alleyne, 2011).

But what did I do?

My Adult ego state, my rational, logical self, who needs to find a route to good outcome, knew the best line of action would have been to request a meeting with the student. This would have provided an opportunity for both of us to reflect on 'diversity in practice'. But my inner Child insisted that I run away from the discomfort, pain and shame that such a conversation would generate inside me. My feedback on her essay was just cowardly:

> You explore the issue of gender within your family and how this has impacted on you with regard to your role as mother and professional. I remember (in one of your triads) you recalled there was significant levels of racism in the family, and wonder if you'd reflected on how this cultural heritage could impact on your own frame of reference, albeit unconsciously?

'Wonder if...' That was cowardly, because I was pretending curiosity, when in actual fact I doubted very much that she'd reflected on whether her father's White supremacy had any negative impact on her own ability to hold all people equal and of value, despite their origin, race or colour. She would never know about the pain she'd inflicted on me, albeit unconsciously, because I couldn't bear to put myself in the line of fire again. I didn't want to have to mop up White women's tears, which I'm sure would have been the outcome. As Eugene Ellis puts it, 'Responding to race hurt is further made more difficult to untangle by the invoked White privilege of not having to feel the uncomfortableness of race' (Ellis, 2021, p.132).

Eric Berne says our inner Child, or archaic Child, replays all the emotional routines we experienced in our childhood (Berne, 1973). But as the teacher – not the taught – I was supposed to lead, nurture, critique, be fair, be self-compassionate and be firm in my teaching. I was supposed to provide and model the core conditions to enable change, growth and learning. But I did not have the capacity to do so. I couldn't deal with the trigger, not in the room or on the page. This student passed, and I had failed again.

My failure to equip her with the insight and knowledge she really would need to practise safely felt to me like a major error. My own internal oppressor is never far away, an inner Critical Parent in constant negative dialogue with my inner Child – that symbiotic seductive relationship that provides constant negative noise and leaves little space for a rational, more Adult appraisal of what the options are, the choices and chances I could have considered and taken. If the external system is always 'right' and the dominant world view is the one I feel I need to fit into, to get by, get paid, get liked, accepted, respected

– then I'm going to beat myself up, because it's easier than railing against a world in which no one can see me.

There was and is a yawning gap here – which I've now experienced as both 'the assessed' and 'the assessor'. The gap is the lack of a safe space in which to have conversations about race. All parties need to become more aware of the feelings this subject generates – and I mean *physically* aware. We need the space to sit with these feelings, to really 'feel' them, with each other, to get past the dysregulation and dissociation that can and does interfere with our practice (Menakem, 2021). Unfortunately, in both the scenarios I've described here, I could not protect my inner Child from the racism being inflicted upon her, and nor could I summon up enough Adult ego state to generate situational learning from the process.

Rewind five years – I resubmitted my assignment to my professional body, making it very clear to any assessor that I'm Black and not very well off, several times throughout the essay. But that's pretty much all I changed. A month later, I learned I'd passed this time. I still feel like a failure.

A better future for Black therapists

What struck me, when writing this chapter, is how hard I am on myself – how much emotional work I expect myself to get through, despite and in spite of the world of uncertainty that I navigate daily, at work and out in the community. It also feels like I'm letting go of a secret and so there's some relief, as well as trepidation, not knowing what the impact will be.

Going forward, it's the triggers that are most problematic – the inner Child being awoken from her concealed acceptance and expectation of racism. In therapy, the client is likely to let it all hang out, and if our inner Child isn't ready for that stuff, we're at risk of being damaged by it, and damaging the client in turn.

Educators and assessors need to reframe difference and diversity; they need to recognise it not as an 'add-on' piece of learning but as an integrative element of the core conditions, so 'acceptance' or being 'non-judgemental' is fully understood in their widest and deepest sense. That would include permission to feel uncomfortable in a race conversation; freedom to analyse regression episodes without fear of being invalidated; giving and taking the opportunity to stop, breathe and notice the dysregulation of our complex racial relationships, and staying curious about how we can move forward with more insight, compassion and intention to heal and/or be healed.

And perhaps, to do that, we must recognise and be more actively intentional about creating boundaried safe spaces for conversations with each other. Safety is the key word. There is danger in the layers of trauma concealed by Black counsellors like me: danger for us, our clients and our students. With no permission to take space in a White world that is also our world, we will miss much needed time and opportunity to explore our new experiences, in the light of old traumas, without fear of further trauma (Ellis, 2021, Chapter 1). Supervision is the place to kick this off. Perhaps all Black counsellors and supervisors should insist on scheduled time to discuss what's been coming up for us, to give our supervisors the chance to feel and notice any dysregulation, and for us, as their clients, to lean into it and explore a better way forward.

We know the human brain didn't evolve for the purpose of thinking, or to give us all a good time. Staying within its 'window of tolerance' (Siegel, 2020) is the default activity of a brain that has a tremendous amount of arguably more important work to do – keeping us alive and breathing. To create these safe spaces, then, we will need to override the default programme; to intentionally plan for dysregulated dialogue where we can support each other, accept each other and learn more about each other; to create a 'here and now' that can withstand all the fears and opportunities that open dialogue will present us with going forward. If we really care about our colleagues, our clients and our professional bodies, then we must insist on widening the gates of dialogue to embrace what we know, as psychotherapists, to be the only way forward – authentic, empathic dialogue, boundaried by deep acceptance and a quest for learning.

References

Alleyne, A. (2011). Overcoming racism, discrimination and oppression in psychotherapy. In C. Lago (Ed.), *The handbook of transcultural counselling & psychotherapy* (pp.117–129). McGraw-Hill/Open University Press.

Berne, E. (1961/2021). *Transactional analysis in psychotherapy: A systematic individual and social psychiatry*. Hauraki Publishing.

Berne, E. (1973). *Games people play: The psychology of human relationships*. Ballantine Books.

Berne, E. (1974/2018). *What do you say after you say hello? Gain control of your conversations and relationships*. Corgi.

Buber, M. (1958). *I and thou* (2nd ed.) (trans. R.G. Smith). T & T Clark.

Clarkson, P. (1995). *The therapeutic relationship*. Whurr.

Dhillon-Stevens, H. (2011). Issues for psychological therapists from black and minority ethnic groups. In C. Lago (Ed.), *The handbook of transcultural counselling & psychotherapy* (pp.105–116). McGraw Hill/Open University Press.

Ellis, E. (2021). *The race conversation.* Confer Books

Hardy, K.V. & Laszloffy, T.A. (1995). The cultural genogram: Key to training culturally competent family therapists. *Journal of Marital and Family Therapy, 21*(3), 227–237.

Menakem, R. (2021) *My grandmother's hands.* Penguin.

Siegel, D.J. (2020). *The developing mind: How relationships and the brain interact to shape who we are* (3rd ed.). Guilford Press.

Smith, L.C. (2015). Alterity models in counseling: When we talk about diversity, what are we actually talking about? *International Journal for the Advancement of Counselling, 37*(3), 248–261.

Steiner, C. (1974). *Scripts people live: Transactional analysis of life scripts.* Grove Press.

6. Racism and coercive control in an NHS counselling service

Anya Amrith and Roshmi Lovatt

What follows are two accounts, one from a trainee therapist's perspective and one from the perspective of her clinical supervisor, of events that took place several years ago. 'A' in this account is, and is not, Anya; what she describes is compiled from her own experiences and from what we know happens, or situations very like it, to so many student therapists of colour as they go through their training. 'R' is, and is not, Roshmi, and what she describes is similarly a compilation of incidents and experiences she has witnessed, heard and held supervisees through in her professional role. We know these things happen from the stories therapists of colour tell each other, but they are rarely, truly heard by white therapists and the white-dominated profession, and we know this too from numerous studies and surveys.

To that extent, the details in these accounts are true, but many have been changed to avoid any individual being identifiable. We hope that those who see something of themselves in these accounts will use this prompt to question their assumptions, attitudes and behaviours, to reflect, and perhaps even take some of the actions we list at the end.

In these accounts, A was completing her training as a therapist and was on a placement organised by her course provider. R was A's clinical supervisor for her private practice, unconnected to the placement, and had supported A over several years, through her previous placements, as she progressed through her learning. A identifies as a cis-gendered woman of colour in her 30s; R identifies as a middle-class, cis-gendered woman of colour in her 50s.

The trainee's perspective (A)

I was in my final year of training. I recall the excitement I felt on receiving the offer of work experience at a specialist counselling service within the

NHS. Following on from my previous experience of placements, and after accumulating precious learning hours as a student, this was going to be my opportunity to further my learning in a service supporting minority ethnic groups in my community. As a Brown female trainee, my enthusiasm for actively supporting people who were under-represented in the psychotherapeutic field could not be contained. I understood I would be joining a team of white professionals, and I relished the prospect of sitting alongside colleagues who all had psychology or psychotherapeutic training. With their level of training in the field of psychology, I expected that the team would be open minded.

The course provider taught us trainees that the learning practice we received was akin to gold dust. We were lucky to receive these opportunities and the real-life experience. So, as I began the placement, I thought nothing of being thrust into group and one-to-one work without a clearly laid-out contract and boundaries that would normally be part of the therapeutic framework. I had trust in a long-established institution and believed that its processes would safeguard me as a student.

M, a white male in his early 60s, was a senior manager in the service, and was also my placement supervisor – a dual role that is flagged up as potentially problematic by BACP (2021). I wondered if it was unusual that my one-to-one client sessions were more like a three-way meeting, in that M insisted that he was also physically in the sessions with me, and intervened regularly. I was assured by M that this was to protect the clients, as I was a stranger to them. When I checked with my course provider, they gave permission for this practice to continue, but just for a month until I had settled in. No other trainee in this setting had seen clients so quickly, but I reassured myself that I was there to learn as much as possible and should make the most of my opportunity.

Each week felt increasingly intense, with more expectations placed on me by M, as I worked with the highest-risk clients. Boundaries were often unclear: for example, I was given client case histories at the last minute before my sessions; I wasn't made fully aware of the clients' levels of risk; timeframes regarding the number of sessions being offered were unclear and not communicated. For group sessions, I was asked to exclude some service users who were deemed inappropriate by M, and to find some way to communicate this to them. I was often undermined during sessions: for instance, if I asked a question to a client, M would quickly intervene and take over the conversation.

The tipping point came when I enquired about a client's culture in a team meeting, as it seemed to me to be relevant to their care plan. M interjected and announced to the team that culture was not a 'thing' and that all families were the same. After the session, he took me aside and told me that referring to culture causes discomfort and isolates people in the room. I was left feeling ashamed and shaken. On the course, we had been taught that our contributions would be valuable, and that we should ask questions about minority groups to ensure that lived experiences and differences could be acknowledged and understood as much as possible. It was confusing, and I felt like I was being silenced for raising culture and diversity, which for reasons unknown to me were not permitted to be discussed.

Johnson and colleagues (2018) discuss microaggressions that occur through posture, gesture and facial expression, and how they can subtly signal disapproval, dismissal or even contempt. In my case, I noticed that M looked at me with disdain, particularly in group sessions and in our one-to-one feedback sessions. His tone of voice would become more abrupt and angry when we were in a room alone together, behind closed doors. If I asked questions in order to learn about his practice, he would ignore me and shift the focus back to my practice. He would ask me to verbally list all aspects of my practice that had not worked well that week but we never looked at what had been effective. He scrutinised my notes and changed them, and frequently told me that my recollection of events was not true. M's questioning was also highly inappropriate: for instance, he would ask me for the full names of professionals and clients I worked with outside of the placement and for very personal details about my private life, including the name of my personal clinical supervisor – R – who was supporting my private practice.

Every idea I came up with was quickly claimed as his own, and he often suggested my own ideas back to me, without acknowledgement. He increased my workload, claiming that he was 'pushing me in at the deep end' because of my enthusiasm. As I reflected with my own therapist on what was happening, I began to understand that, far from trying to help me learn, he was setting me up for failure. Every time I got through one of his tests, his criticism and disdain towards me increased and the next challenge was far steeper. I was exhausted, both mentally and physically, and getting through each day was a challenge.

Yet, because M was both my manager and placement supervisor, my only source of support in my role came from him. There was no one else to whom I could go for help.

This behaviour from M was not exclusively limited to our relationship. I witnessed many injustices from staff towards clients within the service, most of which related to discrimination and oppression.

As the weeks went on, my anxiety increased. I was always on guard against M's discouraging comments and the next test that would be suddenly thrown my way. I could feel the change in my personality, how my presence was becoming smaller to protect myself. The placement consumed a large proportion of my mental energy. I found myself feeling more exhausted in my personal life, struggling to balance life with my children, partner and friends. I stopped engaging in recreational activities and became quieter in my overall presence with people, to the point that my family voiced concerns for my wellbeing:

> In addition to learning how to scan the environment for nonverbal indicators of threat, participants spoke about how their bodies responded and adapted to these hostile social worlds. (Johnson et al., 2018)

I felt a sense of immediate danger and the historical trauma and shame response it reactivated in me. I was reminded of the abuse I had suffered as a child. I felt agitated and became hypersensitive, trying to anticipate the next moment to such an extent that I lost my appetite and ability to sleep through the night. I sought to stay focused on the clients and found that my creativity in sessions could provide them with small amounts of safety. I did this by channelling the parts of me that could remain grounded and provide reflection, even when my own safety felt compromised. In my personal therapy sessions, my therapist and I reflected on the parallel process taking place between me and the clients.

When I raised my concerns to the course provider, I was told that this was my allocated placement and I should stay focused on the work, rather than on personal dynamics. But they did say they would call M to discuss the situation. The week that followed this call was one of worst of the entire experience. I was isolated and belittled by him behind closed doors all week, and formerly friendly colleagues changed in their behaviour towards me, suggesting that M was discussing me with them behind my back. I was excluded from team emails, so M became my sole channel of communication with colleagues. At no point would M leave me alone, to the extent that he insisted that I ate my lunch in his presence. It felt like I was being punished for seeking help from my course provider. From then on, he constantly asked me what I was feeding back to the course provider.

Then, a few weeks later, M's attitude towards me suddenly changed. His tone of voice softened and he began smiling, which was unusual. I thought maybe he had somehow become pleased with my work. A few days later, I received a phone call from R, my external clinical supervisor, who supervised my private practice and had also supervised me in other placements during my training.

R explained that M had come up to her at a conference they both happened to be attending and had spoken openly and unfavourably about me. I was shocked to realise this was around the time his behaviour had changed, and to learn that this conversation with R had taken place without my knowledge or permission. Was he now trying to poison my other working relationships, not only within the placement, but with other professionals, in order to isolate me further? He never raised with me any of the criticisms of my character that he shared with R, even after the conversation had taken place, or mentioned what he had done.

What M did not know was that R had been working with me since the start of my training, and that she and I already had a strong working relationship. Since she had overseen all my work in previous placements and knew my character, R deduced that M was actively attempting to discredit my work. But what kind of damage or repercussions on my professional career would he have achieved if R had not already known me?

I was finally heard when I reported what was happening in my termly meeting with my course tutor and, with R's support, arrangements were made so I could leave the placement. Although M made leaving extremely challenging for me, and the course provider did not, in my view, fully acknowledge the extent of the mistreatment I suffered, I was grateful to have been able to remove myself from this abusive situation.

The supervisor's perspective (R)

I had been A's clinical supervisor since the beginning of her training, having started supervising her work from her initial client hours during her first placement. A had regularly brought recordings of her sessions and artwork for us to explore, and I had been impressed by her organisation, qualities and skills, as well as her personable way of being. A and I had built a strong working relationship in which she and I could both bring 100% of ourselves, in the interests of the client. In supervision, it is important to co-create a safe place where supervisees of all levels can feel safe to bring their triumphs as well as their mistakes, without feeling that they will be judged or criticised. A was keen to learn and appreciated my critiques of her sessions, often showing how she had gone away and applied her learning.

To set the context in brief, I am an experienced psychotherapist and founder and director of a psychotherapy practice offering a range of psychological therapies to the local community. Our ethos actively promotes a social justice model of business and practice. I identify as a woman of colour, as does A, and this is what originally brought A to me for supervision. She was looking for representation of her own racial/ethnic identity in the higher levels of the profession.

When A began her final placement at the organisation described in this chapter, I was excited for her. A had been working in private practice as a trainee, and during this time I continued as her clinical supervisor. Fairly soon into the placement, A began to tell me about some of her experiences there. Although strictly I was not there to supervise her work on this placement, as this was provided by M, I was concerned. I realised that A had nowhere else to take these often-distressing experiences, and as she shared these snippets of information, my unease grew. In particular, I was concerned that all M seemed to give her was negative feedback and micro-management. This was a white, older, senior manager who held sole responsibility for supervising a young, female, trainee therapist of colour. BACP's supervision competence framework (2021) is very clear on the need for great caution in instituting such dual roles within an organisation, and explicitly requires:

> Knowledge and understanding of common dilemmas in organisation-based supervision, including but not restricted to manager/supervisee conflict, dual roles, and issues relating to boundaries, competency, client referral, confidentiality and lines of responsibility and accountability. (2.1, iii: Knowledge and understanding)

I had a deep, embodied reactivation of my own experiences from when I was a trainee. I would feel a surge of anger deep in my core, which I was aware was my own racial trauma, experienced at the hands of previous therapists, tutors and supervisors – people in positions of power. I was holding in mind that the BACP supervision competence framework (2021) also states as one of the core competencies:

> Knowledge and awareness of the significance for the supervisee of feeling respected, valued, and trusted by the supervisor. (3.2, i: Relational skills, qualities and behaviours)

I was also aware of the potential for shame for a trainee on placement:

> Supervisors are responsible for creating an atmosphere within which the experience of shame – and the defenses commonly used to guard against shame – can be identified. (Hahn, 2001)

However, at this stage I wondered if M was perhaps micro-managing A with a view to protecting her interests, as she was so new to this setting. Was he perhaps safeguarding A, as a student, so that she would feel supported and safe? But I continued to keep an eye on the situation.

Two specific incidents brought me to reflect and then act on the racial aspect of the dynamics between A and M. The first was the incident that occurred a few weeks into A's placement, when A inquired about the cultural background of one of the patients and M took her aside and told her not to refer to culture as it could cause discomfort and alienate people. Given that the client demographic of the service was predominantly people of colour, this struck both A and me as odd. With my own supervisor, I reflected on the implications of a practice that pro-actively excludes the naming of culture. What gets missed, invalidated and oppressed? As Hernandez and McDowell write in their paper, 'Intersectionality, Power and Relational Safety in Context':

> Effectively acknowledging and challenging these dynamics offers supervisors and supervisees opportunities to enhance the safety in their relationship and increase their critical social awareness. (Hernandez & McDowell, 2010)

Again, holding in mind the BACP supervision competence framework (2021), I was concerned that A's placement supervisor was not demonstrating:

> Knowledge of the importance of initiating discussions of differences and similarities to enhance safety in the supervisory relationship and depth of dialogue. (BACP, 2021, 4.1, iii: Knowledge and understanding)

I was concerned for A, as a person of colour herself, and I began to wonder about the conscious and unconscious dynamics that might be playing out beneath the relationship between M and A. In taking some of these reflections to my own supervisor, I was able to unravel something about my own responses – in particular, my anger about A's situation, but also my own fear of speaking up about it. I wondered what conscious or unconscious racial prejudices were possibly being enacted in the relationship between A and M. If naming culture was 'taboo' in the setting and could not be spoken about, how were racial dynamics being addressed? How could any cultural bias be highlighted or spoken about? Also, through an intersectional lens, I was concerned that a white male was holding such a position of authority and power over a Brown female still in training. I began to question whether other core competencies were being met within the BACP supervision competence framework (2021):

> Knowledge and awareness of self in relation to others from a perspective of power. (8.3, i: Power)

> Awareness of the ways in which the supervisor occupies and manages the role from the perspective of power. (8.3, ii: Power)

If relational safety through the naming and exploration of diverse cultures could not be achieved, what choices did A have, and how might she learn, grow and flourish in such a placement?

> Relational safety does not refer to blind validation and emotional support. Rather, it refers to development of critical thinking in a caring relational environment. (Hernandez & McDowell, 2010)

I reflected on my role in safeguarding A as a student of colour. Holding in mind cultural competence as a core aspect of ethical practice, I reflected that A's training organisation had a duty of care towards their trainee of colour. I felt it was important that they should be aware of A's difficult experiences, and therefore advised A to speak with her training organisation's placement officer.

The second incident, which finally brought me to act, was my encounter with M at the conference A describes. Recognising me by my name tag, M came over to speak with me during the lunch break. He introduced himself as A's placement manager and ascertained that I was A's clinical supervisor. He did not know at this point the length of my supervisory relationship with A. He began to talk with me about A in ways that I can only describe as undermining, discouraging and discrediting. He spoke aggressively about A's conduct and manner, and questioned whether A should be in private practice at all. The implication I took from this was that A was not competent to set up in private practice.

As I listened to M, I felt extremely uncomfortable. First, there was the issue of talking about A behind her back, which troubled me. Second, the language he used struck me as disparaging towards A. His descriptions of A did not match or resonate with my own impressions of her in the slightest. In retrospect, I wish I had said this out loud, but at the time I found it impossible to stop the conversation. In my reflections subsequently, I have come to recognise that this was in part to do with the power of his white authority in that moment, which effectively silenced me from being an ally to A. Additionally, perhaps my own internalised racism was telling me that I did not have a right to stand up to this white man.

> The term recognition trauma portrays the experience of powerful feelings that occur when an individual becomes aware that they have been a victim of racism… Denial, silence or rage are behaviors that can be associated with this concept. (Mckenzie-Mavinga, n.d.)

I felt that I had a duty of care towards A to inform her of my encounter with M and his comments. This was partly informed by my reflection that, if I had been someone who did not have any prior knowledge of A, then M's words would have put me off: for example, if I had been a prospective employer looking for a reference. This discrediting of A by M to A's own clinical supervisor bothered me, and I was holding information pertaining to A of which A was unaware, which again contravened the recommendations in the BACP supervision competence framework (BACP, 2021) that the supervisor should demonstrate:

> Knowledge and awareness of the potential for misuse of power in the supervisory relationship, for example by violating the boundaries of the supervisory relationship. (2021, section 3.3(iii): Power in the supervisory relationship: Knowledge and understanding)

Again, the issue of safeguarding students of colour came to mind, and I felt a strong imperative to act on this conversation. I knew that students of colour are already at a disadvantage within the profession, having to navigate and survive white spaces, biases and Eurocentric curricula. To then be unfairly discredited by people in positions of authority was another layer of what I began to see as a racially motivated move to sabotage A's progress. Student progression, when viewed through the lens of intersectionality, takes on many nuanced layers that require careful consideration by culturally skilled practitioners. For students to progress in a 'meaningful way requires that supervisors and supervisees have a safe context for learning' (Hernandez & McDowell, 2010).

In my subsequent feedback to A, I could sense her upset and distress. I had considered not telling her, but it felt like a painful yet important step for her to have the evidence of 'harm' being done to her by M. I learned afterwards that M did not tell A that this conversation with me had taken place, and clearly A had not consented to M speaking about her to me.

As a consequence of my disclosure to A, we jointly raised a complaint with A's training organisation, and A eventually left the placement.

Reflections, questions and actions
Reflection 1: Safeguarding trainees of colour

The experience A had with M in an NHS service raises many questions regarding the safeguarding of trainees on placement, and in particular trainees/students of colour. It is important to note that there was no HR department or anti-bullying policies for A to refer to within the placement. She was therefore left in the vulnerable position of having no one within the service to oversee or protect her welfare, as the individual responsible for her suffering was the person who was abusing her. As a trainee on placement, she also had no recourse to employment law.

Questions
- What are the roles and responsibilities of supervisors, training organisations, placement co-ordinators, placement organisations and placement managers in ensuring the safeguarding of students of colour?

Actions
- Training organisations, supervisors and placement managers need to evolve their ability to engage in and model non-oppressive communication that seeks to validate rather than pathologise.
- We need to actively understand how 'actions or inactions amplify or enable the systematic dynamics already in place' (Livingston, 2020).
- We need to educate people within institutions to look at the structural dynamics and how these interact with a person's identity.
- We need to improve our knowledge and awareness of self in relation to others from a perspective of power, including the awareness of the ways in which the supervisor occupies and manages their role.
- We need to be more effective allies to students of colour. This includes speaking up when we notice that another professional – trainee or otherwise – is being discredited, invalidated or brought into disrepute.
- We need to support students of colour to 'feel safe and grounded as a first step toward addressing the bodily hypervigilance, dissociation, and constriction that can result from repeated microaggressions' (Johnson et al., 2018).

Reflection 2: Structural biases

Although the training organisation eventually removed A from the placement, we have to reflect on the tension in the three-way relationship between the training organisation, the placement provider and the student of colour in training. Due to the structural biases of two white institutions, a number of dynamics get played out both consciously and unconsciously in trying to simultaneously support the student and maintain a relationship with the placement provider. Due to this tension, the safeguarding of students like A in this story and an adherence to anti-discriminatory policy may not be as rigorous as we would expect from our profession. Incidentally, and perhaps most sadly, in R's many years of experience as a supervisor of colour, this is just one of a multitude of such situations involving students, trainees and therapists of colour working in white-dominated organisations within the profession.

Questions

- How do people of colour 'prove' that their treatment is racist, as so often this is quickly dismissed any white organisations due to defensiveness and white fragility?
- How can the profession get better at acknowledging, believing and acting on the lived experience of practitioners of colour?
- How can the profession create cultures that make it possible for trainees and practitioners of colour to call out such behaviours without having to go through formal procedural requirements that may result only in further harm due to white fragility, rather than learning?

Actions

- The profession needs to ensure processes between all teams is rigorous. Roles should be clearly defined and a whistleblowing policy should be in place to call out discriminatory behaviour as soon as it arises.
- There should be greater knowledge and awareness of self in relation to others from a perspective of power, including awareness of the ways in which the supervisor occupies and manages the role from the perspective of power.
- Every white professional/practitioner needs to be prepared to step up to be an effective, proactive ally to students of colour – this includes the capacity to speak up when you notice that another professional – trainee or otherwise – is being discredited, invalidated or their competence and professional standing brought into disrepute.
- The processes and communications between all teams should be thoroughly and regularly reviewed for robustness and rigour.

Reflection 3: Power-motivated abuse and coercive control

Specific to this story it is important to reflect on the nuances of an experience that raises the issue of coercive control in the working environment. The UK Women's Aid website describes coercive control as behaviour that is:

> Designed to make a person dependent by isolating them from support, exploiting them, depriving them of independence and regulating their everyday behaviour. (2022, para.2)

Coercive control is a criminal offence (gov.uk, 2022). Much work has yet to be done in aiding people to understand how this form of abuse operates. By its nature, coercive control is extremely difficult to prove. Furthermore, coercive control is still a relatively new concept outside domestic abuse situations. Progress still needs to be made in understanding how this form of abuse is subtly used in the workplace.

Questions
- How can all practitioners be equipped to pick up on cues around racial dynamics, name them and take action to safeguard practitioners of colour?
- How might R have acted earlier to safeguard A?

Actions
- Actively train practitioners in the profession to recognise manifestations of racial abuse, including microaggressions, embodied abuses of power, coercive control and other ways in which racism plays out in professional settings.
- Find ways to support practitioners to become allies, including support around unravelling the silencing of oppression.

Reflection 4: Power and oppression within institutions

Paired with oppression, the use of coercive control becomes an alarming, often invisible danger that is highly present in our society and our institutions. The British Psychological Society has published the Power Threat Meaning Framework (Johnstone & Boyle et al., 2018), which discusses the impact of racism and discrimination within that dynamic:

> Discrimination may also be deeply embedded in the procedures, policies, laws and employment practices of organisations and services (institutional racism) in a way which renders it more or less invisible except to those discriminated against. (Johnstone & Boyle et al., 2018, p.134)

In this case, this form of institutional racism is apparent in the lack of anti-discriminatory policies and procedures or whistleblowing process within this placement, as mentioned above.

This also brings to light an important aspect, which is the operation of power within institutions, organisations, social structures and through the media, social media, education and social and family relations. Using A's experience as an example, as a trainee she held significantly less power than her manager/supervisor, or indeed than an employee. In A's experience, having one person hold the power as well as a dual role (both a manager and a placement supervisor) meant that A could be easily isolated from other colleagues within the organisation. While these dual roles do occur in many agencies and statutory organisations, there is something important about having conversations that support the navigation of such dual roles and boundaries within the counselling and psychotherapy arena. In the case of A, no such conversation was possible with M, given the undermining nature of M's authority. In addition to this, holding in mind that A is a Brown female, with a manager and supervisor who is a white male, this dramatically increased the level of power he held and furthered A's oppression. The situation meant that M was in a position to have complete control over A, without being monitored by anyone else in the service.

Questions

- How do we challenge and dismantle systems of oppression within our profession?
- Whose responsibility is this?

Actions

- People in positions of power in organisations should be actively managed and supervised, especially in circumstances where they are responsible for trainees.
- People in supervisory roles should be fully trained supervisors with a specific skill-set that complies with their professional body's standards and the capacity to challenge systems of oppression.
- The profession needs to monitor the common occurrence of dual roles and responsibilities in supervisory relationships, especially when one person holds a dual position with managerial/supervisory power. For example, placement manager and supervisor roles should be allocated to two individuals, or safeguards put in place that ensure proper protection for students from the potential for abuse within such dual roles and the dissolving of necessary professional/managerial boundaries.

Reflection 5: Intersectionality

The intersectionality framework allows us to comprehend this oppression in more detail. The framework explores how a person's identity markers, including race, gender, sexuality, age, class and able-bodiedness, combine to create different types of discrimination and oppression. The term was developed by Kimberlé Crenshaw in 1989 (Crenshaw, 1994) and draws from a Black feminist perspective. It allows individuals to understand their own position of power, their social location and the cultural capital they hold, before comprehending other people's experiences within society:

> Intersectionality is not just about naming difference, but rather understanding the social structures that give power to some and oppress others. (Kuri, 2017, cited in Eastwood, 2021, p.4)

As Verdonk argues, medical institutions are embedded within power structures. These structures, which were put in place generations ago, still prevail within institutions through transgenerational trauma:

> In western settings, the downstream effects of medical education on doctors and patients are shaped by patriarchal and colonial histories and values. (Verdonk, 2013, cited in Samra & Hankivsky, 2020, p.857)

In A's experience, there were people in the service who witnessed, and even colluded with, the abuse and mistreatment of others. This is a clear symptom of an embedded power structure, steeped in hierarchical patriarchy. It cannot be ignored that our history of colonialism, intertwined with gender, still impacts our systems today. An intersectionality framework and education can be used to dismantle these power structures and confront marginalisation (Samra & Hankivsky, 2020). Adoption of the framework aids organisations and institutions to understand that any two people placed in the same position may not have the same experience. It highlights the use and allocation of power. It is only by identifying an individual's intersectionality markers that we can begin to consider the nuances of power that may be at play. By disassembling power structures, organisations will also prevent people who seek out senior rules so they can enact their trauma cycles while hiding within the prevailing culture.

Questions

- Had R not been a person of colour, with experience in the field of psychotherapy, how might this situation have been different?
- What do we need to put in place in our profession that will ensure the ongoing commitment to viewing our practice through an intersectional lens?

Actions

- Training organisations should embed the use of an intersectional lens into core training.
- Training organisations need to address the under-representation of minoritised groups in mainstream psychotherapy.
- Training organisations need to attract more diversity in students and make it possible for a greater diversity of students to progress to qualification and beyond.
- The profession and NHS need to ensure that more people of colour are employed in managerial roles across higher bands within the NHS.
- Those in positions of power need to be supported to regularly reflect on their own assumptions, attitudes and beliefs about issues relating to equality, diversity and inclusion, and to work sensitively from this awareness.
- Managers and practitioners should maintain ongoing awareness of when shame and silencing merge to collude with the status quo of discrimination.

Conclusion

In this example of racism from a student's perspective, the discrimination and coercive control experienced by A at the hands of M were picked up by R because R shared some of the same intersecting identity markers as A. Additionally, R was familiar with the nuances of anti-discriminatory practice, which meant that A was seen, heard and believed. As the profession of psychotherapy advances, it is essential that more people are educated to use the intersectionality framework, regardless of identity markers, in order to better safeguard our students. Asking pertinent questions, as above, that catch the subtlety of a person's experience and the nuances of systemic injustice is essential. We would recommend that this practice is adopted throughout all our professional organisations and institutions.

The experience described here also further highlights the importance of continued learning for people who hold management and senior positions. If practitioners at any level are not actively continuing their reflective professional development, it prevents us from evolving as a profession and becoming more aware of and responsive to emerging diversity, difference and understandings of oppression as a society. We feel it is only in learning that we can overcome the unconscious processes that create workplace discrimination and so stop the cycle continuing through further generations:

> Anti-oppressive practice is an essential component for the growth, development and self-knowledge of the therapist supervisor and supervisee and is about good ethical professional psychotherapy. (Dennis, 2001, p.163)

We are writing this chapter for future generations of psychotherapists so that our profession does not remain a hothouse for racially motivated harm, conscious or unconscious, towards people of colour in majority white spaces. It is important for the psychotherapy profession to become truly anti-discriminatory. We cannot therefore continue to reproduce the status quo of inequalities that maintain the social and cultural capital of dominant groups and structures. And in particular we need to safeguard our students of colour on their journeys to become professionals of the future.

Reflections from A

As I reflect on my experience with M, I've been struck by how painful and horrific my ordeal was. It came at such a tender stage in my development as a psychotherapist, and for some time afterwards it deeply impacted my confidence. It took time to regain my sense of self in my body and mind. In writing this chapter, the part of me that lived through the experience has gained a voice – she is no longer small or silenced. I am grateful that I had a supportive clinical supervisor in R, and my personal psychotherapist and family to help me work through my feelings of humiliation. This came not only from my experience, but also in witnessing the shaming of clients accessing a service that they vitally needed in their life. It feels important to give them a voice too, to empower us all.

I feel disheartened that experiences like this can take place within the profession of psychotherapy, and that it took so long for me to be heard and then to be removed from my placement. I wonder if other trainees in the same position would have been put off continuing their training. Ours is an occupation where more psychotherapists of colour and diverse cultures are required. We cannot afford to lose trainees through abusive experiences during their training. I now draw upon my life experiences of harm and racism when working with clients of colour, and I use intersectionality as a tool in my practice. Having first-hand knowledge of discrimination and oppression, I can offer empathy, validation and empowerment to clients who encounter similar harmful behaviours and attitudes in their lives. Unfortunately, these experiences are still commonplace. It's important to keep discussing the unconscious processes that take place within all institutions, so that we foster a cultural change in our society so we do not cause harm to clients or to students who wish to enter the profession.

Reflections from R

In writing this chapter I have become painfully aware of how my own internalised racism/oppression can be quick to play out, even after all the years I've worked on understanding and applying an intersectional lens in my practice. My body has felt tight and pained during this process, in part because reading A's written version of her experience lands in the place of my own wounds, and also in part because I come face to face with my own silencing of myself. Reading and re-reading this chapter causes a restriction in my being, and I have to actively find strategies to mitigate against the shame that emerges in me of silencing and being silenced. In some way, the writing of this chapter is a big part of that mitigating, and chimes with my body's need to speak the unspoken. It comes with fear, certainly, but also with a sense of freedom and the knowing that future generations of trainees and supervisors might be more equipped to keep speaking out.

References

BACP. (2021). *Supervision competence framework*. BACP. www.bacp.co.uk/media/10930/bacp-supervision-competence-framework-feb21.pdf

Crenshaw, K.W. (1994). Mapping the margins: Intersectionality, identity politics, and violence against women of color. In: M.A. Fineman & R. Mykitiuk (Eds.), *The public nature of private violence* (pp.93–118). Routledge.

Dennis, M. (2001). An integrative approach to 'race' and culture in supervision. In M. Carroll & M. Tholstrap (Eds.), *Integrative approaches to supervision* (pp.145–163). Jessica Kingsley Publishers.

Eastwood, C. (2021). White privilege and art therapy in the UK: Are we doing the work? *International Journal of Art Therapy, 26*(3), 75–83. https://doi.org/10.1080/17454832.2020.1856159

Gov.uk. (2022). *Amendment to the controlling or coercive behaviour offence*. www.gov.uk/government/publications/domestic-abuse-bill-2020-factsheets/amendment-to-the-controlling-or-coercive-behaviour-offence

Hahn, W.K., (2001). The experience of shame in psychotherapy supervision. *Psychotherapy Theory Research Practice Training, 38*(3), 272–282.

Hernandez, P. & McDowell, T. (2010). Intersectionality, power, and relational safety in context: Key concepts in clinical supervision. *Training and Education in Professional Psychology, 4*(1), 29–35.

Johnson, R., Leighton, L & Caldwell, C. (2018). The embodied experience of microaggressions: Implications for clinical practice. *Journal of Multicultural Counselling and Development, 46*(3), 156–170.

Johnstone, L. & Boyle, M. with Cromby, J., Dillon, J., Harper, D., Kinderman, P., Longden, E., Pilgrim, D. & Read, J. (2018). *The Power Threat Meaning Framework: Towards the identification of patterns in emotional distress, unusual experiences and troubled or troubling behaviour, as an alternative to functional psychiatric diagnosis.* British Psychological Society.

Livingston, R. (2020, September–October). How to promote racial equity in the workplace. *Harvard Business Review.* https://hbr.org/2020/09/how-to-promote-racial-equity-in-the-workplace

Mckenzie-Mavinga, I. (n.d.) . *The challenge of racism in a post racism society.* [Blog]. https://www.ishamckenziemavinga.com/articles.html

Samra, R. & Hankivsky, O. (2020). Adopting an intersectionality framework to address power and equity in medicine. *The Lancet, 397*(10277), 857–859. https://doi.org/10.1016/S0140-6736(20)32513-7

Women's Aid. (2022). *What is coercive control?* www.womensaid.org.uk/information-support/what-is-domestic-abuse/coercive-control

7. Confronting the colonial history of transphobia

Sam Hope

'My name is Aditi,[1] my pronouns are she/her, I'm a trans woman.'

I met Aditi some years ago. I have an impulse to add, 'when I still had a lot to learn,' but I am aware that unlearning racism is an ongoing project, so I know I still have a lot yet to learn.

'I chose the name Aditi for its Hindu associations with liberty,' she tells me in our first session; 'I'm out and living as me everywhere now, apart from at uni, where I still pretend to be a man.'

She tells me about her fears of coming out there: 'A physics PhD is hard enough as a woman, let alone for a Brown, trans woman.'

'Yes, I can understand that anxiety, particularly in an environment dominated by white cis[2] men,' I reflect back.

We talk about her anxieties some more, and her support networks.

'My parents have been great. They're talking about helping me go private for hormones, because waiting times are ridiculous and sometimes...' she trails off.

'Sometimes?' I say gently.

'Sometimes I don't think I'll make it, having to wait that long. It's hard to function, you know?'

As we explore this, it is clear she is not currently at risk of suicide, but there is a real sense that she could be if she has to continue to live with untreated gender incongruence.

---

1. Aditi is a fictional character, a non-identifiable composite representing my own journey as a White therapist working with trans clients affected by racism and colonialism.
2. Cis comes from Latin – it is the opposite of trans.

After the session, I reflect on our first encounter. As well as my concern for this new client, I think about how I experienced Aditi and pick up some biases in my inner responses. I notice I found myself momentarily surprised that her family were supportive. I recognise the thought comes from stereotypes perpetuated by many white LGBTQA+ people and the media. The stereotype positions certain white-dominated cultures as being at the pinnacle of LGBTQA+ acceptance. Reality is so much more nuanced and bound up in colonialism, as I will discuss later. I *know* this, and yet it doesn't prevent less helpful thoughts arising.

I work to recognise the stray thoughts that run through the back of my brain. It is easy to disown those thoughts, to think of myself as not racist, to prevent myself acknowledging the work I still need to do. But I know that, when I disown them, these thoughts can trip me up in unconscious ways. I am comprised of the sedimented layers of all the stories I have encountered in my life, where oft-repeated racist ideas have shaped my thinking. When I am tired, stressed, hungry or approaching burnout, I can start to lose the ability to consciously counteract these notions. They are so strongly embedded that I can revert to them outside of my awareness. My reflexive process encourages me to accept that I have these thoughts and to seek out more up-to-date information so that I can challenge them. It will always be a work in progress.

Structural inequalities in the relationship

This chapter looks at the way racism intertwines with transmisogyny and neurodiversity biases. Therefore, the reader will also need an understanding of each component and how they combine to disadvantage Aditi.

'I can't cope with the ticking clock. Can you get rid of it please?' Aditi says some way into our second session.

I experience her as quite abrupt and forceful and am momentarily taken aback. Because I am experienced in this field, I am aware that neurodiversity is exceptionally common among LGBTQA+ people. I quickly realise that Aditi might be autistic, something that is confirmed by diagnosis later.

'It sounds like the ticking really upset you,' I observe, after taking the clock out of the room. Here, I have resisted my initial impulse to be judgemental and misread her response as bossy or controlling, an 'overreaction', and instead I empathise with her reaction.

'God, yes, it was like hammers in my brain,' she says, looking relieved.

My knowledge and understanding of neurodiversity counterbalance another bias – that this is 'male socialised behaviour' rather than an autistic person close to a meltdown due to anxiety and sensory overwhelm. As Serano (2013, p.28) says:

> When you're a trans woman, you are made to walk this very fine line, where if you act feminine you are accused of being a parody, but if you act masculine, it is seen as a sign of your true male identity.

Bias towards Aditi's autism may well get in the way of her being accepted as the woman she is. Her interests, talents, manner of speaking and profession may be used to undermine her identity by others in ways that are founded in sexist stereotypes about how women should act. This can mean trans women, particularly trans women who also experience racism, are excluded from ideas of who needs safety, protection and care.

Some of my identities overlap with Aditi's but others we don't share. I am white, and I am someone who, as a trans person who was assigned female at birth, does not experience transmisogyny. Transmisogyny is a word for the way the intersection of transphobia and misogyny impacts and endangers trans women specifically, particularly those who also experience racism. My understanding of transphobia and neurodiversity bring to light some of the biases I could fall into here. I see this landscape in more detail because of how immersed I am in trans stories through my work, life and activism. When we see a situation from distance and are more influenced by wider culture's interpretations, it is easier to be swayed by bias, and this takes work to undo. Therapists who experience marginalisation along one axis, as I do, may be lulled into thinking we will automatically understand other oppressions better. This is not so.

I still have to work through internalised ableism and transphobia, even though I am autistic and trans, but I may see this territory more accurately. But even though I've encountered transphobia and misogyny in my life, transmisogyny is something unique that I do not experience, and this can be seen in some of my initial judgements towards Aditi. For example, the projection of maleness onto trans women is how they've been systematically excluded from safety and undermined in their right to be seen as women, and racism can magnify this phenomenon, as I'll discuss later. It takes hard work on my part to notice that I hold these biases.

Aditi has also worked out that she might be autistic, but after a few sessions she tells me she has also been given a diagnosis of 'emotionally unstable personality disorder' (EUPD, formerly borderline personality disorder). She does not believe the label fits her. She tells me that she experienced the psychologist who diagnosed her with EUPD as frustrating, dismissive, and full of microaggressions towards her trans identity as well as her ethnicity.

'He constantly misgendered me,' she says, 'and talked about me having "identity confusion". He told me my culture doesn't accept gay people, and that's why I "thought I was a woman", so I told him "That's a joke because I'm a fucking *lesbian*". He told me I was being aggressive and uncooperative. I never went back to the service, but the discharge letter said I had EUPD.'

'I feel angry on your behalf that you experienced racism and transphobia when you were looking for care,' I say. Something in Aditi unclenches when I say this. I think it is important to name and problematise the oppressive systems that have harmed Aditi in this interaction and not remain neutral. As Archbishop Desmond Tutu said: 'If you are neutral in situations of injustice, you have chosen the side of the oppressor' (Ratcliffe, 2017).

'Yes, I *am* angry. But am I allowed to be? There isn't much room for people of colour to get angry without being seen as aggressive or difficult, right?'

'Right,' I affirm, 'and that's an abuse of power.'

'Yeah, if I was a white man rather than a Brown trans woman, it would be much more acceptable for me to express anger.'

'Yes, and there's so much injustice in that,' I reflect.

The strands of Aditi's identity cannot be separated from one another. She is not separately a neurodivergent person, trans, a woman and a person with British South Asian heritage; she is all of those things together. They interrelate and complicate each other in many ways: the legacy of colonial attitudes towards LGBTQA+ people; the way misogyny interacts with transphobia to undermine trans women's identities, with additional violence, exclusion and undermining directed at trans women who experience racism; the way ableist attitudes towards neurodiversity combine with oppressiveness towards her identity to pathologise her difference and distress.

Familiarity with the landscape

I have noticed a common misapprehension among counsellors that we are able to offer the core conditions to our clients no matter what their story or their background, without any training specific to their identities. Experience tells me that we are not always aware of the ways in which we have internalised inaccurate ideas about certain groups of people from wider culture, such as those promulgated in the media and popular opinion and by politicians, which unconsciously shape our experiences of clients from those groups.

Soto and colleagues (2018) explore the way therapists' self-assessments of their own cultural competence are often inadequate. If I am meeting my client with biases that I'm not aware of, how many of the core conditions remain intact? Can I deeply empathise if I am encountering notions I absorbed from the world around me, instead of seeing my client clearly, unclouded by pre-existing biases and assumptions? Can I be fully congruent if I'm unaware of my biases? How can I offer unconditional positive regard if I am making judgements without realising?

A therapist, supervisor or mental health worker who has specific knowledge of an identity can have more accurate awareness of the landscape a client is traversing and see past mainstream biases. A shared identity can sometimes be more helpful still.

'It sounds like you were experiencing sensory overwhelm,' I offer, when Aditi tells me she couldn't cope with the texture of a meal in a noisy restaurant and started to feel panicky and irritable. We explore ways to accommodate her sensory needs better. Much of this is about acceptance and self-compassion; she is not 'fussy' or 'difficult', although she has internalised those labels through her experiences. Later, when Aditi cannot understand why she is seen as very sociable in certain situations but in others comes across as abrupt, we identify that she struggles with small talk.[3] I spot these details because I am attuned to neurodiversity and have devoted considerable learning to the subject, as well as having lived experience. A less neurodiversity-aware therapist might have missed quite a lot of this detail and projected different stories onto Aditi's behaviours.

Contrast the depth of understanding I have around neurodiversity with the relative shallowness of my understanding of what it is like to be racialised in the culture we both live in. I am aware it takes continual hard work to see the impacts of racism and white supremacy that I have been taught from birth *not* to see. I might, for example, miss how some of Aditi's autistic traits would probably be accepted and understood better in a white, cis man.

Rupture in the relationship

A couple of sessions on, Aditi circles back to her anger at the racist psychologist who diagnosed her with EUPD.

'Stupid fucking white man with his white supremacist hot takes,' she says. 'Like we need any more colonial impositions on us. It wasn't just gay people the British Empire screwed over.'

I am appreciating Aditi's uncensored anger and her trust in me that I believe it shows. 'I realise you would have been just as badly criminalised as a hijra,' I say, believing at the time that hijra is simply a term in India for trans women.

'I'm not a hijra!' Aditi says angrily. 'I'm a trans woman!'

I confess, I'm not appreciating Aditi's anger so much now that it is turned

---

3. It is worth noting the high emotional cost of 'masking' here – autistic people can hide their differences by, for example, learning to fake 'small talk', but it is very stressful and tiring, so it is helpful if therapists catch any impulses to encourage their clients to assimilate better. There are parallels here with expectations of clients to 'fit in' with the dominant culture around race and gender.

towards me. I experience a fear and shame response; my cheeks flush, my pulse quickens, and my body prepares itself for defence from perceived attack. I am terrified of being thought of as racist and want to fight back against the implication that I've said something ignorant, even though I realise I have. I feel I've really tried to learn about the LGBTQA+ context in South Asia. I've read articles, blogs and books that have touched on this subject, and I've also had an extensive conversation with an Indian colleague. Unfortunately, she is cis and straight, and it so happens that her understanding was not terribly accurate.

My mistake had been to think situated knowledge about a marginalised community could be learned from one person just because they share the same ethnic heritage. This was, I think, a racist assumption. The person I consulted did not know the difference between the terms trans woman and hijra either, because both are significantly outside of her experience.

In the session with Aditi, I ground myself, breathing through my inner defensive response and refocus on how Aditi is feeling. My response is useful information about work I need to do, but Aditi's experience needs to be my focus. So often in interactions over racism (or any kind of oppression), the oppressing person focuses on themselves and their own feelings (Saad, 2020). Even if I were not in a professional, therapeutic role, this is something I need to unlearn as a white person. It matters to me that, as a white counsellor, I am capable of receiving a client's anger towards a racist misstep. A rule I live by in these situations is that, if I feel the anger is disproportionate to what I believe has occurred, it is likely that I'm lacking some of the story, because this is not within my lived experience.

'I'm sorry,' I say to her, 'I think I've really missed some nuance in what I've learned about hijras. I apologise for hurting you.'

'Is that how you see me? As third gender?' Aditi's voice is tight.

'No, I...' This is not the time to say I know enough to know that not all people who identify as hijra want to be thought of as third gender. I recognise that Aditi feels othered. 'I think of you as a woman, Aditi, but I had not recognised the implication of hijras being seen collectively as "third gender".'

'You can't understand if you're not from my background,' she says, sinking in on herself a little, her arms crossed.

'I think perhaps that's true,' I say, 'but I promise to go away and learn more, and I apologise for thinking I knew more than I did.'

My self-concept as the good, anti-oppressive therapist is at question. I have gone from a trusted trans therapist to an uninformed white therapist. We talk it through carefully, but I have been made aware of my limitations as a white trans person in this conversation (although, as we have seen, a cis, straight person who shares Aditi's heritage can also misstep, but perhaps for different reasons).

Why should a British woman, born and raised in this country, necessarily feel more affinity towards a highly stigmatised group from another continent, with their own internal culture and traditions, than she would towards an identity formulated through the wider culture in which she grew up? In imagining her identifying with hijras, as well as not understanding the complex cultural history and stigma around that term, I have unconsciously thought of Aditi as more Indian than British. It constitutes a version of asking someone 'Where are you from?' on the assumption that they are not from *here*.

In retrospect, I should have been much more careful not to conflate different cultural ways of thinking about gender diversity, and I should have taken more care to stay close to the client's chosen self-description. But as well as that, I rolled together some of the infinite variability of gender divergent experiences. This is somewhat comparable to the unaware and racist psychologist who could only imagine one kind of LGBTQA+ person, and so projected racist assumptions of cultural homophobia onto her and erased her identity as a woman.

I've made a series of oversimplifications in my thinking – a mistake therapists often make when looking at a situation from the outside. We do not see the fine detail if it is not our lived experience. I missed so much of the nuance in my client's experience as a British South Asian trans woman.

'Aditi,' I say later, 'if I feel I've caused a client to do unnecessary labour because of a difference between us, it's my practice to offer a free session in which we can talk things through, because I don't believe my clients should pay for something that's my responsibility.'

She accepts my offer, and I take this to supervision and do a lot more reading and reflecting before we meet for the free session. The session is not for me to be educated but to give her space to talk about how I have impacted her. In the session, I take pains to legitimise her anger towards me. It would be so easy to pathologise it, particularly when she already has the EUPD label that was given to her, and given how racialised transmisogyny can conjure up a false story of aggression. In between the sessions, I have taken time to process my shame and defensiveness so that I can be sure to centre Aditi's feelings and not my own. I try not to shy away from talking about the ways in which I, as a white person, unconsciously uphold racism, even though I do not wish to.

'I'm glad you were able to tell me that I got it wrong for you and show me that you were angry,' I say. 'I'm grateful for what you taught me here, but you should not have had to do this labour.'

'I feel like… I thought you really got it, and you really didn't, and now I don't know how much I can trust…' her voice trails off.

'I can understand your trust in me has been shaken,' I say. 'It makes sense that you'd feel that way.'

I'm not going to tell Aditi right now that she can or should trust me; that's something I hope I can re-establish over time. I hope the process of attending to the rupture and my willingness to face my mistake is helpful to Aditi, but I know I need to go into this work without expectations of getting something back from the person I have harmed (Saad, 2020).

Reflections

I have noted in spaces where counsellors come together a tendency to respond to anger about oppression with *tone policing* (Saad, 2020). The danger is that we miss the structural violence inherent in what has been said originally, and which the person who challenges it is focused on, as their response is problematised for not being sufficiently well-mannered. I can still be tempted to tone police in relation to racism, even though as a trans person I know society has gone to inordinate lengths to paint my community as unreasonable, aggressive, dangerous, touchy and oversensitive (Baker, 2019). My experience of oppression could help me understand and notice my own impulses when I am challenged on racism, but that's not automatic, and white LGBTQA+ people can sometimes overlook our capacity to oppress as white people, since we are marginalised in other ways (binaohan, 2014). I can see the importance of trying to exceed my clients' often understandably low expectations of white therapists. It is also important that I practise humility when I get things wrong, and that I am able to maintain my empathic connection with clients' anger and the impact of structural violence, and not lose it through my own shame response and defensiveness.

I would like to think of myself as a person who isn't racist. For a very long time when I was younger, I thought myself so, comparing myself favourably with my overtly racist parents. The bar was very low, so it wasn't hard. But that self-concept does not serve me as a therapist, and during my training I underwent a painful awakening to the ways in which I still was influenced by racist ideas. That work is ongoing. If I as a white person am benefitting from an unequal structure, then I am, however unintentionally, participating in racism. Until racism has been dismantled, I understand myself as a racist person who is doing their best not to be by continually working at it. In particular, I have found it unhelpful to compare my own levels of racism favourably with that of others who are more blatantly racist than me. Focusing on the excessively racist other can be a way to avoid the inner-self work. Sometimes it is subtle and unaware prejudice from people who consider themselves allies that can be most corrosive, because it happens within spaces and relationships that purport to be trustworthy, and so can disrupt trust and safety that much more.

One issue I take to supervision is a paradox. I know that lived experience of an identity makes a difference to the nuance of understanding that a therapist can provide, and marginalised clients will often seek out therapists who share their identity; yet recent research has found that trans clients who also experienced racism reported difficulties finding therapists who fully matched their identities, and felt let down by white trans therapists and cis therapists who shared their racial heritage in terms of competency and therapist microaggressions (Holti et al., 2023). I am left with a sense that to be a good enough therapist in this regard, I need to fully understand my inadequacy as a white therapist and hold that inadequacy with both acceptance and full determination to continue to do better. Deepening my cultural awareness and understanding of racism and colonialism will be an unending task, but clients who seek out my specialisms need me to keep doing this work.

Understanding the context of colonialism

A legal binary of gender and sex has become so established in the colonised world that it is hard, perhaps, to understand how many precolonial cultures, India being but one, thought about these topics somewhat differently, acknowledging and accepting diversity in biology, sexuality and identity (Agrawal, 1997). Hijra were criminalised under British rule, as were homosexual acts, where prior to colonisation both were more accepted (Ahmed, 2017). Hijra are now referred to and have legal status as a 'third gender', which reflects colonisers' imposition of a legal sex binary that hijras could not fit into, and many view this term as a problematic patch for a more systemic problem (Agrawal, 1997).

Anti-LGBT laws across the globe originate almost entirely from European colonisation, and the British Empire was the worst offender, portraying itself as a 'civilising' force (Ahmed, 2017). Commonwealth countries are still responsible for disproportionate amounts of LGBTQA+ oppression (Ahmed, 2017).

Now, anti-LGBTQA+ attitudes that are the legacy of colonialism are sometimes held up as evidence of the cultural superiority or progressiveness of white nations, in both subtle and blatant ways (Ahmed, 2017). If I am working around LGBTQA+ issues, particularly but not only cross-culturally, it feels important to be aware of the colonial history of homophobia and transphobia:

> The danger here is that the rhetoric of 'civilisation' could take hold once again. Empire was often justified as a means of enlightening, and thereby saving, the populations of the colonial outposts. If Western neoliberalism

and paternalism can be reframed as liberating tendencies, that false narrative will return with force. (Ahmed, 2017)

Aditi's British South Asian ethnicity added to the psychologist's pathologisation of her and undermining of her trans identity. One myth that abounds in anti-trans campaigning is that trans people are gay people transitioning to avoid the stigma of being gay. The (repealed) criminalisation of homosexuality in India is framed to serve the idea that homophobia is more prevalent outside of white-dominated nations (Ahmed, 2017). Transness can then be misrepresented as an attempt to escape from homophobia, and the legacy of colonialism is thus used in further racist ways that also overlook the equally violent repression of gender diversity under colonialism (binaohan, 2014).

The trans community is diverse, with widely varying experiences and no 'one, true story'. Sometimes, our story is about our relationship with our own bodies. Sometimes, it is more about our relationship with our culture: for example, with this oddly rigid system of gendered names, pronouns and legal, binary sex that Europe and the Anglosphere decided on. Equally, the hijra community are not a monolith. Towle & Morgan (2006, pp.674–677) point out the way 'one type of gender variation is posited per nation or per culture', and how ludicrous this is. In other words, the huge variation of gender diverse experiences is erased by dominant and colonising cultures, and I unfortunately replicated this process to a degree with Aditi. But it may also be true that Aditi herself had a flattened-out perception of the stigmatised hijra community. 'Hijras exist in a completely different context and constellation of meanings', Towle & Morgan go on to say – a context and meanings that are specific to Indian culture and history, including religion, colonialism, and the caste system (2006, pp.674–677).

Understanding the context of racialised transmisogyny

There is currently a strong global conservative movement to portray trans women as a danger to cis women, despite the evidence that trans women pose no greater risk than cis women (Hope, 2019a). Trans women, and in particular trans women from racialised groups, are subjected to considerable violence, while being seen as a threat to others and therefore not in need of protection (Ilga Europe, 2021). The history of racism sadly gives us plenty of examples of the ways in which white women are often also seen as the only women in need of protection and safety (Phipps, 2021), dating back to Sojourner Truth (1851).

Relegating a trans woman, particularly one who is also at risk of higher levels of violence due to racism, to a third-gender identity, is othering and endangering in our current cultural context, as well as inaccurate in reflecting her experience. Excluding trans women from the category 'woman' is a way of exempting them from belonging to a category in need of special protection from violence, and in particular, male violence (Phipps, 2021).

As someone not subject to these specific forms of violence, I want to hold an awareness of the danger that trans women, particularly trans women who experience racism, are in, and how my language might contribute to the exclusions that perpetuate that risk.

Understanding neurodiversity in the context of racism and transmisogyny

There is a known significant overlap between being LGBTQA+ and being autistic (Kaleidoscope, 2021). I do not have the space here to set out how we know this is not a causal link but a population cluster that also includes left-handedness, hypermobile joints and many other quirks – I explore this in more detail in my book (Hope, 2019b, pp.105–106). Interest in knowing why this is the case tends to come from a place of wanting to 'fix' these differences. I wish for this diversity to be acknowledged, embraced and celebrated.

Aditi's style of communication, her sensory overwhelm, coupled with her anger towards people guilty of racist and transphobic microaggressions and macroaggressions, might make her seem 'difficult' and hard to empathise with. Milton (2012) talks about the 'double empathy problem' in which it is understood that autistic people do not lack empathy so much as allistic[4] people fail to empathise *with* us (and vice versa, but to no greater degree). There are also interesting studies that show that people's perceptions of anger depend on who is displaying it and can be racially biased: racialised people, particularly women, are often perceived as being more aggressive than they are objectively behaving (Walley-Jean, 2009). Other studies show how the media has persistently influenced people to believe trans people are 'touchy' or 'oversensitive' (Baker, 2019).

Although it is not my job to diagnose or challenge diagnoses, I am aware of the over-diagnosis of LGBTQA+ people with EUPD (Eubanks-Carter & Goldfried, 2006). Racialised people and women are much less likely to get a diagnosis of autism, ADHD or other neurodiversity when it is warranted (Cascio et al., 2020). And there is increasing understanding that people previously diagnosed with EUPD often meet the diagnostic criteria for autism (Engelbrecht & Bercovici, 2023).

These kinds of biases, alongside a lack of awareness of phenomena such as minority stress, complex trauma and neurodiversity, could feed

---

4. Allistic means non-autistic.

into stigmatising and pathologising perceptions of Aditi and her distressed responses. Once the EUPD diagnosis has been applied, it becomes easy to question the reasonableness of Aditi's feelings when she challenges the structural violence of racism, transphobia or ableism. Thus, it can become very easy to gaslight this client into believing that *she* is the problem, if a therapist finds it hard to understand, or stay with, her feelings and reactions or does not fully see or accept her identity. She might be mislabelled aggressive, and this could be used to judge her as failing in expected (transmisogynistic) feminine standards of passivity (Serano, 2013). Such standards might also be added to by white cultural expectations of British South Asian women.

In 2019, the World Health Organisation (WHO, 2021) made the long overdue decision to treat trans identities in the same way that it treats gay identities: that is, no longer listing them as a mental illness (homosexuality was declassified in 1990). Sadly, the legacy of trans people being treated as mentally ill endures, and this will also feed into how Aditi is treated. If your very identity is pathologised and undermined by services that should support you, you are going to be subject to iatrogenic harm (Holti et al., 2023).

I am not immune to these biases, even ones that affect me personally, but I perhaps did more work to unlearn ableism and transphobia than racism and transmisogyny because those systems of oppression affected me directly. But they are not separable, they feed into one another, and I have to keep working to bring all of these structures and the ways in which they operate into my conscious awareness and notice how they tell false stories about my clients. This means reminding myself that my instincts and gut reactions in relation to this client might be responses rooted in racism and transmisogyny, as well as ableism.

Interlocking oppressions

White people may assume Aditi would find more acceptance for her LGBTQA+ identity in 'mainstream' UK culture – an idea that is steeped in hidden ideas of white superiority that we are constantly drip-fed. These narratives fail to talk about the persistent racism and transphobia that resides within white British culture or the persistent racism that resides within the white LGBTQA+ community, including the parts of it that are trans inclusive. In the UK, Aditi is unlikely to find a safe haven among white people and is highly likely to face extra barriers in healthcare and therapy due to racism (Holti et al., 2023). Equally, it does not make sense to presuppose negative attitudes from people of South Asian heritage, even if we cannot ignore the colonial legacy our British South Asian clients may still be impacted by.

> I feel that there's an assumption in society that the communities I'm a part of don't all fit together, but actually my gender is never going to be separate from my race, and my race is never going to be separate from my faith. I think we have to smash the assumption that you have to lose a part of yourself to find the rest. (Choudrey, 2015)

This means a sobering responsibility falls to those of us working with multiply marginalised people to be as faithful as we can to our clients in all aspects of their identities, including those we do not share. Even though I continue to work on raising my own and others' awareness of the legacy of colonialism on my profession and specialisms, I am still tripped up by racism, because it is not one obvious thing but a web of powerful stories woven in countless ways throughout my culture and into how I learned about the world. There is no simple method of unlearning racism. The only pathway I have been able to identify is to keep working – read more, learn more, listen more, think more, reflect more. Keep noticing those threads of oppressive ideas that are woven into the fabric of my culture, and my resistance to noticing and naming them.

I've found it's particularly important to read those intersectional stories, to think of the ways racism combines with other oppressions. I believe we can understand how oppression works more clearly and marginalised stories more accurately when we hear voices from the margins of the margins. Learning from trans people impacted by racism has taught me so much more about both racialised and gender diverse experiences than I ever could learn from more privileged members of either community. The privileged voices that often are invited to speak for their entire communities can be insulated from the more common experiences that come from occupying multiple marginalised identities. In other words, I urge people not to listen only to white voices on the subject of neurodiversity and LGBTQA+ issues.

References

Agrawal, A. (1997). Gendered bodies: The case of the 'third gender' in India. *Contributions to Indian Sociology, 31*(2), 273–297. https://doi.org/10.1177/006996697031002005

Ahmed, I. (2017, March 20). Debating the British Empire's 'legacy' is pointless – this is still an imperial world. *The Conversation.* www.theconversation.com/debating-the-british-empires-legacy-is-pointless-this-is-still-an-imperial-world-74222

Baker, P. (2019, November 26). *Representing trans people in the UK press – a follow-up study.* [Blog]. ESRC Centre for Corpus Approaches to Social Science. http://cass.lancs.ac.uk/representing-trans-people-in-the-uk-press-a-follow-up-study-professor-paul-baker/

binaohan, b. (2014). *decolonizing trans/gender 101.* Toronto: biyuti publishing.

Cascio, M., Weiss, J. & Racine, E. (2020). Making autism research inclusive by attending to intersectionality: A review of the research ethics literature. *Review Journal of Autism and Developmental Disorders, 8*, 22–36. https://doi.org/10.1007/s40489-020-00204-z

Choudrey, S. (2015, December 6). *Brown, trans, queer, Muslim and proud.* [Video]. www.youtube.com/watch?v=w6hxrZW6I9I&ab_channel=TEDxTalks

Engelbrecht, N. & Bercovici, D. (2023, February 21). *It's not BPD; it's autism.* Embrace autism. https://embrace-autism.com/its-not-bpd-its-autism/

Eubanks-Carter, C. & Goldfried, M.R. (2006). The impact of client sexual orientation and gender on clinical judgments and diagnosis of borderline personality disorder. *Journal of Clinical Psychology, 62*(6), 751–770. https://doi.org/10.1002/jclp.20265

Holti, R., Callahan, E., Fletcher, J., Hope, S., Moller, N., Vincent, B. & Walley, P. (2023). *Improving the integration of care for trans adults: Final report.* Health and Social Care Delivery Research (in press).

Hope, S. (2019a). *Creating a lie: How trans women are portrayed as predators.* A feminist challenging transphobia. https://feministchallengingtransphobia.wordpress.com/2019/05/10/creating-a-lie-how-trans-women-are-portrayed-as-predators/

Hope, S. (2019b). *Person centred counselling for trans and gender diverse people: A practical guide.* Jessica Kingsley Publishers.

Ilga Europe. (2021, November 20). *Say their names: The trans and gender diverse people whose murders were reported in europe and central asia last year.* [Blog]. Ilga Europe. https://www.ilga-europe.org/blog/say-their-names-trans-gender-diverse-people-murders-reported-europe-central-asia/

Kaleidoscope. (2021). *The overlapping spectrums of ASD and LGBTIQA+.* [Blog]. Kaleidoscope. www.kaleidoscopelgbtq.org/the-overlapping-spectrums-of-asd-and-lgbtqia

Milton, D. (2012). On the ontological status of autism: The 'double empathy problem'. *Disability & Society, 27*(6), 883–887.

Phipps, A. (2021). White tears, white rage: Victimhood and (as) violence in mainstream feminism., *European Journal of Cultural Studies, 24*(1), 81–93.

Ratcliffe, S. (Ed.). (2017). *Oxford essential quotations* (5th ed.). Oxford University Press. www.oxfordreference.com/view/10.1093/acref/9780191843730.001.0001/q-oro-ed5-00016497

Saad, L. (2020). *Me and white supremacy: How to recognise your privilege, combat racism and change the world.* Quercus.

Serano, J. (2013). *Excluded: Making feminist and queer movements more inclusive.* Seal Press.

Soto, A., Smith, T.B., Griner, D., Domenech Rodríguez, M. & Bernal, G. (2018). Cultural adaptations and therapist multicultural competence: Two meta-analytic reviews. *Journal of Clinical Psychology, 74*(11), 1907–1923.

Towle, E.B. & Morgan, L.M. (2006). Romancing the transgender native: Rethinking the use of the 'third gender' concept. In: Stryker, S. & Whittle, S. (Eds.), *The transgender studies reader* (pp.666–684). Routledge.

Truth, S. (1851). *Speech entitled 'Ain't I a Woman?' by Sojourner Truth delivered at the 1851 Women's Convention in Akron, Ohio.* https://thehermitage.com/wp-content/uploads/2016/02/Sojourner-Truth_Aint-I-a-Woman_1851.pdf

Walley-Jean, J.C. (2009). Debunking the myth of the 'angry black woman': An exploration of anger in young African American women. *Black Women, Gender and Families* 3(2), 68–86.

World Health Organisation. (2021). *WHO/Europe brief – transgender health in the context of ICD-11*. World Health Organisation. www.euro.who.int/en/health-topics/health-determinants/gender/gender-definitions/whoeurope-brief-transgender-health-in-the-context-of-icd-11

8. (Inter)racial transference: A case of projective identification

Jaspreet Tehara

In sharing an experience of part of my training through this chapter, I am looking to communicate some of my thoughts and feelings around being psychologically attacked in a therapeutic setting because of my race, and to share some reflections on how I was left following it. I will introduce a White British patient, Richard,[1] and discuss how the relationship between us highlights a case of projective identification, where I was left holding his projection to an unsatisfactory end. The vignettes span the first three sessions of our therapeutic engagement and highlight how I perceived Richard as a threat through his antagonistic stance toward me.

I explore our interactions from a relational perspective (Mitchell, 2014), tracking their evolution from a perceived boundary violation through to Richard's attack on the process of therapy, his attack on me, and how I reacted. My aim is to explore my thoughts on some psychoanalytic concepts and how they can be used to consider the experiences of minority ethnic therapists with White British patients when race is brought into a room aggressively or with hostility. The chapter will conclude with some further thoughts on the process and what was learned. I hope there is plenty of food for thought for the reader in how the experience affected me.

Transference and projection

Transference is experienced as a common phenomenon in the therapeutic relationship. Gelso and Bhatia (2012) define transference as:

---

1. Richard is a composite based on several of my encounters with patients in my therapy room. All details are completely fictionalised.

the patient's experience and perceptions of the therapist that are shaped by the patient's own psychological structures and past, involving carry-over from, and displacement onto the therapist of feelings, attitudes and behaviours belonging rightfully in earlier significant relationships. (p.385)

Transference can be experienced by the patient in both positive and negative ways, in terms of spectrums of healthy to unhealthy transferences. Healthy positive transference would indicate that the therapist is seen as a helpful, interested person; unhealthy positive transference can indicate that a patient idealises the therapist (Kernberg, 1989; Levy & Scala, 2012), and it may have to be addressed to enable the patient to integrate both the good and bad parts of the therapist. Negative transference can be characterised by feelings of mistrust, upset and anger. Again, it can occur along a spectrum from healthy negative feelings that arise through the therapeutic work to feelings of intense hatred towards the therapist (Gelso et al., 2013).

Gelso and Hayes (2007) define countertransference as:

the therapist's internal and external reactions that are shaped by the therapist's past and present emotional conflicts and vulnerabilities. (p.25)

Gelso goes on to explain that countertransference reactions are reflections of a therapist's own unresolved issues that have been brought to the surface by the patient (2014).

Briefly, projective identification (Klein, 1946; Sandler, 2018) is a two-part phenomenon, whereby a person (person A) uses the defensive method of projection – that is, they assign *their own* unwanted thoughts, feelings and affects onto another (person B). Person B then introjects (unconsciously adapts) their own beliefs, thinking or behaviour to fit person A's expectations and predictions. Often, the unexpected changes in person B appear to arrive from nowhere, and with little warning. In the encounters I am exploring in this chapter, projective identification occurred due to repeated psychic attacks during the beginning of the therapeutic intervention and culminated in my (r)ejection of the patient from our sessions in a manner that was out of character for me. My thoughts at the time were that I had acted appropriately, but as time has passed, I have been left with a sense of incompleteness, and I now acknowledge this was a missed opportunity to explore the pain for both of us of a racialised incident within the bounds of a therapeutic relationship. I hold that working with someone relationally means that therapists may need to engage in processing the patient's position in a racialised dynamic, as well as

Race and development of the other

Regarding issues of racism in the therapeutic milieu, a litany of theoretical and research papers pontificate on the nature of the encounter, predominantly centring on the therapeutic engagement from a perspective of a minority ethnic patient being 'done to' by a White practitioner in the therapeutic space. These papers, building from a feminist and anti-colonial praxis, discuss issues of power dynamics and intersectionality (Crenshaw, 1989; Collins & Bilge, 2020), clinical faux pas (Leary, 2000; Layton, 2006) and inadequacies in cultural alignment, often born from a misunderstanding of cultural nuances (Laungani, 2004).

Some psychological and sociological research seeks to address issues such as intersectionality and contemporary theories of oppression, including multiple minority stress theory (Cyrus, 2017; Meyer 2003), as well as highlight how compounding stressors result in poorer health and wellbeing outcomes for people with minority status. Literature such as Fanon's *Black Skin, White Masks* (1967) looks to understand how analytic theories may not be appropriate when addressing the trauma inflicted on colonised peoples. This is because psychoanalysis, tied as it is to individualised processes, fails to recognise how largely oppressive societies built in a Eurocentric image use economic power to subjugate and create a sense of subjective inferiority (in Fanon's terminology, 'epidermalisation').

More recently, there is emerging literature and discussion from White ethnicity therapists addressing issues of race and systemic privilege with their White patients (Drustrup, 2020), with an attempt to focus on acknowledging the structural and societal influences of which these patients may or may not be aware in their interactions with people of colour (King & Borders, 2019). This emerging trend is, however, open to critique as there is ongoing discussion about the contextual need to explore these issues in therapy, if they are not part of the patient presentation. Presently, there is no academic literature on this critique but there are ongoing discussions that have been published in magazines such as *The Psychologist* and *Therapy Today* (the membership journals of the British Psychological Society and the British Association for Counselling and Psychotherapy, respectively) from various practitioners querying the validity and purpose of these discussions in the therapy room between White therapist and White patient. However, there appears to be less written or reported about minority ethnic therapists in therapeutic relationship with White patients. Even less has been written about the experiences of minority ethnic therapists when they are subject to racism in the therapeutic encounter, and this is the focus of my chapter.

Broadly speaking, we can look to understand racial issues as ones of visible difference and otherness that lend themselves to group and social exclusions based on cultural and biological assumptions of superiority and inferiority (Said, 1978; Clarke, 1999). More recently, we can observe the discussion at the beginning of the Covid-19 pandemic where socio-economic factors that led to the lack of protection for many minority ethnic groups were reframed as biological deficiencies in these people (Paradies et al., 2015; Platt & Warwick, 2020). Such arguments sought to dehumanise people from minority backgrounds (Devakumar et al., 2020, 2022), and follow a long historical pattern of so doing (White, 2020).

To think and understand 'the other' as both *different to* and *separate from*, however, draws on psychoanalytical theories about the nature of the object and our relationship to it from one's subjective position (see Chapter 3 in Bollas (2017) for more discussion around the topic of the subject and the object).

It is pertinent to explain the rationale for addressing these complicated mechanisms of defensive procedure as this chapter will focus on and explore the events that occurred between Richard and me during my training as a counselling psychologist.

Enter Richard

Richard presented to me during my second year of a training placement. He had self-referred to the service, seeking help with problems with anger management. The referral form said that his employer had suggested he seek help after a falling out with his line manager. It did not offer much further information. As was the practice of the service, I telephoned Richard two days before his appointment for the initial assessment, to confirm his attendance. He answered the phone sounding irritable, as though I was interrupting something, and I noted tension in his voice. I asked him if this was a good time to continue speaking, due to my perception of his tone, and he said it was 'fine' and that he would be coming to the appointment and then abruptly ended the call by hanging up.

Richard was a lower middle-class, cis-gendered White male in his mid-50s. He looked flushed and scowling as he arrived in the reception area, where I met him. The therapy room was on the second floor of the building, and I liked to meet and greet patients, rather than leave them to follow the receptionist's directions. I told him the room number and he brushed past me and marched up the stairs, with me following behind. In the room, he immediately took the chair nearest the door, without invitation. Once we were seated, I mentioned the referral and how little information was in it and invited him to say more about what had brought him to therapy. He dismissed my questioning and launched into talking about my telephone call two days before. In the following vignette taken from the session, we can explore some of the anger evident towards me in Richard's reaction to what he perceived as a boundary transgression.

Session one

Richard: I don't understand why you called me two days ago.

Jaspreet: Why do you think I called you?

Richard: I don't know, but I don't like people calling me unexpectedly.

Jaspreet: Okay. I understand that. I get a sense, listening to how you're talking about it, that you're upset by me calling you. What is your experience of people calling you unexpectedly?

Richard: Well, it's usually cold callers and people that want something out of you.

Jaspreet: So how did you experience our call?

Richard: I found it strange you'd call me to confirm our session slot when you knew I'd be here.

Jaspreet: Why would I know that?

Richard: Why did you think I wouldn't turn up? I don't appreciate unsolicited telephone calls. I said I'd be here. I'm a man of my word.

Jaspreet: We do normally call people before we see them for the first session, as a courtesy and as part of the introduction process. We do it to check whether or not they would still like therapeutic work. I noticed it has been some time since you made your self-referral.

Richard: So, you're checking to see if other people still think I'm crazy then.

Jaspreet: People think you're crazy?

Richard: That's what the person on the phone was hinting at when she was asking me all those personal questions.

Jaspreet: You sound quite angry about that.

When I think back, this initial exchange offered clues to what would later transpire in subsequent sessions. For instance, when Richard stated that he experienced people who called him as 'wanting something out of you', this was the first clue to his experience of other people as extractive. His comment, 'I'm a man of my word' offered another point to explore because I could read it as either people finding it difficult to trust him or Richard distinguishing himself as better than other people who do not keep their word. Third, there were clues to how others experienced Richard and his behaviour in his statement that other people thought him 'crazy,' when I experienced him in the room as being extremely upset, possibly due to his feeling interrogated by the person doing the initial telephone assessment. My transgression may have been to have failed to address his upset and hurt and instead to call him 'angry'. Anger is often a reactionary expression of pain, and through exploration of the pain we may come to understand more about the causes rather than simply address the symptoms. However, in the session I felt under pressure to address the frustration expressed in Richard's manner toward me, so I labelled it as anger.

Session two

The second vignette comes from the second session between us. We were discussing Richard's family background and, at this point, his relationship with his sister, through an exploration of his developmental family genogram (McGoldrick, 2011) (a drawing of the developmental family matrix, stemming from more systemic approaches to understanding psychological work with a patient). This is an approach I would often use as part of my initial assessment.

At this point, Richard launched into an attack on the process of therapy.

Richard: What's the fucking point of all this?

Jaspreet: Is something upsetting you?

Richard: This whole process. I seem to be answering the same questions over and over, again and again! Do you think it's fun to drag up all your family history?

Jaspreet: I can understand this may be difficult; I was looking to understand the relationship between you and your sister a little more.

Richard: This whole process is shit. You're all as thick as shit. It's the same questions over and over again. First you tell me the information you were given wasn't enough and then you make assumptions that I actually want to talk about my family. That is not why I'm here. I'm here about something different. I was sent here to talk about what happened between me and my boss at work. You haven't even mentioned that.

Jaspreet: What would you like to tell me about that? I wonder if you feel as though you do not get heard when you speak in other contexts too, so please, tell me.

Richard: He was always telling me how to do my job. From day one. He waltzes into the job, over my head, with his fancy degree in computer claptrap, no experience, no knowledge of the business. I've worked there for 20 years. Never missed a day and never lost a single item. No recognition of that when they advertised the post. And then he has the cheek to say I'm maybe stressed because of my marriage breaking down and that I should do some effing course and 'get help'. I know what this is about. It's just this positive discrimination thing – the company wants to look good by having Black people in middle management so they can tick boxes – at my expense.

Jaspreet: I can see you are very upset by this. It seems something very hard for you to have experienced this and to feel you have been slighted when you have given so much.

Reviewing the interaction between us, the attacks on me during the first vignette had now widened out to attacks on the process of therapy. I asked him if he was upset, as a way of naming a feeling I was observing, but I could also have asked him what he was feeling in the moment and explored his capability to express his emotions. With hindsight, I would have chosen this second option as it was more exploratory and less assuming.

It was also through this session that Richard brought in the information about his relationship with his line manager, and that the manager was both younger and Black, which had not been mentioned in the referral information. Richard's outburst occurred when the manager was trying to explain a new process of digitally recording goods in and out of the warehouse, which Richard had previously completed manually. Richard was unfamiliar with computer software packages and digital technology and was of a generation where this was not taught in school. I would have liked to ask Richard if he held concerns about me because of his experience with this manager, making a direct link between this relationship and his therapeutic relationship with me in the immediate moment. However, as will be highlighted, the possibility of Richard accepting an interpretation from me was low.

Session three

The third vignette comes from our last session. During the session, there was an eruption between us, and I ended the session by (r)ejecting Richard from the therapeutic space. I was caught in an enactment that appeared to replicate the breakdown of his relationship with his manager, resulting in an ending of a relationship that was thought to be (and was possibly experienced as) transactional and complicated by racial dynamics. In the moments preceding this part of the session, I listened to Richard again express some of his annoyance and anger towards his manager, which was now also placed in the context of a discussion about his manager's experience, age and race.

Jaspreet: So, you've spoken previously about the relationship between yourself and your mother, in relation to how she expected you to be contributing to the household budget from your earnings when you were 16. I'm wondering how you experience me, as a non-White therapist, asking you for money, weekly, in therapy?

Richard: See, that's the problem with you all. I don't particularly like the idea that I have to give money to you at all. The only reason I do it is because this is a counselling service, for a charity, but I should never have been signed up with you at all.

Jaspreet: Do you have a sense that this is a scam, that you are being done out of what is rightfully yours, like the job?

Richard: Something about it is off. I would never come to you if I had the choice.

Jaspreet: Why? What makes you say that?

Richard: I don't think I can trust you all. At all.

Jaspreet: You all? Meaning?

Richard: Pakis, Niggers. You're all the fucking same.

Jaspreet: Excuse me?

Richard: You're all a bunch of scammers. What's in this for you? Pakis, you're always into some scam.

Jaspreet: I think this session is over. You need to get the fuck out of my room. We're done here. You don't need to pay for the fucking session. Get out.

In the immediate aftermath of this session, I was left with a very strong sense of annoyance and upset at what had just occurred. I felt as though I had not been seen for who I was, but rather as an emotional punching bag and a proxy for the feelings Richard had towards his boss. I believe his rationale for this was my race, age and experience. I highlight my age as I was also younger than Richard, much like his new boss.

I was left shocked by my own reaction toward Richard – my swearing at him and demanding that he leave the therapy room. Partially that shock arose from my letting go of my professionalism, but it also came from an annoyance that Richard had activated in me a sense of threat that I felt I needed to address through reverting to language and a vulgarity that I thought I had outgrown. I had experience of de-activating such behaviour in my patients, but in this instance, I was not able to maintain my critical distance, professional objectivity and self-composure.

Analysis

I recall how threatened I felt by Richard's aggression during the course of the sessions, knowing that he was becoming increasingly antagonistic towards me. I felt physically taut, with knots in my stomach, as the sessions progressed. I also recall a low, ongoing sense of anxiety, which made it hard for me to concentrate and sit still as the time for the sessions drew nearer on my clinical diary. I had other patients to see on those days, and we trainees can feel pressured to continue with our clinics even after an upsetting incident such as this, because we need to gain the necessary clinical hours of face-to-face contact. As a counselling psychologist in training, I needed to complete 450 clinical hours in three years, together with attending lectures and completing demanding academic and research work. The capacity for such disruptions were limited and there was a strong pull to bracket negative experiences and explore them later in supervision, either with the placement supervisor, peers or my course tutor.

I was angry, and I was hurt, and I couldn't understand what had happened between us in those moments. I felt disorientated as I had engaged in something I had never, until that point, contemplated could occur – I had thrown a patient out of the therapeutic space and terminated a relationship prematurely. As the session had ended so abruptly and early, I had enough time to write my notes, make a cup of tea and put the episode to one side to review it later. But in the moment, I felt unsupported because I did not feel I had anywhere to address this experience. I was not able to contact my placement supervisor, as my clinical diary was full. I knew I had to contain and package my feelings and deal with them when the working day was over, and I would then have time to fully process my feelings by contacting my peer group.

Through discussing what happened later, in my own therapy, I have explored my own transference issues around parental-type figures and what it means to have to make myself vulnerable to people offering me support in a hierarchical structure and what it means to accept that support. Indeed, I spoke to my peer group first because I found it difficult to express myself to supervisors who were representative of structures that are notoriously backward in identifying, validating and acknowledging the harm of racialised incidents (Fernando, 2017). What made the peer group safe was partially its diversity: I was in one of the most ethnically diverse cohorts of trainees our course had taken on at the time of my attendance, with a similar diversity of ages and sexualities. It was a place of relative safety and acceptance where I could express my thoughts about the experience.

My cognitive processes in the immediate moment were thoughts around my failure to communicate and interpret Richard's pain in a safe and contained way. Through my processing of what occurred, I was able to hold the thought that Richard may have also been so hurt and in pain that he was not yet ready to process his feelings in any way that I could have contained.

I was able to process my experience through critical distance and appropriate supervision, and develop my understanding that the anger I exhibited was secondary to the hurt I had experienced in being reduced in Richard's eyes to a part-object.[2]

Following some time thinking about the interactions in the first two sessions, my attempt to build a space where we could discuss issues of race came through my trying to make a total transference interpretation[3] through which we could have explored Richard's sense of conditional worth (Joseph, 1985). When I tried to help Richard think about the parallels between his relationship with his mother when he was younger, his relationship with his boss, and the relationship between me and Richard in the here-and-now, I was hoping he would take the opportunity to reflect on what I was giving back to him from the content he had provided.

It appears he was unable to hold or stay with what I had said to explore the interpretation further, and as such, went on to perform what Bion would describe as an attack on linking (1984). Bion (1984) describes this as a process of splitting (into 'good' and 'bad') in which part-object relationships dominate the mind of the patient. This process occurs not only to the external objects (like the therapist), but inwards, towards the self also. As such, the inability to hold and examine the uncomfortable part of the self is turned outward into projection. In this instance, Richard received a countertransferential reaction from me that was neither considered nor well thought out, as I rejected him in the session in a way that possibly mimicked how he wanted to reject me. In the moment, I was not able to see that the feelings Richard expressed toward me, and that I reacted to, were not my own, or of my own making – they

---

2. In psychoanalytic thinking, a part-object is a partial mental representation of a person, object or body-part that is separated from its whole or from its context. Infants, for example, are not yet able to understand people as complete entities and only perceive items for the binary experiences of pleasure or frustration (see Klein (1946) for further discussion). As a child develops, they are then able to integrate parts in to a whole and create a fuller understanding of the world and the people around them.

3. A total transference interpretation is a type of interpretation that uses the analyst and the present time to indicate and make a fuller interpretation of the experience of the patient, to the patient in the moment. It consists of three parts: 1) The relationship of the patient with a person in the past, outside of the room; 2) the relationship of the patient with a person in the present, outside of the room, and 3) the relationship between the patient and the analyst in the present, in the room. The purpose of this interpretation is to assist the patient in understanding their reoccurring unconscious dynamics and relational patterns in an attempt to make the patterns conscious and to make different experiences actionable for the patient.

ostensibly came as a reaction to his rejection of me. On review, I am able to hold that my intentions were to engage with him in an exploratory manner, but there was also a reactive element in my interpretation that arose from a sense of threat and the anxiety that accompanied it.

Richard stated that he did not want me, that he would not have paired with me for therapeutic work, that he did not want to pay for the work with me, and he would not be in the session with me if he had the choice. Overall, this left me feeling as though I was of no value and no worth to him. Richard then went on to sever the connection as best he could by using racialised slurs, which compounded that sense of rejection.

Reflection

I spent time processing the interactions in supervision over the following months to better understand my actions in throwing Richard out of the session and why this occurred.

In retrospect, my anger with Richard reflected my disgust that Richard had used racial slurs in my presence. Racism is dehumanising and Richard's words exemplified this. It was also totally unexpected. I had experienced racism previously when I was working as a healthcare assistant in mental healthcare settings, but this was my first experience of it in a therapy setting. My experience had been that therapeutic relationships are intimate and far more intense that those in my previous care roles, and therefore racism was not something I had been expecting to experience so overtly. I had been insulted because of my ethnicity, and compared to someone operating a scam. In that moment, I was so angry that I could do nothing else except shout at Richard to leave. But once I had processed my anger, I was left with more questions than answers, which became wholly unsatisfactory, as there would be no resolution with him.

From a personal perspective, I experienced many mixed emotions over the next weeks and months as I worked through the process of what had occurred. I was left with some professional shame for having handled the episode as I did – for being unable to separate my professional self from my personal self. This left me with questions about when and where that is possible, if at all, when faced with racism in such a direct manner. To deny one's ethnicity in the encounter is to fail to offer a full and authentic experience of 'being with' the patient, and when something is immediately obvious, like ethnicity, it cannot be ignored in the therapeutic milieu, as minority ethnic peoples wear our ethnicity on our skin. Ideally, the issue of race can be a fruitful ground for exploration, to contribute to greater education of difference *and* similarity in a common humanity in therapeutic work. However, I think that curiosity around what race means for both patient and therapist often can be missed, due to uncontained negative feelings when race is brought into the room in an antagonistic manner.

Retrospectively, I now feel that this was a missed opportunity to work with someone on their attitudes towards people of colour. This has come from my position of having less structural pressure to perform and achieve targets at the expense, even, of my own wellbeing, and my reflections on the processes of othering and dehumanisation that occurs through racism. Coming back to the idea of negative transference, I can see that Richard may have been looking to channel his negative feelings towards something that he could harm – a younger, minority ethnic therapist – as he couldn't express them towards his mother or his boss. There may be an alternative reading, but I may not ever be able to explain it due the termination of our therapy together.

I find this an incredible statement to make because I am aware of the contradictory and complex feelings I am exploring in this chapter, and I am also aware that there may be some disagreement among readers, due to the affective nature of racism. But I believe I lost sight of one of the core objectives of therapeutic work, which is to provide a reparative relationship. Moreover, I recognise that I felt unable to provide my patient with containment, which called into question my own internal sense of competency, and I experienced this as far more hurtful than anything Richard had said. Richard was extremely hurt by experiences he'd had and found an object in me that he could channel his anger, pain and upset into. It is my understanding now that I was, at that time, not robust enough to hold his feelings in a contained manner, or in a way that could facilitate him to explore them.

But this by no means absolves Richard of responsibility for his actions. I can now hold that there may have been such a desire to get rid of that feeling through projection into our relationship that I acted out and identified with what had occurred before, effectively cutting off the relationship before it had time to develop and evolve any further. Living through this episode offered me valuable experience in terms of how to approach issues such as this in the future. I also spent time thinking about links between Black African and South Asian cultures, reading about social theories of the peoples of both continents (Ikuenobe, 2006; Singh, 1990), and exploring more about communalism and the hangovers from colonialism (Judge, 2002). However, I was offered the interpretation in supervision that this may be too intellectualised an approach as I was searching for an answer that would explain the situation rather than sit with my feelings of upset. The second interpretation is that possibly Richard had a transference reaction to a younger mentor of colour trying to guide him through a process of self-exploration, because it echoed his previous experience of his younger boss guiding him through a new and unfamiliar activity at work. My countertransference through the process was one of anger towards Richard for the psychological attacks on me, and a total transference interpretation could be viewed as the retaliation whereby I banished him from the room. In being split off and unable to reflect on himself, Richard's process prompted me to split as well – I was unable to think clearly in the moment. I accept that I may have been premature in my assessment of Richard's ability to embrace and reflect on a total transference interpretation, and instead acted out my feelings of frustration with him in the countertransference (Winnicott, 1949). Paula Heimann writes:

> From the point of view I am stressing, the analyst's counter-transference is not only part and parcel of the analytic relationship, but she is the patient's creation; it is part of the patient's unconscious. (1950, p.83)

Richard had been openly antagonistic in the first session following his perceived boundary violation, dismissive of the process of therapeutic work in the second, and, finally, attacking in the third when seemingly he was unable to hold an interpretation. My interpretation of the splitting off that occurred with Richard is partially what led on to my own sense of fragmenting in the work with him and not feeling able to hold parts of myself together, resulting in reactive outburst. Heimann goes on to state:

> The analyst's countertransference is an instrument of research into the patient's unconscious. (1950, p.84)

I also considered the process of projective identification. This had been my first experience of being so overwhelmed by another that my own ability to think was severed. Fanon (1967) explores the concept of the phobogenic (meaning an object that causes fear in the White person), and in processing my interactions with Richard, I have pondered the ways in which he may have been fearful of the rejection he eventually elicited through projective identification. He was faced with a younger man of colour in a position of relative professional expertise, from whom he may have sought support for psychological harm, and this is a subversion of the paradigm of Eurocentric superiority to which he was very likely accustomed. Perhaps this was too much for him to bear in consideration of his experiences with his young, Black boss.

Finally, there was also an opportunity to think about castration and the anxieties that could have arisen in the relationship between us. In a relational sense, and in considering the role of the father (Thomas, 2010; Stern, 2007), I may have castrated Richard, rather than being able to spend some time with him considering together what it meant to have said the words he used and the way we arrived at that point. Instead, in the moment, he experienced the wrath of my direct reaction to his words through my expulsion and cutting off his therapy.

Conclusion

I wish to state that I am not advocating that a minority ethnic therapist sits with being racially attacked, be that psychologically, verbally or physically. However, the ability to examine and learn in a reflexive capacity may halt descent into some of the pitfalls that could occur when issues of racism enter therapeutic spaces. Jonathan Bradley (2018) writes about the ways in which patients are driven by parental and reparative drives. Bradley suggests that empathy and insight are gained by the therapist being able to recognise their own early self in the patient and to gain some form of understanding for their plight. In looking back to my own actions, I am left wondering if I had an identification with the aggressive feelings and, in acting out, sided myself with aggressive behaviours to feel safe. This was not reparative to Richard, or to me, in the work.

One of the ways of thinking about how my own sense of threat could have been interpreted is through a compassion-focused lens (Gilbert, 2009, 2010) and by understanding that clear thinking is not likely to be achieved in a state of threat or anxiety. In my immediate reflection on the interactions with Richard, I was able to understand the sense of threat that I felt through active use of supervision, although I was not able to process the ways in which threat blocks clearer thinking in a multifactoral manner. In this chapter, I have talked about a sense of threat from the patient and also from the institute, which I had assessed as unable to hold my feelings. This is something I would highlight as important for minority ethnic therapists who work with threat and antagonisms in their therapeutic environments, as well as their day-to-day environments in Western societies. Being attuned to the sensations of threat and what they can mean in a physiological manner can highlight flight-fight-freeze instincts, blockages in thought and process, and ultimately transference–countertransference interactions that are the bedrock of psychodynamic and psychoanalytic therapy. My experience at the time indicated I needed to think through the various issues that show because of being a minority ethnic trainee, and the structural support I felt had been missing.

Richard spoke to me in ways that suggested he felt fearful and upset, and this was not something I was able to connect to, due to the pervading sense of threat he elicited in me. At the same time, there is no need to express complete benevolence in the face of racialised content. Perhaps there was opportunity enough to explore this further while also holding my feelings towards Richard in a way that wasn't so disconnected and rejecting.

References

Bion, W.R. (1984). Attacks on linking. In, W.R. Bion, *Second thoughts: Selected papers on psychoanalysis* (pp.93–109). Routledge.

Bollas, C. (2017). *The shadow of the object: Psychoanalysis of the unthought known*. Routledge.

Bradley, J. (2018). Being 'black' in the transference: Working under the spectre of racism. In F. Lowe & M.F. Davids (Eds.), *Thinking space* (pp.85–108). Routledge.

Clarke, S. (1999). Splitting difference: Psychoanalysis, hatred and exclusion. *Journal for the Theory of Social Behaviour, 29*(1), 21–35.

Collins, P.H. & Bilge, S. (2020). *Intersectionality*. Polity Press.

Crenshaw, K. (1989). Demarginalizing the intersection of race and sex: A black feminist critique of antidiscrimination doctrine, feminist theory and antiracist politics. *University of Chicago Legal Forum, 1*(8). http://chicagounbound.uchicago.edu/uclf/vol1989/iss1/8

Cyrus, K. (2017). Multiple minorities as multiply marginalized: Applying the minority stress theory to LGBTQ people of color. *Journal of Gay & Lesbian Mental Health, 21*(3), 194–202.

Devakumar, D., Selvarajah, S., Abubakar, I., Kim, S.S., McKee, M., Sabharwal, N.S., Saini, A., Shannon, G., White, I.R. & Achiume, E.T. (2022). Racism, xenophobia, discrimination, and the determination of health. *The Lancet, 400*(10368), 2097–2108.

Devakumar, D., Shannon, G., Bhopal, S.S., & Abubakar, I. (2020). Racism and discrimination in COVID-19 responses. *The Lancet, 395*(10231), 1194.

Drustrup, D. (2020). White therapists addressing racism in psychotherapy: An ethical and clinical model for practice. *Ethics & Behavior, 30*(3), 181–196.

Fanon, F. (1967). *Black skin, white masks*. Grove Press.

Fernando, S. (2017). *Institutional racism in psychiatry and clinical psychology*. Palgrave Macmillan.

Gelso, C. (2014). A tripartite model of the therapeutic relationship: Theory, research, and practice. *Psychotherapy Research, 24*(2), 117–131.

Gelso, C.J. & Bhatia, A. (2012). Crossing theoretical lines: The role and effect of transference in nonanalytic psychotherapies. *Psychotherapy, 49*, 384–390.

Gelso, C.J. & Hayes, J. (2007). *Countertransference and the therapist's inner experience: Perils and possibilities*. Routledge.

Gelso, C.J., Palma, B. & Bhatia, A. (2013). Attachment theory as a guide to understanding and working with transference and the real relationship in psychotherapy. *Journal of Clinical Psychology, 69*(11), 1160–1171.

Gilbert, P. (2009). Introducing compassion-focused therapy. *Advances in Psychiatric Treatment, 15*(3), 199–208.

Gilbert, P. (2010). *Compassion focused therapy: Distinctive features*. Routledge.

Heimann, P. (1950). On counter-transference. *International journal of Psycho-Analysis, 31*, 81–84.

Ikuenobe, P. (2006). *Philosophical perspectives on communalism and morality in African traditions*. Lexington Books.

Joseph, B. (1985). Transference: The total situation. *International Journal of Psycho-Analysis, 66*, 447–454.

Judge, P.S. (2002). Religion, caste, and communalism in Punjab. *Sociological Bulletin, 51*(2), 175–194.

Kernberg, O. (1989). *Psychodynamic psychotherapy of borderline patients*. Basic Books.

King, K.M. & Borders, L.D. (2019). An experimental investigation of white counselors broaching race and racism. *Journal of Counseling & Development*, 97(4), 341–351.

Klein, M. (1946). Notes on some schizoid mechanisms. *International Journal of Psycho-Analysis*, 27, 99–110.

Laungani, P. (2004). *Asian perspectives in counselling and psychotherapy*. Routledge.

Layton, L. (2006). Racial identities, racial enactments, and normative unconscious processes. *The Psychoanalytic Quarterly*, 75(1), 237–269.

Leary, K. (2000). Racial enactments in dynamic treatment. *Psychoanalytic Dialogues*, 10(4), 639–653.

Levy, K.N. & Scala, J. (2012). Transference, transference interpretations, and transference-focused psychotherapies. *Psychotherapy*, 49(3), 391.

McGoldrick M. (2011). *The genogram journey: Reconnecting with your family*. W.W. Norton.

Meyer, I.H. (2003). Prejudice, social stress, and mental health in lesbian, gay, and bisexual populations: Conceptual issues and research evidence. *Psychological Bulletin*, 129(5), 674.

Mitchell, S.A. (2014). *Relationality: From attachment to intersubjectivity*. Routledge.

Paradies, Y., Ben, J., Denson, N., Elias, A., Priest, N., Pieterse, A., Gupta, A., Kelaher, M. & Gee, G. (2015). Racism as a determinant of health: A systematic review and meta-analysis. *PloS One*, 10(9), e0138511.

Platt, L. & Warwick, R. (2020). *Are some ethnic groups more vulnerable to COVID-19 than others?* Institute for Fiscal Studies.

Said, E.W. (1978). *Orientalism*. Pantheon Books.

Sandler, J. (2018). *Projection, identification, projective identification*. Routledge.

Singh, R. (1990). Communalism and the struggle against communalism: A Marxist view. *Social Scientist*, 18(8/9), 4–21.

Stern, D.N. (2007). A felicitous meeting of attachment and relational psychotherapy. *Attachment: New Directions in Relational Psychoanalysis and Psychotherapy*, 1(1), 1–7.

Thomas, L.K. (2010). Relational psychotherapy: The significance of father. *Psychodynamic Practice*, 16(1), 61–75.

White, A.I. (2020). Historical linkages: Epidemic threat, economic risk, and xenophobia. *The Lancet*, 395(10232), 1250–1251.

Winnicott, D.W. (1949). Hate in the counter-transference. *International Journal of Psycho-Analysis*, 30, 69–74.

9. Diunital[1] healing: A multi-dimensional approach to therapy

Oye Agoro

The poison with no chemical formula

I can't see it, smell it, or taste it
But I know it's there
Its invisibility makes me vulnerable, fragile
I can feel it seeping into my pores
Decimating my flesh
Chain sawing my spirit
Shredding my self esteem
Infantilising me, rendering me numb, mute
Leaving me traumatised, emotionally fractured, paralysed
Nevertheless
I have no choice, but to pick myself up
Dust myself off
Await my next encounter
With the poison with no chemical formula

Oye Agoro (2018)[2]

As a cis woman of Yoruba ancestry, a darker-skinned African woman born in London during the 1960s, the era of signs on pub doors saying 'No Irish, No Coloureds, No Dogs', my experiences of racism and the violence of intersecting oppressions have been numerous. I have lost count of the times that I have been spat at and verbally abused on the street.

---

1. Diunital is an ancient belief based on African philosophy that there can be more than one way of understanding things. It is a system of logic based on seeing the whole in terms of dualities as opposed to dichotomous opposites – both and logic, rather than either or (Wright, 1997; Nichols, 1986).
2. All my poems can be read at https://oyeagoro.wordpress.com/poems

Three months after my birth, I was transracially fostered with a white family. Transracial fostering is a complex issue: some people have positive experiences; for others, their experiences are more mixed, and some of us are still living with the consequences of the multi-layered trauma of the experience. Seeking out talking therapy has been one of the ways that I have attempted to heal the wounding, loss and trauma that I have felt.

The journey to therapy

Getting off a bus in an affluent suburb of my home city, I was about to walk the last few hundred metres to my therapist's office when a nondescript, middle-aged white man in a brown leather jacket walked past me and said: 'Black n***** bitch whore, go back to where you belong.'

Then he spat on me.

I was left speechless, bewildered and immobilised. I watched him walk down the street and turn the corner before any words formed in my mind. I felt shame and humiliation at my inaction. I wanted to retreat immediately, to return to the safety and cocoon of my own home, but it was miles away.

Hesitantly, I proceeded to my therapy session. I had been seeing a white female therapist for several months. I made the decision to start the session by telling her about what had just happened.

As I spoke, I was aware of anger and rage rising in my body – hard knots of radiating pain in my stomach, chest and lower back, in conjunction with fragmented and unsettling thoughts: does this white man do that to every Black woman he sees in the street? What level of rage and disturbance must he be holding internally to do that? Spitting at, or worse, *onto* another person has never entered my head.

My therapist gave me space to speak uninterrupted for several minutes. Then she proceeded to repeatedly ask what I had been doing before the incident, asking detailed questions about how I had been walking down the street, and what had been said. I was left with the impression that my therapist thought I had provoked or imagined the attack. Meanwhile, I was wondering, could anything justify that man's behaviour? I started to question if it was naïve of me to bring the incident to therapy with a white therapist. But it felt so raw; I needed to try to make sense of it, to process what had happened.

But I could see my therapist becoming angry; red blotches were appearing on her face, and I wondered if her outrage was related to the fact that it happened so near to her house. She became insistent that I report the incident, and started to get up from her seat with what I assumed was the intention to escort me to the police station. I said that I would think about it – although I had no intention of doing so, since I knew it was only likely to add to the trauma of the incident. My therapist sat down with an air of indignation and disbelief that I was not accepting her 'help'. Shaking her head, she said that I was not taking responsibility for myself by choosing not to go to the police station immediately.

With hindsight, I feel that the space my therapist initially gave me to explore what happened was helpful. The therapeutic alliance formed between us over several months of therapy had been 'good enough' for me to risk bringing it into the therapeutic space. It allowed me to reflect further on what level of internal dysfunction must be present for a person to misogynistically and racially abuse another human being, unprovoked, while casually walking down a street, and on how verbal assaults say so much about the internal world of the person perpetrating the violence.

In that moment I became aware that, although I rationally understood the abhorrent nature of the intersection of racism and sexism, of *misogynoir* (Bailey, 2010), there had still been a small part of me that felt I was to blame for that violence, that something about me had caused it. The full realisation of this man's complete responsibility for the incident and the anger and hatred he expressed towards me as an anonymous Black woman impacted me in a visceral way, which I experienced as a body blow to my chest that took my breath away. It then felt like a physical integration of my thinking mind and body, which moved me into a deeper and slower breathing pattern – to an understanding that went to the bone and the marrow.

But my therapist's persistent questioning, initial reluctance to accept my experience and her expectation that I report the incident to the police immediately inhibited my ability to fully connect to my emerging feelings of anger and rage and reduced my sense of personal agency in deciding what was best for me. The tone of the questioning about what happened before and during the incident created a dynamic where I felt I was expected to evidence the validity of my experience. This effectively closed down further exploration of what I thought and felt about the incident, along with my past and ongoing experiences of racism and misogynoir in my life. I experienced this as especially painful given my past experiences of racism within my white foster family and predominantly white schools and work environments. The response and attitude of my therapist substantiated my instinct that my therapist had little awareness of racism, and so struggled to hear, acknowledge or appropriately hold the emotional distress of my experience.

My problem with talking therapies

The diligent search for the right therapist
A hope of relief for my fractured soul and psyche

> *But my healing mirage is abruptly shattered*
> *By the endless need for explanations about my social location*
> *Persistent denial of my reality*
> *Casually delivered microaggressions*
> *If I'm lucky – banal expressions of outrage on my behalf*
> *Hotly pursued by white liberal paternalistic benevolence*
> *How does it make me feel?*
> *A rage and pain so deep that it's hard to verbally articulate!*
>
> Oye Agoro (2021)

My journey through racism

For most of my childhood, I lived with a white foster family, in a primarily white area in England, with intermittent periods in Nigeria with my biological family. At both primary and secondary school, I was generally the only child of colour, and always the only African child.

At school, it was a common happening for me to be called a monkey, with accompanying monkey chants. On a bad day, in school and in town, I would be chased by youth members of the National Front, who would hurl banana skins, sticks and stones at me and spit on me, if they had the opportunity.

My white foster mother took care and attention to knit me school cardigans for the winter and sewed my school dresses for the summer. Alongside, she never missed an opportunity to have me photographed with a monkey. She was always eager to tell me, 'Sticks and stones may break your bones, but words can never hurt you.' My recollection is that she never seemed to hear me when I said that other children had thrown things at me in the playground. To my knowledge, she never felt a need to intervene at school. I believe my foster mother viewed racism as a form of 'teasing' and expected me to rise above it.

As a child, I had no understanding of racism, and consequently internalised what most white people around me were saying and thinking about Africa and African people. With hindsight, I can see that these experiences were what brought me to therapy in my adult life.

Experiences of talking therapy

I have experienced helpful therapy from Black and white therapists. However, many of my encounters with white therapists have left me feeling that the challenges I have encountered from living in predominantly white racist and misogynistic spaces were my personal psychological failing: that they were nothing to do with the white supremacy culture and racism within and dysfunction of society at large around me.

An important part of my healing journey has been understanding and accepting that racism is an inherent consequence of white supremacy culture. White supremacy has been defined as:

> An historically based, institutionally perpetuated system of exploitation and oppression of continents, nations, and people of colour by white people and nations of the European continent, for the purpose of maintaining and defending a system of wealth, power and privilege. (Martinez, 1998 p.16)

I have come to understand the legacy of white supremacy from my lived experience and through discovering the work of Franz Fanon, bell hooks and Na'im Akbar, along with many other Black writers. It is an ideology that has at its core a belief that white skin tones are more beautiful and embody superior traits such as purity, intelligence and civilisation. By comparison, darker skin tones are considered negative, inferior – a marker of being primitive, unintelligent, uncivilised, sexually promiscuous and evil (Adams, 1996).

Using an understanding of white supremacy, we can hypothesise that the man who physically and verbally assaulted me aligned himself to white supremacy ideology and believed himself to be superior because of his skin colour. The words he used to abuse me reference significant events in British and North American history. The use of the 'n' word signifies to me a direct connection to the history of empire, enslavement, lynching and the colonisation legacies of the British state. The words 'Black whore bitch' allude to the belief in the animal-like status of Black people under brutal colonial and plantation systems, where we were viewed in terms of our worth as labourers or for our sexual or reproductive value. The 'whore' reference links with how enslaved Black women were sexualised and labelled as promiscuous to justify systemic rape. 'Go back to where you come from' evokes the era of Enoch Powell and his 'Rivers of Blood' speech. This is a widely acknowledged and recurring racist positioning in British politics that views the immigration of darker-skinned peoples as a threat to the perceived rightful entitlements and privileges of white working-class people in Britain (Andrews, 2019).

A critical analysis of racism, centring its relationship to white supremacy, history and the understanding that racism comprises individual, institutional and systematic components, is necessary to throw light on the impact that racism has on individuals, communities and the environment (Schell et al., 2020).

Individual racism can be seen as interpersonal acts of racism, prejudice and discrimination, ranging from microaggressions and being spat on in the street to the maiming and killing of Black people. Institutional racism can be observed in the stark pay differentials and health inequalities between Black and white communities (Office for National Statistics, 2020; Burgoyne, 2021). Systemic racism can be seen as evident in the way that white people, especially white males, control the political, economic and legal power bases of society (Bell, 1995).

This framing has helped me to externalise my experiences of racism, which has in turn facilitated a move towards greater self-compassion and an understanding that my experiences are connected to a wider and historical struggle against injustice. I have also observed this process happening with many BIPOC clients that I have seen during my 30 years practising as a talking therapist.

Bringing a critical and historical understanding of racism to my experience of transracial fostering has enabled me similarly to frame my initial entry into the care system in Britain within the context of historical racial health inequalities in Britain. My mother endured a traumatic labour and post-partum experience, where she nearly died, in a prestigious London hospital. Decades on from my birth, Black women are still four times more likely to die in childbirth than white women (RCOG, 2020).

The black hole of white supremacy

Unprocessed whiteness is so exhausting
Whatever it touches it destroys
Leaving behind a carcinogenic wake
Aversely consuming everything to satiate its own need
Devoid of all self-awareness
The human equivalent of a black hole
Extracting, absorbing, accumulating all light and energy from Mother Earth and humanity
The modern frontier of white supremacy attempts to obscure
Masking itself behind a veneer of sophistication and benevolence
But all eyes are upon you
We see the way you devour all our humanity and Mother Earth with your pathology

Oye Agoro (2022)

Intersectionality

As an African woman with mixed religious and class heritage, intersectionality has provided a valued way of naming and describing my experience of the world.

Intersectionality is defined as:

> Ways of understanding how aspects of a person's social and political identity combine to create different modes of discrimination and privilege. (Runyan, 2018)

Kimberlé Crenshaw (2016) has played a pivotal role in developing an intersectional understanding and analysis of oppression that recognises how different forms of discrimination are not stand-alone inequalities but are often intertwined.

Using an intersectional framework has helped me as a therapist to understand my own and other people's social positions and locations in relation to privilege – an understanding that our social locations connect us to systems of discrimination and oppression (see Figure 9.1).

We could hypothesise that my therapist's social location as a white, middle-class woman may have impacted her ability to acknowledge my experience of a verbal racial and sexist assault near her home and to understand my reluctance to report the incident. I did not trust that the police station would be a place of safety; I believe my therapist assumed that it would be. I was mindful of the number of Black people who have died in police custody (Faro, 2020).

Racial trauma

Naming my experiences of racism as racial trauma has played a powerful role in facilitating my healing journey. Racism and other oppressions are increasingly seen as a form of trauma. Trauma can be defined as a threat to your personal safety and security and to that of your family, your lineage and your community (Ojelade, 2019). Racism is increasingly understood to produce chronic stress responses, resulting in trauma and, in some cases, intergenerational trauma (Mckenzie-Mavinga, 2009). Intergenerational trauma has been described as what happens when an individual, family or a group of survivors of extreme adverse conditions, such as institutional racism, colonisation, enslavement and genocide, pass on the unprocessed trauma of the experience to subsequent generations (Degruy, 2017; Berube, 2015; Alleyne, 2022).

I have come to understand that, when we become aware that we have experienced social trauma, it opens up the possibility of naming and exploring the experiences and narratives around it. This exploration can allow for the identification of past and current survival strategies, as well as areas of resilience. It also offers the opportunity to collaboratively explore the strengths and disadvantages of such strategies and resilience practices, and to identify others that may be valuable. These collaborative processes

Figure 9.1: Intersecting axes of privilege, domination and oppression (Natalya D., 2014)

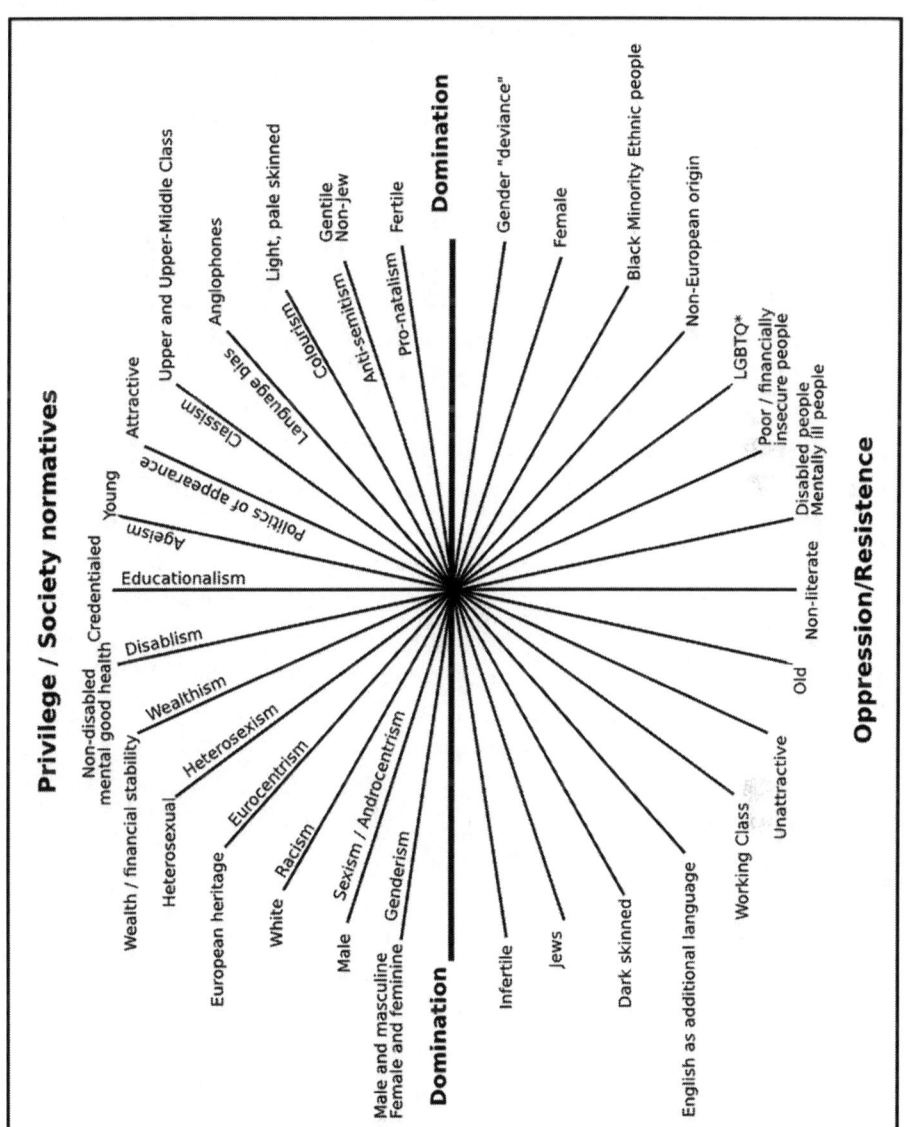

are likely to promote safety, resilience and wellbeing, which are important protective factors in coping with and resisting ongoing oppression and structural inequalities and, I believe, central to working within a decolonising and intersectional framework (Mullan, 2023). Without conscious awareness of social trauma, the opportunity for consideration and exploration of this area in therapy can be easily missed.

Internalised racism

Based on my experience of being transracially fostered and my work as a therapist and supervisor with BIPOC communities, I have concluded that no understanding of inequalities and oppression from a therapeutic perspective can be effective without an understanding of internalised oppression.

Internalised oppression is the process by which we take on and act out some of the negative stereotypes and myths about social groups often promoted by dominant cultural groups, which Gramsci (1999) has described as 'ruling class hegemony'. Franz Fanon clearly describes the effects of internalised racism in his book *Black Skin, White Masks* (1967), where he outlines the dehumanising and psychologically damaging effects of colonial racism on those who are colonised by white supremacy.

This internalisation process can result in feelings of self-hatred, shame, low self-esteem and conscious and subconscious feelings of not being good enough, and can lead to false negative stereotyping becoming self-fulfilling prophecy (Lipsky, 1987).

Developing an understanding of internalised racism was a pivotal point in my healing journey. This conceptualisation helped me to put words to how I felt, growing up in a white family. As a child in Britain, I never felt good about having short curly black afro hair, dark brown skin and full lips. I internalised the message that white beauty standards were the natural norm and something to aspire to – long blonde hair that blows in the wind, blue eyes, slim lips and a slender body.

Intermittent periods at home in Nigeria, where Black beauty was the norm, played an important role in helping me to feel good about my skin colour. As an African child living in Britain, during the 1960s and 1970s, I rarely felt celebrated for who I was. The script I internalised was that any value I had came from working hard, educational success, behaving well and taking care of people, especially white people.

The ways we all consciously and subconsciously act out dominant discourses around ability, age, class, gender, patriarchy and race are complex and diverse (David, 2013). Bringing knowledge of different forms of oppression into our therapeutic work can have a significant impact on the way we conceptualise clients' narratives and experiences of distress. This awareness supports a historical, contextual and multi-dimensional understanding of the causes of distress, 'disease' and wellbeing, rather than a Western, individualistic approach and cognitively focused understanding of illness, symptoms and treatment (Nobles, 2006). We know that many presentations of distress, such as depression and self-harm within marginalised populations, can be viewed as expressions of lived experience of oppression (Chesler, 2018; hooks, 1996; Clarke & Yellow Bird, 2021; Maté & Maté, 2022)

Internalised oppression and domination strategies

Having an awareness of internalised oppression and domination strategies has been important in enabling me to reflect on my responses to racism and understand domination behaviours in others and myself.

In considering the psychological consequences of oppression and internalised oppression, a knowledge of behaviours that are associated with oppression and domination can provide an important starting place for disrupting and dismantling oppressive behaviours and practices. Vanissar Tarakali (2010) outlines identifiable strategies adopted by those in privileged positions and those experiencing oppression.

Internalised domination describes how members of dominant privileged groups adapt and accept the denigration, subjugation and marginalisation of, and discrimination against, a particular group as natural and inevitable. Internalised dominance strategies include denial, dissociation, numbness, being unaware of oppression, defensiveness, attacking, blaming and avoidance of marginalised groups, refusal to take responsibility for oppression and self-absorption.

Internalised oppression describes how those in groups experiencing oppression find ways to endure their oppressive circumstances. Internalised oppression survival strategies include appeasing, caretaking of dominant members, staying silent or attempting invisibility, withdrawal, isolation from dominant group members, dissociating, numbing, hypervigilance, and interpreting anything in the social environment as a threat.

My therapist's focus on interrogating me about what I was doing and saying before I was assaulted could be recognised as denial and blaming aspects of internalised oppressive strategies. After feeling silenced by my therapist, I made a conscious decision to withdraw and remain silent about issues related to racism and race, as a deliberate coping strategy. Reni Eddo-Lodge describes this position so clearly in *Why I'm No Longer Talking to White People About Race* (2017).

Racism and other oppressions are often seen as only impacting and affecting the group directly experiencing racism: namely, members of BIPOC communities. However, racism and other oppressions can also be seen as affecting those in positions of power and dominance. By being complicit in oppression within our positions of privilege, we not only dehumanise those being oppressed, we also dehumanise ourselves in becoming perpetuators of oppression/intersectional violence. Diminishing our humanity has emotional, psychological, and spiritual consequences. In his book *Healing Collective Trauma*, Thomas Hubl (2020) describes how unprocessed ancestral trauma and dominant oppressive ideologies and culture cut us off from having fully integrated relationships with ourselves. He details how this fuels modern conflicts and warfare, as well as humanity's destructive relationship with the earth (Hubl, 2020).

As therapists, being aware of internalised oppression, oppression survival strategies and internalised dominance strategies can provide an important lens for considering and analysing the therapeutic alliances we form with people for whom we are providing healing spaces. I consider these to be important tools for deconstructing oppressive ideologies such as white supremacy and patriarchy. Consciously deconstructing oppressive hegemony provides a fertile soil for developing therapeutic alliances across privileged and marginalised communities. A compassionate and non-judgemental awareness of these dynamics can provide space and opportunity for us to unpack and deconstruct these narratives if we choose to. This may encourage clients to bring more of themselves into the therapeutic space, rather than feeling the need to self-censor to avoid experiencing further social trauma through the therapeutic relationship.

Deconstructing cultural imperialism

As a therapist I have found that having a conscious awareness of dominant, white, neoliberal cultural values can help us ensure these values are not being consciously or subconsciously transmitted in our therapeutic practices. The dominance of white cultural values around the world has often led to an assumption that these values are superior, universally applicable and to be aspired to (Sue et al., 2019). White Western culture has been identified as having some of the following markers (Jones & Okun, 2001; Barndt & Crain Major, 2023; Katz, 1985):

- individualism – independence, autonomy and self-reliance are viewed as desirable states and the individual is seen as having supreme control over their own life and destiny
- rigid beauty standards – blonde, blue eyed, thin and youthful archetype for women; athletic ability, social status and economic status for men
- competition – winning is everything and a win/lose dichotomy exists
- action orientation – emphasis on being master of and in control of nature, and the expectation that something can always be done in a situation

- time – rigid adherence to time; a view of time as a commodity, with an emphasis on the importance of deadlines
- family structure – cis-heterosexuality and the nuclear family perceived as the ideal unit.

During my training as an intercultural therapist, I learned how understanding different worldviews, and especially a critical comprehension of the biases of Western culture, enables therapists to make more discerning and ethical choices about therapeutic approaches and interventions that are compatible with clients' belief and values systems.

A central part of my healing journey has included processing the impact of being transracially fostered and my experiences of racism on my identity as an African woman living in Britain.

Over the last 60 years, there has been an increasing interest in researching racial and ethnic identity formation, which has led to the emergence of several models and frameworks. Identity models have provided a useful tool for me in thinking about how racism has shaped my identity. They give a name to the processes that I went through while living with a white family.

I believe that working with the idea that our identities are impacted by the ruling hegemony and that the ruling hegemony is informed by white supremacy values provides an important starting place for naming and consciously thinking about what can help to dismantle oppressive ideologies such as white supremacy, racism and the impact of internalised racism.

In my opinion, an understanding of identity formation within cultures where systems of institutional oppression and disempowerment operate is important when facilitating a healing or therapeutic space.

There are many racial identity models developed in America (Cross, 1995; Helms, 1995; Atkinson et al., 1993; Rowe et al., 1994). Identity models typically have various phases that are dynamic and not always linear, as we can enter and move out of identity phases fluidly, depending on what's happening in our lives, externally and internally. The fluid nature of identity also means that we can experience different identity phases simultaneously across gender, sexuality, religion/spirituality, class and race. Understanding the external influences on our identities can open up an awareness of a multitude of conscious and unconscious choices.

Minority identity model

I have adapted the racial and minority identity development models described by Adler (1986), Cross (1995) and Atkinson and colleagues (1993) to outline an intersectional model that is more directly relevant to the UK context.

Conformity phase

The conformity phase is when we downplay our own group identity and seek actively to emulate and assimilate into the dominant culture and institutions. We are unlikely to see ourselves in a cultural or racial way, regarding social differences as unimportant and preferring to conform to dominant cultural values. For example, in thinking about white supremacy, racism would be seen as unimportant, but we would be likely to believe in, and defer to, white supremacy values. This phase is also identifiable by a deprecation of self and others in the same minority groups(s) and a need for acceptance and approval from the majority group. We are likely to act out various dynamics around internalised oppression, such as cis women supporting and colluding with patriarchal power and violence, queer people remaining in the closet and people of colour embracing colourism, as well as changing accents and patterns of speech and behaviour to gain acceptance.

Dissonance – conflict phase

During this phase there is a growing acknowledgment of our own cultural group and ancestry/community traditions, and an awakening of socio-political consciousness. We may question previous identifications and begin to regard our own cultural group positively. At this stage, we may experience conflict between appreciation for own cultural/community heritage and a desire to conform to dominant cultural norms. Under patriarchy, this might look like recognising the inequity of gender pay disparities, while at the same time deferring to male authority and acting out gender stereotypes in everyday life.

Realisation and immersion phase – 'separatism'

There is a complete surrender to the values of one's own group/community and a rejection of dominant group values. We are likely to have negative attitudes towards the dominant culture and to idealise our own cultural group. Typically, we may feel uncomfortable with difference and struggle to see or acknowledge oppressions other than our own. We may have trouble forming interpersonal relationships and alliances with people from dominant majority groups because of the anger we feel about our experiences of discrimination and oppression from those who hold privileges and power due to their dominant-group status.

Introjection phase

During this phase we find comfort and security in our own group/communities and develop a solid minority identity. We may question our previous hostility towards the dominant culture and increasingly understand it within the wider historical and present contexts. We are likely to come to appreciate some aspects of the dominant culture. We typically will use our anger about discrimination positively and creatively for the benefit of our own social group/communities. For me, this has involved selectively adopting some of the positive elements of Western talking therapy in my work with Black communities in London, while rejecting other aspects, such as the violence the profession has perpetrated against LGBTQIA+ communities, disabled people and women, and its historical association with eugenics.

Synergetic articulation and awareness phase – 'freedom'

We have a sense of fulfilment with our own group/community and have a positive regard towards ourselves and our own group/communities. We are likely to embrace our minority/marginalised identities as among the most important aspects of our life. We are likely to have a high level of personal autonomy, along with an appreciation and respect for other groups, cultures and communities. Characteristically, we will seek to eliminate all forms of oppression and to make alliances with members of dominant cultures who are similarly committed to ending oppression.

Within the frameworks of these identity models, I have a personal commitment to social justice and have developed an intention to maintain a dynamic identity, ideally around synergetic articulation and integrative awareness – the 'freedom' positionings outlined in the identity models. I'm aware that when I experience racial and gender-based trauma, such as the incident described earlier in the chapter, I tend to move back into a more 'separatist' position.

From my lived experience, I have come to understand that I am more likely to maintain self-awareness about my identity and to sustain a fluid and expansive identity positioning within the synergetic articulation and integrative awareness outlook within these models, when I am mindful of the following:

- minimising contact with what I believe to be the most problematic aspects of dominant culture, such as white supremacy and misogynistic ways of being, to minimise my exposure to racial and gender-based trauma
- immersing myself in the magnificence, richness and diversity of BIPOC culture by listening to and watching films, TV, podcasts, music and literature, which all helps me disrupt dominant oppressive narratives
- being in community with like-minded people.

The self-awareness that I have gained through reframing my personal experiences within a historical and critical understanding of racism, along with an awareness of identity development under oppressive ruling hegemony/

culture, and the different values and beliefs between African and white cultures, have all helped me to gain greater self-compassion and listen to myself. By creating the space to listen to myself, I've been able to hear and connect to the ancestral wisdom and resilience that I hold in my body and DNA. Reconnecting to and developing a closer relationship to my body have made me aware of the ways that I hold distress and trauma in my physical body, and how gentle movement, along with talking about my feelings, can help me to self-regulate and process feelings and situations. I regularly swim and practise qigong. Reconnecting to my body has also reconnected me to nature, the earth and the land. I've developed an interest in gardening, planet-based medicine and walking my dog in green places. All these are central elements of African wisdom (Mason-John, 2021).

Mother Earth

No need to over think it
I can just be
Because I am of the earth

Oye Agoro (2021)

Healing – therapy praxis

During my own healing journey and while working as a talking therapist, I have drawn on several explorations and approaches to develop a multidimensional therapeutic practice. It is continually evolving, as I continue to decolonise myself from internalised oppression and residual internalised dominance strategies, while also learning from the therapeutic space that I offer as a therapist. Some of these approaches are outlined here.

Critical analysis of structural inequities

I have taken time to gain an understanding of 'disease', distress and healing within an intersectional justice-allied framework through adopting a historical and holistic approach. I hold onto how, in many indigenous wisdom traditions, healing includes an awareness of our personal, family and ancestral histories, and the importance of attending to our bodies and our spiritual, emotional and psychological wellbeing. This recognises that we are not just isolated individuals but depend on wider networks of interpersonal relationships, communities and society, and our relationship with nature. This critical understanding requires us to make space for the development of healing rituals and traditions that acknowledge the significance of our own family and ancestral histories and legacies of intergenerational trauma, and that we reconnect with resilience skills and helpful coping strategies that may be available from our ancestral lineage and wider communities. Tricia Hersey and her organisation, The Nap Ministry, provide a wonderful example of the power and importance of rest as a resilience strategy, which she learned from her grandmother (Hersey, 2022). The Nap Ministry's motto is 'Rest is Resistance',[3] and its aim is to seek to redress the ancestral and lived experience among Black people of over-working under white supremacy, slavery, plantation economies and present-day racism. It argues that 'rest is a form of resistance' and sleep deprivation is a racial and social justice issue. Thus, rest should be regarded as an intentional self-care practice and disruptor to overworking.

Externalisation

My understanding is that within any social justice-allied healing approach, any 'disease' and distress caused by the violence of structural inequities needs to be unequivocally named and attributed to its causes within society, rather than interpreted as individual pathology. To do otherwise perpetrates victim blaming and adds a further layer of trauma to the original social trauma(s) (Akbar, 1996; Nobles, 2006; Mullan, 2023). Research has evidenced that racism has a detrimental impact on mental health, causing depression, stress, anxiety trauma and suicidal thoughts (Synergi Collaborative Collective, 2018). Discrimination has also been shown to trigger high blood pressure and a weakened immune system and inflammation, which can lead to chronic health conditions (Thames et al., 2019).

Understanding cultural imperialism

An intersectional, multidimensional healing approach requires a critical analysis of cultural imperialism to ensure that any therapy offered (in the broadest sense of that word) is not inadvertently promoting neoliberalism, cis-heteronormativity, the patriarchy or ableism. Otherwise, as healers, we will be reinforcing institutional oppression (Mullan, 2023).

Deconstructing ruling hegemony (decolonisation)

Capitalism and neoliberalism have at their core a drive towards the accumulation of profit and a belief that market forces should govern how societies are organised (Wilson Gilmore, 2022).

Given the multitude of ways that capitalism and neoliberalism have colonised the planet and our bodies and minds, it can be argued that social justice-allied therapists have a moral responsibility to hold space for the deconstruction of neoliberalism within any healing process. I believe this means

---

3. https://thenapministry.wordpress.com/about/

holding in mind that capitalism/neoliberalism actively promote overwork, materialism and over-consumption, binary gender identification, ableism, cis-heteronormativity, white beauty standards, aggressive competition, binary and hierarchical thinking, individualism, narcissistic personality traits, and white supremacy (Hersey, 2022).

An understanding of identity formation

I have found that an important element of decolonised, multidimensional therapy is an understanding of dominant group and minority group identity formation under ruling hegemony and structures of oppression. Talking therapy can play a key role in creating a non-judgemental space for us to explore and unpack our personal and family stories. Holding space for our personal and family stories, or whatever narratives we choose to create, can be a powerful way of facilitating an exploration of our identities, particularly when this is done with the intention of promoting personal and community growth, autonomy and freedom.

Embodied healing from trauma

My own healing and ongoing recovery from past intergenerational and personal social traumas has been complex. Being in talking therapy has undoubtedly helped, providing a space to express and reflect on my emotions and life story. Other practices, such as meditation, restorative yoga, massage, mindful rest, the use of essential oils and compassionate movement such as swimming and qigong, have helped me to process and release the trauma and distress that I often hold in my body. I'm increasingly coming to understand that healing generally, and healing social traumas more specifically, can take many forms.

Diunital healing

I have come to value healing that encourages integration between our minds and our bodies, promotes and nurtures our creativity, and celebrates our unique identities. The term 'diunital thinking', also known as diunital logic or diunital reasoning, has been used to describe an African worldview (Jones & Nichols, 2013). It is an understanding that we can experience and feel more than one thing at a time. One of the core foundations of a diunital worldview is the belief that there are multiple ways of doing things, or multiple parts to the whole. This opens the possibility that we may need to draw on a combination of approaches and practices to support our healing and growth.

I have observed that most healing journeys are not binary but diunital, encompassing a multitude of rituals and practices. For me and the people I have offered healing spaces for, these have included the following:

Being in nature	Listening to music	Reflexology
Breath work	Aromatherapy	Reiki
Forest bathing	Yoga	Hydrotherapy
Friends and family	Rituals and ceremony	Activism
Swimming	Cooking nutritious food	Comedy
Tai qi	Journalling	Clearing clutter
Meditation	Retreats	Gardening
Martial arts	Acupuncture	Dancing
Running	Plant based remedies	Shamanic healing
Cycling	Writing poetry	Steam baths
Breathwork	Sport	Massage
Qigong	Singing	Cinema/film
Being creative	Novels	Affirmations
Jogging	Saunas	Talking therapies
Mindfulness	Audio books	Walking in nature
Art	Climbing	Making music

Radical self-care

Increasingly, radical self-care, self-compassion and love for our ourselves and others in the communities that we live in, are being seen as a cornerstone of sustainable activism. They play a key role in decolonising us from ruling hegemony (Lorde, 1988; hooks, 2016; Davis, 2016; Taylor, 2021; Hersey, 2022.)

Radical self-care and love directly challenge the patterns of violence endemic in the world today. They are in complete contrast to the dehumanisation and trauma that many of our ancestors experienced through chattel slavery, colonisation, and other forms of violence. Consequently, radical self-care and love have the potential to be the ultimate forms of political resistance and activism in themselves and have the transformative power to ensure a different future for the generations that come after us.

As Audre Lorde writes: 'Caring for myself is not self-indulgence. It is an act of self-preservation and that is an act of political warfare.' (1988)

Healing

Steaming, jacuzzi, sauna, swimming
Finding my calm, returning to being
Swimming, steaming, sauna, jacuzzi
Finding my equilibrium
Returning to equanimity

Oye Agoro (2018)

In summary, I have outlined the key elements in my multidimensional healing journey and practice, which I describe as diunital healing. It is a practice that I use to disrupt and heal the wounding caused by the legacies of white supremacy, patriarchy and capitalist neoliberal culture. Diunital healing reflects a symbolic returning home to my ancestral lineage and community. It is a remembering and reconnecting to a way of being that is present in many indigenous wisdom traditions, a way of being that values the importance of self-awareness and the interconnectedness of all life on this planet (Some & Some, 1999).

In the words of an African proverb: 'To be able to love other people you must be able to love yourself.'

References

Adams, M.Y. (1996). *The multicultural imagination: Race, colour and the unconscious*. Routledge.

Adler, N.J. (1986). Cultural synergy: Managing the impact of cultural diversity. In J.W. Pfeiffer (Ed.), *1986 Annual: Developing human resources* (pp.229–238). Pfeiffer & Co.

Akbar, N. (1996). *Breaking the chains of psychological slavery*. Mind Production & Associates.

Alleyne, A. (2022). *The burden of heritage: Hauntings of intergenerational trauma on black lives*. Confer.

Andrews, K. (2019). *Back to black: Black radicalism for the 21st century*. Zed Books.

Atkinson, D.R., Morten, G. & Sue, D.W. (1993). *Counselling American minorities*. Brown & Benhmark.

Bailey, M. (2010, March 14). They aren't talking about me. [Blog]. The Crunk Feminist Collective. www.crunkfeministcollective.com/2010/03/14/they-arent-talking-about-me

Barndt, J.B. & Crain Major, B. (2023). *Deconstructing racism: A path toward lasting change*. Fortress Press.

Bell, D.A.A. (1995). Who's afraid of critical race theory? *University of Illinois Law Review, 4*, 893–910.

Berube, K. (2015, February 16). The intergenerational trauma of First Nations still runs deep. *The Globe and Mail*. www.theglobeandmail.com/life/health-and-fitness/health-advisor/the-intergenerational-trauma-of-first-nations-still-runs-deep/article23013789

Burgoyne, B. (2021). *Medical racism: Decolonising healthcare*. Inne. https://www.inne.io/en/blog/article/medical-racism-decolonising-healthcare

Chesler, P. (2018). *Women and madness*. Chicago Review Press.

Clarke, K. & Yellow Bird, M. (2021). *Decolonizing pathways towards integrative healing in social work*. Routledge.

Crenshaw, K. (2016). *The urgency of intersectionality*. [Video]. https://www.ted.com/talks/kimberle_crenshaw_the_urgency_of_intersectionality

Cross, W.E. (1995). *The psychology of nigresence: Revising the Cross model.* In J.G. Ponterotto, J.M. Casas, L.A. Suzuki & C.M. Alexander (Eds.), *Handbook of multicultural counseling* (pp.93–122). Sage.

David, E. (2013). *Internalized oppression: The psychology of marginalized groups.* Springer Publishing Company.

Davis, A.Y. (2016). *Freedom is a constant struggle: Ferguson, Palestine, and the foundations of a movement.* Haymarket Books.

Degruy, J.A. (2017). *Post-traumatic slave syndrome: America's legacy of enduring injury and healing* (Revised ed). Joy DeGruy Publications Inc.

Eddo-Lodge, R. (2017). *Why I'm no longer talking to white people about race.* Bloomsbury Publishing.

Fanon, F. (1967). *Black skin, white masks.* Grove Press.

Faro, K. (Dir.). (2020). *Ultraviolence* (Documentary film).

Gramsci, A. (1999). *Prison notebooks.* Q. Hoare & G. Nowell Smith (Eds. & trans.). Elecbook.

Helms. J.E. (1995). An update of Helms's White and People of Colour racial identity models. In J. Ponterotto, M. Casas, L.A. Suzuki & C.M. Alexander (Eds.), *Handbook of multicultural counseling* (pp.181–198). Sage.

Hersey, P. (2022). *Rest is resistance.* Aster.

hooks, b. (1996). *Killing rage: Ending racism.* Penguin.

hooks, b. (2016). *All about love: New visions.* William Morrow.

Hubl, T. (2020). *Healing collective trauma: A process for integrating our intergenerational and cultural wounds.* Sounds True.

Jones, B.A. & Nichols, E.J. (2013). *Cultural competence in America's Schools: Leadership, engagement and understanding.* Information Age Publishing.

Jones, K. & Okun, T. (2001). *Dismantling racism: A workbook for social change groups.* ChangeWork.

Katz, J.H. (1985). The socio-political nature of counselling. *Counseling Psychologist, 13*(4), 615–624.

Lipsky, S. (1987). *Internalised racism.* Rational Island Publishers.

Lorde, A. (1988). *A burst of light.* Dover Publications Inc.

Martinez, E. (1998). *What is white supremacy?* Catalyst Project. www.collectiveliberation.org

Mason-John, V. (2021). *Afrikan wisdom: New voices talk black liberation, Buddhism, and beyond.* North Atlantic Books.

Maté, G. & Maté, D. (2022). *The myth of normal: Trauma, illness and healing in a toxic culture.* Vermilion.

Mckenzie-Mavinga, I. (2009). *Black issues in the therapeutic process.* Palgrave.

Mullan, J. (2023). *Decolonizing therapy: Oppression, historical trauma, and politicising your practice.* W.W. Norton.

Natalya D. (2014). *Intersecting axes of privilege, domination and oppression.* https://sites.google.com/site/natalyadell/home/intersectionality

Nichols, E.J. (1986). Cultural foundations for teaching Black children. In O.M.T. Rattery (Ed.), *Teaching mathematics. Volume 1: Culture, motivation, history and classroom management* (pp. 1–7). Institute for Independent Education.

Nobles, W. (2006). *Seeking the Sakhu: Foundational writings for an African psychology.* Third World Press.

Office for National Statistics. (2020). *Ethnicity pay gaps: 2019*. ONS. https://www.ons.gov.uk/employmentandlabourmarket/peopleinwork/earningsandworkinghours/articles/ethnicitypaygapsingreatbritain/2019

Ojelade, I. (2019). *Advocating for the advocate: Identifying, preventing and recovery from Secondary Trauma*. Race Matters II: The Impact of Race on Criminal Justice. NACDL 2nd Annual Seminar. January 10–11. www.nacdl.org/Media/Identify-Prevent-and-Recover-from-Secondary-Trauma

Rowe, W., Bennet, S. & Atkinson, D.R. (1994). White racial identity models: Critique and alternative proposal. *Counseling Psychologist, 22*(1), 120–146.

Royal College of Obstetricians & Gynaecologists (RCOG). (2020, March 6). *Racial disparities in women's healthcare*. https://committees.parliament.uk/writtenevidence/8498/pdf

Runyan, A.S (2018). What is intersectionality and why is it important? *Academe, 104*(6). www.aaup.org/article/what-intersectionality-and-why-it-important

Schell, C.J., Dyson, K., Fuentes, T.L., Des Roches, S., Harris, N.C., Sterud Miller, D., Woelfle-Erskine, C.A. & Lambert, M. (2020). The ecological and evolutionary consequences of systemic racism in urban environments. *Science Reviews, 369*(6510), eaay4497.

Some, M.P. & Some, L.M. (1999). *The healing wisdom of Africa: Finding life purpose through nature, ritual, and community* (Reprint ed.). Jeremy P. Tarcher.

Sue, D.W., Sue, D., Neville, H.E. & Smith, L. (2019). *Counseling the culturally diverse: Theory and practice* (8th ed.). John Wiley.

Synergi Collaborative Collective. (2018). *The impact of racism on mental health: Briefing paper*. https://legacy.synergicollaborativecentre.co.uk/wp-content/uploads/2017/11/The-impact-of-racism-on-mental-health-briefing-paper-1.pdf

Tarakali, V. (2010). *Surviving oppression; healing oppression*. [Blog]. Tarakali Education. https://vanissarsomatics.com/surviving-oppression-healing-oppression/

Taylor, S.N. (2021). *The body is not an apology: The power of radical self-love* (Revised 2nd ed.). Berrett-Koehler.

Thames, A.D., Irwin, M.R., Breen, E.C. & Cole, S.W. (2019). Experienced discrimination and racial differences in leukocyte gene expression. *Psychoneuroendocrinology, 106*, 277–283.

Wilson Gilmore, R. (2022). *Abolition geography: Essays towards liberation*. Verso Books.

Wright, W.D. (1997). *Black intellectuals, black cognition and a black aesthetic*. Praeger Publishers.

10. My journey to visibility: Using congruence to explore racial microaggressions within the supervisory relationship

Rajita Rajeshwar

> You cannot reflect on being congruent if you do not experience and consider diversity. (Merry, 2012, p.218)

I wish to begin this journey by sharing my ethnic identity. However, I am already lost in the mental gymnastics of defining myself. Shall I describe myself as BAME (Black, Asian or Minority Ethnic)? I find this acronym problematic. Am I an anonymous member of a homogenous group, or is my identity only positioned in relation to white people? Maybe I should define myself as a member of the 'global majority' – a collective term to represent the 80% of the world's population who are non-white: that is, Black, Asian, dual heritage and indigenous to the Global South? Maybe I should adopt a term used by minority groups, such as person of colour? Or perhaps use my own, self-selected term: second generation Tamil Indian psychotherapist and supervisor. However, I have no deep affiliation with any of these terms; they all appear insipid and nebulous. Therefore, I will use them interchangeably to describe myself in this piece of writing.

In my role as Tamil Indian integrative creative supervisor, I have predominantly engaged in 'cross-cultural' supervision. By this I mean that my experiences have frequently/mostly involved supervising white British trainee counsellors. During my time supervising, I have often experienced a particular type of racial microaggression that has left me silent, puzzled and feeling stuck. Solórzano and Yosso (2002) describe racial microaggressions as subtle, automatic or unconscious insults, verbally or non-verbally expressed, and directed toward people of colour. I have often dismissed this discomfort hanging in the air, for fear of jeopardising the relationship. I also have struggled to find the words to communicate what felt complex, layered and highly sensitive.

I wondered too, if my silence, my minimising of the experience due to shame and confusion, and my brushing off this 'hot potato' had been experienced by other supervisors and therapists of colour engaging in cross-cultural work. It is my hope that sharing my reflective process relating to my own rocky journey of responding to microaggressions will enable others to name, identify and explore their own experiences.

I have created a fictitious supervisee, 'T'. T is a composite of interactions with trainees I have supervised where the issue of racial microaggressions has surfaced in sessions. I also share how I've responded to these tricky moments and what I might have said on further reflection. I draw on person-centred theory, in particular the use of congruence, critical race theory, intersectionality and positionality (a fluid, ever-changing position, where personal values, views and location in time and space influence one's understanding of the world) to share my path forward. The aim is to explore in more depth the relationship between supervisor and supervisee.

Congruence

When I think of the meaning of congruence, I imagine it to be an inner wisdom, a deep knowing of one's way of being. Rogers (1990) defines congruence as 'being dependably real and genuine'. The foundation of congruence, Rogers asserts, is based on psychological contact, empathy, presence and unconditional positive regard. I wonder as I write this how easy it is to be honest and genuine in the supervisory relationship when themes of power, privilege and cultural difference are at play. How does one professionally and authentically manage moments of conflict, difference and possible attack arising spontaneously in the session?

Baljon (2002) states that supervision is a place for learning congruence. Furthermore, Lambers (2007) highlights how 'the process of supervision facilitates the therapist's congruence to the client' (p.371), arguing that congruence is the foundation of ethical practice. I began to realise how essential the exploration of congruence was in supervision. It's a fundamental touchstone, enabling the therapist to fully see the client.

Segment 1

T: I'm worried about working with this next client.

Me: I can feel you getting smaller as you say this, somewhat restricted in your body.

T: Yeah, my shoulders feel frozen. The whole thing feels big, like I won't know how to relate to her.

Me: Tell me more about this feeling of bigness. Your fears, concerns about relating.

Mearns and Thorne (1988) highlight that congruence begins with 'self-involvement' – the process of appropriately communicating personal sensations, feelings and experiences in response to concerns raised. In these early moments with T, I felt in tune, in psychological contact with her. I could see and feel her both shrinking and worrying. Congruence is also about accessing visceral sensations. Therefore, drawing on Gendlin's focusing model (1978), I offered to T my own felt responses – the tightness in my chest in this moment. My intention was to help T listen inwards, and also to communicate an attitude of care, concern and respect for her, to enable her to feel safe enough to reveal the more vulnerable aspects of herself.

Segment 2

Me: Does this create some fear in you?

T: Yes. She's from Pakistan, or Nigeria maybe.

Me: (Pause) Okay. (Pause).

T: It's fine. She's just a person.

Me: (Pause) Okay, I see. (Silence).

As the session with T continued, I was struck by how my somatic responses may have related to T's fear of racial/cultural differences. I became conscious of the difference between the very visible dark Brownness of my South Indian heritage and her taut white exterior. I felt exposed. Had I fallen through what Morris (2015) calls the 'trap door of racism', described as the unexpected slip of the tongue? Was T subtly expressing her prejudice or was I experiencing a parallel process? I was full of doubt. I'd lost my footing and did not have the words to express what I was experiencing. As a result, a discomfort between T and myself ensued.

Cain (2010), in his guidelines for congruence, argues that strong reactions may result from one's own biases, blind spots or relationship challenges. I wondered if my own reactions were based on an inherent prejudice towards T's whiteness. I allowed myself to acknowledge the strength of this internal collapse within me, triggered by my inner critic shaming me for my professional inability to regard others positively. I began to acknowledge that this sense of deflation had touched my own experiences of being the 'other', the foreigner, and the feelings of uncertainty it encompassed. This alerted me to a feeling of risk around T, as I felt guarded and vulnerable in my fragility. I instantly distanced myself from the relationship. I realised this defensive response was the result of psychological wounds blocking my ability to 'see' and be 'seen' in the relationship.

Furthermore, I felt wary of T's statement, 'She's just a person'. A flood of memories and statements heard from many other students rippled through my mind: 'We are all the same deep down, we are all part of the human race.' To me this was a simplistic and glossed-over version of diversity. However, I questioned again whether my biases were at play, or was I experiencing further racial microaggressions? I was struggling with this challenge.

I pushed down these undercurrents of doubt and fear. I recognised that my 'acculturated conditions of worth', the internalised value and beliefs shaped from the first-generation South Indian immigrant diaspora, involved me suppressing feelings of personal discomfort and attack in order to survive in a foreign country. Also, being likeable and agreeable was another defence from being attacked as a foreigner. As a result of these internal wranglings, I offered a casual, closed response to T, eliciting no further exploration.

Avoiding these uncomfortable moments was a skill I'd honed throughout my life. I did this by adopting a position of colour blindness. Becoming as good as 'white' had been my modus operandi. I was adept at sacrificing the 'culturally different' parts of myself by prioritising the emotions and values of the dominant class over mine. How else could I be acceptable and palatable, and by extension, safe? Ginsberg (1996) defines this process as 'racial passing'. This involves the disowning of one's racial identity before the racial majority to protect oneself from hostile environments. Morrison (2020) intuits these escape strategies as ancestrally linked – 'a knowing so deep it is like a secret' (p.230).

Being incongruent with my cultural self was the only way I survived my training. I disappeared the most visible part of me so as not to rock the otherwise untroubled boat. Taylor-Muhammed (2001) highlights how people of colour are often scapegoated as difficult or angry when they raise issues of race. This incongruence, playing at being invisible, was an adapted survival response. It was another acculturated condition of worth. This time I internalised the messages from the dominant culture: not to challenge and to be grateful for the position I held. Sue and Capodilupo (2008), in their research on coping strategies used by people of colour towards racial microaggressions in America, shed light on common maladaptive responses to these stressors.

Typical reactions noted were hypervigilance, censoring one's true feelings, frustration, anger, fatigue and hopelessness.

I hoped my avoidance and censoring were perceived by T as professionalism. However, I knew I was masking and that the trust we had built together was in jeopardy. I felt the stakes were high if I were to risk revealing myself. At the same time, I did not want to stunt T's own cultural competence and ethical development. Personal supervision and therapy had helped me acknowledge my fear related to race-based stress in the supervisory relationship. Through it I was able to begin to explore how my racial differences contributed to my experiences of alienation and discrimination. Harper (2000) explains how this discomfort manifests as an unintelligible 'felt intuition'.

Meyer's minority stress model (2003) names this felt experience as the accumulation of multiple layers of discrimination experienced by minority groups. These different overlapping layers of stress within the lived experiences of racial minorities may involve rumination on previous experiences of prejudice and discrimination; fear and silencing of one's racial identity; the continued expectation of rejection; internalised de-valuation, and mistrust in others.

More recently, there has been an understanding that pervasive structural discrimination embedded in structural systems, laws and policies negatively impacts the mental health of ethnic minorities (Paradies, 2006). The Commission on Race and Ethnic Disparities (2021) details how BAME communities have greater financial and housing insecurity, the poorest employment opportunities, poor educational outcomes, the highest contact with the criminal justice system and less access to health resources. To add, people of colour who experience racial microaggressions have higher levels of anxiety, post-traumatic stress disorder and impaired psychological wellbeing (Williams et al., 2018; Forrest-Bank & Cuellar, 2018).

These often unseen perspectives were invited into my reality, giving a much-needed context and grounding to my thoughts and feelings. Personal therapy during this supervisory experience allowed me to go further into my process, to connect with the memories I had learnt to bury. It was here that I noticed how the interaction with T had re-awoken a traumatic childhood experience from when I was 10 years old, recently arrived in England from India. Below is a diarised extract of this memory, written as an adult after a therapy session.

The girl before
I remembered the laughter of the group in my school class. It was unabandoned, unashamed, raucous, infectious laughter. The strength of

the bond between them like a powerful force field. I desperately wanted to be part of this electricity, this fusion. I tried to join the chatter, but I didn't understand the small talk. I tried to laugh but was always offbeat. Inside, I felt awkward. It was an excruciating discomfort. The strain of having no place emanated from my being.

There was a momentary pause in the laughter. Spontaneously I responded, 'I can help, I can find out what you want.' I said it enthusiastically to one of the boys. I was so desperate to please, to be part of this. My inner voice shouted, 'I can serve, let me be anything you want.' Instead of engaging, they began huddling closer together. Their backs became an impenetrable wall. I was confused, I tried to intercept. 'Why is that Black girl getting so excited? Step back, Black girl!' I heard their voices shout.

Were they referring to me? I wasn't Black. I was from India. I knew I didn't fit in – was this the reason? I felt the sound of the group's laughter. The echoes signalling a clear dismissal.

In response to this rejection, my mind no longer existed in the present. Instead, it fled to a liminal space. Here I experienced fragments of thought, images, sensations. I'm a blot, I'm a stain. I am nothing, I thought. I wilfully began leaving my body. Keep going, I thought, until you burst, disintegrate; this is how I will keep safe. I will dissipate and exist in the minute particles surrounding others. Move only when other forces guide me. I will exist through the image of others.

'STEP BACK, BLACK GIRL' pervaded my psyche forever more.

This became my truth, my reality. From then on, only slivers of the girl before were seen. Sometimes when the light refracted against the dust, for a moment, in the glimmers, she appeared like gold.

This memory unearthed buried layers of shame, concealment and disconnection around my race identity. Mckenzie-Mavinga (2018) refers to this as 'recognition trauma', which describes how wounds of racism and prejudice can trigger such feelings. My racial identity was also bound in other intersectional frames of migration, assimilation, class and gender, creating other unique stressors and further compounding the feelings of difference I was experiencing. As Audre Lorde (1982) declares, 'There is no such thing as a single-issue struggle because we do not live single-issue lives' (p.138).

In contacting these cut-off, felt senses of fragility and regression, I began opening to further layers of my otherness. I noticed that my feelings of confusion and silence with T were related to layers of both difference and privilege that I was holding, and these nuanced experiences were entwined with my racial identity. I was privileged by being an educated, non-disabled professional, but simultaneously the realities of my non-white immigrant identity contributed to me feeling adrift and powerless in this dynamic. How could I find a path through this to reconnect with T? Perhaps, I needed an honest conversation with her?

A vital step to congruence is self-awareness. In excavating the buried stories of my race identity, in naming my pain, something transformative was happening. Slowly, I began to create space inside myself to hold in mind all these intersecting experiences, with their complexities and confusion. However, this time without dismissal or shame, I felt compassion towards these hurt, confused parts of myself; they felt like small, unloved beings, left in the dark for too long, which I could observe with tenderness. Guided by this empathy and positive self-regard, I noticed something softening in me. I began to feel open and curious about T's lived experiences. My gaze shifted from a state of vulnerability and defensiveness to enquiry.

With this insight, I revisited these initial moments with T. I wanted to create an open space for her; a place where her experiences were seen and held. I wanted to acknowledge that T's unique way of relating to the world would also be informed by her racialised conditions of worth. Chantler (2005) describes this as the societal values, beliefs and expectations shaping one's self-image. For T, this would be her socially constructed identity, based on her skin colour. Hawkins and Shohet (1989) highlight that supervision is a space for personal reflection of the 'how and then' affecting the 'here and now' – how past experiences inform our present. Now, with further thought, perhaps the honest conversation I could have had might have gone like this:

Me: Does this create some fear in you?

T: Yes. She's from Pakistan, or Nigeria maybe.

Me: Tell me more about your fears around this situation. You sound like you are having concerns, worries about relating. Do you know what this is about?

Hycner and Jacobs (1995) describe this position as offering presence: 'the turning of the whole self to the other, turning away from the preoccupations of oneself and offering one's whole being to the other' (p.52). Lewis's (2017) view of 'presencing' seems pertinent here, describing this as a process of here-ness, aliveness, making space to reclaim the vulnerable, fearful and shame-based parts of myself related to difference.

I notice from these reflections that the state of congruence was becoming my ally, supporting and challenging me to deepen my therapeutic practice with self and other. I began to lean further into its meaning. How could I appear more fully in the relationship? How could I attend to the unspoken undercurrents, mirroring processes that may happen with clients? My supervisor's description of congruence rang through my ears; 'If you take risks to be yourself, it will deepen the relationship.'

I began to feel freer. I wanted to be more honest with myself and my supervisee. Mearns and Thorne (1988) state that mindful self-disclosure, relevant to the supervisee's concerns, can be a way of expressing congruence. Cornelius-White (2016) describes congruence as 'involving an awareness of feelings, thoughts, and stories about oneself. Stories influenced by cultural variables' (p.127).

Subsequently, what surfaced were my memories of first coming to England. I felt strange, exposed and small; disconnected from the colours and smells around me. My senses were dulled. I had no reference points for what I was experiencing. I was fearful of the whiteness around me, which was reinforced by my parents, who told me to stay away from those people. *They* had bad ways! For the first time, I was seeing women's bare legs. I was used to seeing women in saris.

I felt trepidation in sharing my story with T, due to my own fears of her judgement. However, I hoped my personal memory would give her permission to bring her own cultural and personal stories to the room. Hopefully my sharing would minimise any feelings of uncertainty, vulnerability and fear she might have about doing this.

Anthias (2008) presents identity as a dynamic process of 'belonging', where one's identity takes many forms dependant on where you are, when, and in what context. This fits with my own experiences of identity as being shaped in multiple contexts. As a child in India, I lived with my cousins, mother and several aunts, in my grandmother's house. Looking back, I felt truly Indian then. The language, expressions and intentions of the people around me made sense to me; the colour of my skin was mirrored in that of others. As a result, I felt a huge sense of belonging. As a teenager in England, I felt unsteady in my identity. I was desperate to be Western, to be white; I rejected Indian food, clothes and music for British alternatives. Now, as an adult still living in England, I am undergoing a process of integration. I now celebrate my skin colour, as it reflects the history and richness of my South Indian roots. I also acknowledge the good and bad experiences of co-existing in both cultures.

Anthias (2008) discusses the notion of hybridity: the intermingling of cultural style and values. This too connects to my experiences as a second-generation South Indian. As a result of these definitions, we can access 'multiple racial configurations of self'. This view moves away from rigid, essentialised views of identity as encapsulated in the classifications defined by the majority, like

'Indian Other' or 'BAME'. Instead, we are freed to acknowledge the fluid, shifting nature of our identity. Therefore, being congruent is acknowledging that we are all in a process of self-exploration. This is echoed by Whelton and Greenberg (2001): 'Our selves are continually in a process of construction' (p.92).

I can now appreciate that my diverse experiences are a positive quality, to be prized. Sue and Capodilupo (2008) argue that sharing one's personal stories in the face of racial microaggressions creates self-belief, strength and hope. Sharing my story with my supervisee would offer a bridge to a different perspective and an opportunity for T to deepen her cultural empathy. Me telling my personal story might enable her to explore what I have described as her racialised[1] configurations of self and her own experiences of belonging. Through this interaction, I would be opening myself to my client's reality.

Indeed, when I invited T to talk about her own childhood and upbringing, she told me she was raised solely by her father in a small village, and had only recently connected with her mother and older siblings. She shared her own struggles of fitting in and finding her place in the world.

> It is through the depths of difference that we make contact with ourselves and others. (Nepo, 2015, p.95)

It can be difficult to put into words personal stories relating to one's cultural identity when it is bound up with one's first language or early childhood experiences. Therefore, in my role as supervisor with T, I could foster safety by using approaches that were not talk-based or cognitive – creative methods, such as psychodrama (exploring culture-based roles, their meanings, and influence at different stages of development) and objects (visual representations, symbolisation of feelings, experiences). I find that this way of working offers a diverse and dynamic way of processing material that arises in supervisory sessions with all supervisees.

I see person-centred supervision as a creative, facilitative and congruent process of sharing and discovering. I am guided by Cooper and McLeod's (2010) pluralistic framework, offering T agency to choose what might be meaningful to explore collaboratively and through dialogue.

I also see my role of supervisor as being about normalising the not-knowing spaces without fear or shame. Another person's frame of reference may simply be outside of our experience. How can we truly step into the uniqueness of another's multipositional, intersectional (race, gender, sexuality, age, class,

---

1. I use the term 'racialise' here in the dictionary definition: to offer a racial interpretation; to perceive, view, or experience in a racial context; to categorise or differentiate based on membership in a racial group.

ability, spirituality, neurodiversity) frames of identity? I could support T to claim statements like, 'I don't know, it's something I haven't experienced, but I am curious,' allowing her to be the expert on her experience. My modelling of this in supervision would look something like this:

Me: Does this create some fear in you?

T: Yes. She's from Pakistan, or Nigeria maybe.

Me: As you can probably imagine, my life as a second-generation, Westernised, South Indian therapist is different to yours. I don't have the experiences of fear you mention. I really want to know what this situation means for you.

Congruence and communication

Having explored the use of congruence through the process of self-involvement, self-awareness and self-disclosure, I will now focus on the importance of congruence and communication. Rogers (1961) elucidates that congruence involves transparency – the explicit communication of thoughts and feelings that are present in the moment. What persisted for me with my supervisee T was an uncomfortableness that Rogers (1990) would describe as 'something being twisted in the relationship'. I believe that the discomfort I felt was related to my concern about T's approach to diversity – her colour blindness, as expressed in her comment:

T: It's fine. She's just a person.

Me: (Pause) Okay, I see. (Silence).

I can clearly see my incongruent response in which I disown my feelings and minimise my experience. The truth was that I didn't 'see'. For me, colour blindness neutralises differences. Sue and colleagues (2007) describe colour blindness as a microinvalidation as it negates, silences and minimises the thoughts, feelings and lived experiences of people of colour. Such microinvalidations are:

> communications that exclude, negate, or nullify the psychological thoughts, feelings or experiential reality of a person of colour. (Sue et al., 2007, p.274)

Asare (2017) asserts that colour blindness acts as a device to disengage from conversations around race and racism. Arguably, this perpetuates the status quo of white power and privilege as it 'whitewashes' the racial inequities, histories of racial violence and the current trauma perpetuated by racism (Williams et al., 2010). I concur with Turner (2020, p.3) when he refutes Rogers' assumption that 'we reside in the same cultural container': Rogers is speaking from his comfort zone of power and privilege as a white, middle-class, male professional – a cultural container that does not include people like me or Turner.

Being unaware of the presence of power and privilege in the therapeutic relationship can lead to us unwittingly imposing onto the other our view and experience of the world as the norm. This is echoed by Neville and colleagues (2001): 'If race[2] is not on the table, then whose frame of reference is being used?' (p.279). It can result in cultural gaslighting. Stern (2009) describes gaslighting as the use of power to deny a person's reality, memories or experiences. The recipient is likely to feel unheard, and to doubt and deny their experiences to avoid conflict in the relationship. Whether this is done knowingly or unconsciously, I have witnessed this result in real harm to clients who are vulnerable. The client's own stressful experiences of institutional structures, in employment and education, for example, may be dismissed.

Therefore, recognising whiteness as a racialised identity is essential, not to elicit feelings of guilt but to acknowledge the unearned privileges that come with having white skin, and to gain insights into historical and current racial oppression. It is my view that limited exploration of one's personal meaning of whiteness leads to a gap in both self-understanding and the understanding of the other.

This invisibility of the racialised identity may lead to the belief that white superiority is the norm. This attitude describes a form of racial microassaults – the acting out of racist attitudes, or 'good old-fashioned racism' (Sue et al., 2007, p.274). I experienced continual microassaults in a previous work role, where my colleagues would hide their personal possessions when I walked into a room. I found this overt act of racism an unsettling, disparaging and hurtful experience. Microassaults form part of a bigger picture of macroaggressions. Gorski (2014) highlights how macroaggressions occur at a structural level encompassing actions that purposefully exclude individuals. My experiences of repeated searches at airport security and being followed by security guards in department stores reflect this type of overt racism on an individual.

Donovan and colleagues (2012) write:

> Macroaggressions occur in the nebulous space between microaggressions and institutional/structural racism. They move past the subtle,

---

[2]. Race is used here to mean a socially constructed form of identity to categorise individuals into groups based on physical characteristics.

unconscious aspects of microaggressions and microinvalidations into a more overt space. (p.186)

Examining the wider white hegemonic spaces where painful everyday experiences of racial inequity occur is our professional ethical responsibility as therapists and supervisors.

In Sue and Capodilupo's words (2008):

Being unaware of the impact of whiteness, one remains part of the system that upholds an unjust racial hierarchy. (p.170)

Chantler (2005) critiques the ethics of congruence, stating: 'The generalisation of the term congruence can avoid, obfuscate issues of intersect, power and politics' (p.246). I concur with this, and with Proctor (2017), who criticises person-centred theory for focusing predominantly on the internal world and how this impacts the therapeutic relationship, but overlooks how the individual is positioned in the external world. Social inequalities could cause the client further disempowerment and harm by thwarting their journey of personal growth.

As I sit with the injustice of this, I notice my social equality muscles flexing. I no longer wish to collude with what Taylor-Muhammad (2018) calls the 'protection of complexion', which is the shield/armour that white privilege offers, allowing such conversations to be avoided. Eddo-Lodge (2017) names these denials 'awkward cartwheels' and 'mental acrobatics'. My commitment here is to the values of BACP's *Ethical Framework for the Counselling Professions* (2018), as stated in the first clause of 'Our commitment to clients': We should 'Put clients first by making [them] our primary concern while working with them'. Supervision is about helping supervisees to focus on the values of non-maleficence and beneficence, human rights and social justice, so as to be more congruent with their clients. This includes ensuring that what's distinctive in the client's life is not overlooked (BACP, 2018). As Carroll (2014) states, the crucial task of the supervisor is to help supervisees develop their ethical antennae so they can attune sensitively to these issues. Therefore, an awareness of self as a racial being can contribute to ensuring that the boundaries of ethical practice are maintained (Sue, 2015).

In my view, the challenge here is to balance these supervisory roles (with this self-reflection?), while offering congruence, empathy and non-judgemental positive regard. T needed to feel understood, accepted and supported to develop her awareness of the boundaries of competency and ethics. I thought about my relationship with T. I had known this trainee for nearly a year. T was deeply committed to the course, wanted to do the best for the client, but was still new to processing, and vulnerable to feeling exposed and not good enough.

Carroll (2014) advises: 'What is paramount is that the supervisor is congruent in their invitation to dialogue' (p.22).

Grounded in this ethical principle of mindfulness for T's wellbeing and her professional developmental needs, I offered T a supportive space to strengthen our bond. I reflected on my own experience of meeting my vulnerabilities and blocks with compassion. This had been a powerful, healing and transformative process for me. So, in turn, I wished to offer this to T. I wanted to create a supportive and containing environment through my care and transparency. I also sought to enhance my communication through meta-awareness (what is felt about being felt), highlighting T's thoughtfulness. Throughout, I maintained a genuine belief in T's capacity to find her own way.

This brief exchange with T had initially struck me at my core. However, through deepening my own sense of racial identity, my understanding of congruence and my clarity about my role as a person-centred supervisor, I finally found the words to describe my experiences and respond to T. I've noted a few of my possible responses below:

T: It's fine. She's just a person.

Me: I'm not sure if you felt you had to rescue me in your response just now, or felt uncomfortable about something?

Me: I'm also wondering if you are responding to my stepping back. I apologise. I think the root of my reaction is a feeling that we may be overlooking something important.

Me: I worry that your statement might imply that you are overlooking the client's colour and hence their unique experience related to this. This may be replicating previous oppressive experiences. I hope this doesn't come across as a criticism of you as a person. I experience you as a thoughtful student.

Me: I don't know if you are aware or not that the colour of our skin will be linked to all kinds of privileges and feelings of difference. This will affect, in many ways, the power dynamic in your relationship with your client.

Me: This is ethically important to look at, so we don't say things unwittingly that may lead the client to feel devalued, invalidated or misunderstood.

Me: There's a lot here to think about. What's happening for you? I'd like to support you to think about these issues. Can we explore this together?

Based on my thoughts and experiences, I have consolidated my reflections of congruence in this poem:

> I fear congruence less.
> Congruence begins with courage and truth with oneself. A commitment to an honest relationship with self.
> Congruence is intimacy, knowing, seeing the insecure, unacknowledged, unaccepted parts of self.
> Congruence is a never-ending process of unravelling, revealing, reclaiming, retelling.
> Congruent is expansive! It leads to new ideas, new ways of looking at things. It puts experiences into words and meaning.
> Congruence is compassion for self and others.
> Congruence is welcoming one's own otherness, therefore your otherness.
> Congruence is a continual commitment to being seen.
> Congruence is creative, dynamic.
> Congruence cannot grow without core conditions.
> Congruence needs relational depth, presence, transparency to survive.
> Congruence can only be offered when the wider political, social, and cultural, intersectional, positional context is embraced.
> Congruence is rooted within an ethical and competency frame. The client is always at the centre of process.
> Congruence involves communicating, welcoming, strengthening, learning, challenging, accepting disagreement.
> Congruence is dialogue, conversation, connection.
> Congruence means having confidence in exploring issues of power culture and difference in the relationship.
> Congruence is emotionally demanding.
> Congruence belongs to everyone, especially when issues of power, privilege and diversity come into play.
> Congruence is reflecting, learning, growing, supporting, being seen, taking risks letting go, trusting.
> Congruence has helped me grow in my intersectional racial visibility and voice.
> Congruence in turn has helped me strive for the racial equality of other therapists and supervisors alike.
> Congruence is empowerment.

Post-reflection

This experience demonstrates that microaggressions are not small or subtle. Rather, they can be deeply damaging to our sense of self. Looking back, I am struck by the complex mental and emotional manoeuvres I was involved in – the layers of personal and professional holding: the responsibility I shouldered alone to create bridges of racial understanding and sharing and the unacknowledged emotional burden of race. This is often a tiring, exhausting and lonely experience.

During my professional and academic career, I have personally witnessed how few people of colour join the counselling profession and how acknowledgement of issues of difference in counsellor training are often marginalised or tokenistic. Now, in my role as a lecturer in counselling and psychotherapy, my congruence is expressed through challenging the systemic blocks to racial equality that result in the invalidation or lack of visibility of people of colour. Williams and colleagues (2010) describe these as environmental microaggressions. My aim, through the continued authentic sharing of my race-based experiences in supervision and teaching, is to increase awareness of such diverse experiences.

Fighting for racial equality also involves dislodging dominant cultural scripts in counselling and psychotherapy, which are often based on white, middle-class discourses. At the same time, I seek to strengthen trainee counsellors' cultural humility through promoting continued reflection on their racial and intersectional identities. Hook and colleagues (2016) define cultural humility as the therapist's ability to adopt an interpersonal stance and attune to the aspects of cultural identity that are most important to the client. I found exploring my own race story, using self-reflective questions (see below) helpful in cultivating my own cultural humility and developing curiosity towards others' race stories.

My visibility has also gathered allies (professional academics and other therapists/supervisors in practice) to collectively challenge systemic inequality. Research into the experiences of students of colour in higher education indicate that one in four experience discrimination and harassment, often leading to repercussions for their mental health and a feeling that it is not safe to express their experiences (EHRC, 2020).

Finally, my journey to visibility has led me to set up independent groups for counselling and supervision students of colour to engage in self-care and make sense of their racial experiences. Here, students can disentangle themselves, where possible, from the roles of cultural educator and cultural interpreter, and from holding the emotional load of racism.

I believe that taking risks so we can have meaningful dialogues within our profession around race/racial difference and its intersectional threads is fundamental to our personal growth. As a result, we can be visible to ourselves, congruent in our practice and deepen our relationship with others.

I want to end with a brief self-reflective exercise. I ask the reader to:

- Describe a moment when your skin colour took a particular meaning for you?
- How do you benefit/miss out because of your skin colour?
- How do you feel about this?

References

Anthias, F. (2008). Thinking through the lens of translocation positionality: An intersectional frame for understanding identity and belonging. *Migration and Social Change, 4*(1), 5–20.

Asare, M. (2017, April 13). Debunking the myth of color blindness in a racist society. *The Bowdoin Orient.* https://bowdoinorient.com/2017/04/13/debunking-the-myth-of-color-blindness-in-a-racist-society

BACP. (2018). *Ethical framework for the counselling professions.* BACP. www.bacp.co.uk/ethical_framework

Baljon, M. (2002). Focusing in client-centred psychotherapy supervision: Teaching congruence. In J.C. Watson, R.N., Goldman & M.S. Warner (Eds.), *Client centred and experiential psychotherapy in the 21st century: Advances in theory, research and practice* (pp.315–324). PCCS Books.

Cain, D.J. (2010). *Person-centred psychotherapies.* American Psychological Association.

Carroll, M. (2014). *Effective supervision for the helping professions.* Sage.

Chantler, K. (2005). From disconnection to connection: Race, gender and the politics of therapy. *British Journal of Guidance and Counselling, 33*(3), doi:10.1080/03069880500132813

Commission on Race and Ethnic Disparities. (2021). *Commission on Race and Ethnic Disparities: The report.* www.gov.uk/government/publications/the-report-of-the-commission-on-race-and-ethnic-disparities

Cooper, M. & McLeod, J. (2010). *Pluralistic counselling and psychotherapy.* Sage.

Cornelius-White, J. (*2016*). Learner-centered teacher-student relationships are effective: A meta-analysis. *Review of Educational Research, 77*(1), 113–143. https://journals.sagepub.com/doi/10.3102/003465430298563

Donovan, R., Galban, D., Grace, R., Bennett, J. & Felicié, S. (2012). Impact of racial macro- and microaggressions in Black women's lives: A preliminary analysis. *The Journal of Black Psychology, 39*(2), 185–196.

Eddo-Lodge, R. (2017). *Why I'm no longer talking to white people about race.* Bloomsbury.

EHRC (2020). *Racial harassment in higher education: our inquiry.* EHRC. www.equalityhumanrights.com/en/inquiries-and-investigations/racial-harassment-higher-education-our-inquiry

Forrest-Bank, S. & Cuellar, M.J. (2018). The mediating effects of ethnic identity on the relationships between racial microaggression and psychological well-being. *Social Work Research, 42*(1), 44–56.

Gendlin, E.T. (1978). *Focusing.* Everest House.

Ginsberg, E.K. (1996). *Passing and the fictions of identity.* Duke University Press.

Gorski, P. (2014). Consumerism as racial and economic injustice: The macroaggressions that make me, and maybe you, a hypocrite. *Understanding and Dismantling Privilege, 4*(1), 1–21.

Harper, P.B. (2000). The evidence of felt intuition: Minority experience, everyday life, and critical speculative knowledge. *GLQ: A Journal of Lesbian and Gay Studies, 6*, 641–657. http://dx.doi.org/10.1215/ 10642684-6-4-641

Hawkins, P. & Shohet, R. (1989). *Supervision in the helping professions.* Open University Press.

Hook, J., Farrell, J., Davis, D., Deblaere, C., Van Tongeren, D. & Utsey, S. (2016). Cultural humility and racial microaggressions in counseling. *Journal of Counseling Psychology, 63*, 269–277. Hycner, R. & Jacobs, L. (1995). *The healing relationship in Gestalt therapy: A dialogical/self psychology approach.* The Gestalt Journal Press.

Lambers, E. (2007). A person-centred perspective on supervision. In M. Cooper, M. O'Hara, P.F. Schmid, & G. Wyatt (Eds.), *The handbook of person-centred psychotherapy and counselling* (pp.366–378). Palgrave Macmillan.

Lewis, G. (2017). Questions of presence. *Feminist Review, 17*(1), https://journals.sagepub.com/doi/10.1057/s41305-017-0088-1

Lorde, A. (1982). Learning from the 60s. In *Sister outsider: Essays and speeches by Audre Lorde* (pp.1345–144). Crossing Press.

Mckenzie-Mavinga, I. (2018). *The challenge of racism in therapeutic practice.* BAATN podcast. Spring seminar series: Therapeutic practice that speaks across cultures. https://uk-podcasts.co.uk/podcast/baatn-podcast/spring-seminar-2018-the-challenge-of-racism-in-the

Mearns, D. & Thorne, B. (1988). *Person-centred counselling in action.* Sage.

Merry, T. (2012). Classical client-centred therapy. In P. Sanders (Ed.), *The tribes of the person-centred nation* (2nd ed.) (pp.21–46). PCCS Books.

Meyer, I.H. (2003). Prejudice, social stress, and mental health in lesbian, gay and bisexual populations: Conceptual issues and research evidence. *Psychological Bulletin, 129*, 674–697. doi:10.1037/0033-2909.129.5.674

Morris, W. (2015, June 24). *Dumber than your average bear.* Grantland. https://grantland.com/features/dumber-than-your-average-bear/

Morrison, T. (2020). *Mouth full of blood: Essays, speeches, meditations.* Vintage.

Nepo, M. (2015). *The endless practice of becoming who you were born to be.* Atria Books.

Neville, H.A. Worthington, R.L. & Spanierman, L.B. (2001). Race, power, and multicultural counseling psychology: Understanding white privilege and colour-blind racial attitudes. In J.G. Ponterotto, J.M. Casas, L.A. Suzuki & C.M. Alexander (Eds.), *Handbook of multicultural counseling* (pp.257–288). Sage Publishing.

Paradies, Y. (2006). A systematic review of empirical research on self-reported racism and health. *International Journal of Epidemiology, 35*, 888–901.

Proctor, G. (2017). *The dynamics of power in counselling and psychotherapy: Ethics, politics and practice* (2nd ed.). PCCS Books.

Rogers, C.R. (1961). *On becoming a person*. Constable.

Rogers, C.R. (1990). A client centred/person centred approach to therapy. In H. Rogers, C.R. Kirschenbaum & V.L. Henderson (Eds.). *The Carl Rogers reader* (pp.135–152). Houghton-Mifflin.

Solórzano, D. & Yosso, T. (2002). Critical race methodology: Counter-storytelling as an analytical framework for education research. *Qualitative Inquiry, 8*(23), 22–44.

Stern, R. (2009, March 19). Identify 'the gaslight effect' and take back your reality! *Psychology Today*. https://www.psychologytoday.com/gb/blog/power-in-relationships/200903/identify-the-gaslight-effect-and-take-back-your-reality

Sue, D. W. (2015). *Race talk and the conspiracy of silence: Understanding and facilitating difficult dialogues on race*. John Wiley & Sons.

Sue, D.W. & Capodilupo, C.M. (2008). Racial, gender, and sexual orientation microaggressions: Implications for counseling and psychotherapy. In D.W. Sue & D. Sue (Eds.), *Counseling the culturally diverse: Theory and practice* (pp.217–240). John Wiley & Sons.

Sue, D.W., Capodilupo, C.M., Torino, G.C., Bucceri, J.M., Holder, A.M.B., Nadal, K.L. & Esquilin, M. (2007). Racial microaggressions in everyday life: Implications for clinical practice. *American Psychologist, 62*(4), 271–286.

Taylor-Muhammad F. (2001) Follow fashion monkey never drink good soup. *Counselling and Psychotherapy Journal, 12*(6), 10–13.

Taylor-Muhammad F. (2018). Cited in Jackson, C. Why we need to talk about race. *Therapy Today, 29*(8), 8–13.

Turner, D. (2020). Race and the core conditions. *Therapy Today, 31*(8), 34–37.

Whelton, W. & Greenberg, L.S. (2001). The self as a singular multiplicity: A process-experiential perspective. In Muran, J.C. (Ed.), *Self-relations in the psychotherapy process* (pp.87–110). American Psychological Association.

Williams, D.R., Mohammed, S.A., Leavell, J. & Collins, C. (2010). Race, socioeconomic status and health: Complexities, ongoing challenges and research opportunities. *Annals of the New York Academy of Sciences, 1186*(1), 69–101.

Williams, M.T., Kanter, J. W. & Ching, T.H.W. (2018). Anxiety, stress, and trauma symptoms in African Americans: Negative affectivity does not explain the relationship between microaggressions and psychopathology. *Journal of Racial and Ethnic Health Disparities, 5*(5), 919–927. https://doi.org/10.1007/s40615-017-0440-3

About the contributors

Oye Agoro is of Yoruba ancestry, and practises as a BACP senior accredited social justice-allied, trauma-informed, integrative, intercultural therapist and supervisor, with more than 30 years' experience of working as a therapist and supervisor in a range of community, NHS and social care services. Oye has a BA in Sociology and Social Anthropology and trained at University College London/Nafsiyat Intercultural Therapy Centre. Alongside her clinical role, Oye has managed nine therapy services in London and been the director of the Lorrimore, a charity based in Southwark, providing therapy and social support to people with mental health difficulties. She was also director of The African Family Mediation Service, a charity providing a range of support services to people in Lambeth. In addition, Oye has worked as the community services manager of Kush, a Black housing association in northeast London that provided a range of housing, community support and respite therapeutic services for Black communities. Oye co-founded the Multi Ethnic Counselling Service (MECS) in south London and previously worked as a social action psychotherapist at The Forward Project, a Black mental health resource in west London. Oye currently has her own therapy practice, based in south London and operating internationally. www.waddonpondstherapy.com

Anya Amrith (artformsthemind.com) works in a trauma-informed way that is gentle and compassionate. She is passionate about creative communication and how we can use this in our society to grow, develop our thinking and improve mental health. Anya works across the voluntary and private sectors, supporting people who self-harm, are actively suicidal or experience dark thoughts. She works with people from a wide range of backgrounds, using intersectionality as a lens in her approach as she continues to learn and develop. Anya resides in the countryside with her two children and partner, and forms part of a co-parenting family.

Rachel Jane Cooke (she/they) is a queer, integrative psychotherapist, supervisor and educator from Ireland, in practice since 2009. She is based in London, runs an online therapy platform (p-therapy.com), consults to charities and social enterprises, and has a long-standing weekly radio segment on sex and relationships, where she often discusses identity, privilege and oppression. She regularly speaks on podcasts and hosts talks and workshops for the public, for therapists and for organisations on topics such as intersectionality, trauma, attachment, health and wellness under neoliberalism, embodiment, feminist therapy and gender, sexuality and relationship diversity. Rachel is passionate about training therapists committed to social justice, particularly through embodied and relational practice. You can read more about her work at racheljanecooke.com

Anita Gaspar is a psychotherapist, clinical supervisor and trainer, working from a relational integrative perspective. She is accredited with UKCP and registered with BACP, and is a member of BAATN and The Relational School. She is also a freelance editor, having worked for many years in the publishing industry.

Sam Hope is a white, transmisogyny-exempt, queer, trans, disabled and neurodivergent accredited therapist of 20 years' experience. They are the author of the book *Person-centred Counselling for Trans and Gender Diverse People: A practical guide*. With a background working with survivors of abuse, they have been offering training to therapists and organisations on LGBTQA+ topics, disability, neurodiversity, trauma and minority stress for more than a decade, alongside their private therapy and supervision practice. They are also a keen photographer and nature lover. Further resources can be found on their website (sam-hope.co.uk).

Roshmi Lovatt, MA, UKCP is a UK-based integrative arts psychotherapist registered with UKCP. She has worked in a number of settings, including within statutory, charity and private sectors. She is the founder and clinical director of BodhiSpace Ltd (www.bodhispace.co.uk), an organisation that offers psychological therapies to the local communities of North Buckinghamshire. She is a course leader and tutor at the Minster Centre, London, as well as a trainer and consultant specialising in the use of creative and embodied methods to explore themes such as race, diversity, power and difference. Her passion is to encourage a paradigm shift in the practice of psychological therapies in order to create a social justice-led model of working that is inclusive and anti-discriminatory.

Dr Ohemaa Nkansa-Dwamena is a registered and accredited counselling psychologist and a senior lecturer on the Professional Doctorate (DPsych) in Counselling Psychology at City, University of London. She is also an advanced accredited schema therapist. Her research interests lie in the use of qualitative methods to study a range of applied counselling psychology topics. Particular interests include multiple identity negotiation and issues related to race, culture and mental health. Dr Nkansa-Dwamena works primarily in private practice with former clinical positions in NHS, higher education and third sector settings.

Rajita Rajeshwar is a lecturer in counselling and psychotherapy at Salford University and a practising integrative psychotherapist, psychodramatist and clinical supervisor. She has more than 15 years of clinical experience working with adults with complex needs in the NHS and charity sector. Her work has focused on supporting refugee and asylum seeker groups. She currently works at Thriving Autistic, a charity offering therapy to neurodivergent adults. She is interested in adapting therapy for clients with cultural and neurodivergent intersects. As a human rights activist, researcher, creative practitioner, supervisor and educator, she has a life-long commitment to tackling racism, oppression and inequality.

Jaspreet Tehara is a senior counselling psychologist currently working in the NHS and private practice, following graduation from the University of Roehampton in 2020. He has research interests in the experiences of sexuality for people of colour, having completed his thesis on the topic of bisexuality experiences in South Asian men. Presently, he is working with older people, and is co-leading an NHS equity of access project for therapeutic engagement with minority ethnic older people across Northamptonshire. Previously, he has worked in forensic settings with 18–24-year-old men. Jaspreet is also a sessional lecturer on the topics of counselling and psychodynamic psychotherapy. jaspreet.tehara@nhs.net

Joanna Traynor is the founder partner of *senseia*, a consultancy specialising in culture change, with a focus on emotional safety, toxic behaviours and transition skills. Joanna is also an award-winning novelist, short story writer and TV producer. She is a keen researcher and won a Winston Churchill Fellowship to extend and deepen her understanding of Britain's role in the American Civil War. Joanna's psychotherapy practice is based in Devon.

Neelam Zahid is an integrative counsellor, psychotherapist and clinical supervisor accredited by BACP. She has practised as a therapist since 2003, having previously worked in higher education for more than a decade, and currently has her own private practice. She is also the Deputy Course leader for the Foundation Year at the Minster Centre and teaches on the Introduction to Counselling Skills course. In addition, she is currently a visiting lecturer at the University of Westminster, teaching on the BSc Psychology and Counselling and Introduction to Counselling Skills courses. Her areas of interest are intersectionality, difference and diversity and she has contributed to several publications, including *The Handbook of Transcultural Counselling and Psychotherapy* (2001) and *Black Identities + White Therapies: Race, respect + diversity* (2021).

Name index

A

Adams, M.Y. 158
Adler, N.J. 165
Agoro, O. 154, 157, 159, 168, 171
Agrawal, A. 131
Ahmed, I. 131–132
Akbar, N. 158, 169
Allen, T.W. 52
Alleyne, A. 78, 81, 83–84, 84–85, 100, 160
Allport, G.W. 18
Andrews, K. 63, 158
Anthias, F. 182
Aqil A.R. 57, 58
Archer, L. 20
Armstrong, T. 34
Asare, M. 184
Ashley, W. 62
Ashwood Garvey, A. 45
Atkinson, D.R. 165
Audet, C.T. 34

B

Bailey, M. 156
Baines, D. 57
Baker, P. 130, 133
Baljon, M. 176
Baran, M. 77, 79
Barndt, J.B. 164
Bates, S. 84
Bean, G. 45
Bell, D.A.A. 159
Bercovici, D. 133
Berne, E. 95–96, 101
Berube, K. 160
Bhatia, A. 138–139
Bhui, K. 63, 73–74

Bilge, S. 140
binaohan, b. 130, 132
Bion, W.R. 147
Black Lives Matter 5, 51, 62, 63, 65
Bollas, C. 141
Borders, L.D. 140
Boyle, M. 116
Bradley, J. 151
British Association for Counselling and
    Psychotherapy (BACP) 2–3, 72,
    106, 110, 111, 113, 140, 186
British Psychological Society (BPS) 72, 116,
    140
Brüne, M. 32
Bryant-Davis, T. 70
Buber, M. 99
Buchanan, N.T. 32
Bukhari, N. 79
Burgoyne, B. 159

C

Cain, D.J. 177
Capodilupo, C.M. 178, 183, 186
Carroll, M. 186, 187
Carter, R.T. 63
Cascio, M. 133
Chantler, K. 181, 186
Charura, D. 73
Chesler, P. 163
Choudrey, S. 135
Clarke, K. 163
Clarke, S. 141
Clarkson, P. 97, 98
Coates, T.-N. 52
Collins, P.H. 140

Comas-Díaz, L. 58, 63, 70
Commission on Race and Ethnic Disparities 179
Connell, N. 40
Cooper, M. 80, 183
Cornelius-White, J. 182
Cousins, S. 19
Crain Major, B. 164
Credit Suisse 45
Crenshaw, K.W. 70, 118, 140, 160
Cross, W.E. 165
Crowell, C. 71
Cuellar, M.J. 179
Curry-Stevens, A. 57
Cyrus, K. 140

D

Dabiri, E. 45, 49–50, 52, 53–54
David, E. 162
Davies, J. 47
Davis, A. 45, 171
Degruy, J.A. 160
Degruy-Leary, J. 63
Del Giudice, M. 32
Dennis, M. 120
Devakumar, D. 63, 141
Dhillon-Stevens, H. 98
Diamond, B. 19
DiAngelo, R. 23, 85, 87
Ding, H.T. 34
Donovan, R. 185–186
Drustrup, D. 140
Dunbar, E. 70

E

Eastwood, C. 118
Eddo-Lodge, R. 52, 163, 186
EHRC 189
Ellis, E. 21, 22, 83, 85, 88, 101, 103
Engelbrecht, N. 133
Eubanks-Carter, C. 133
Extinction Rebellion 32

F

Fannen, L. 39, 41, 46, 47, 48, 49, 52
Fanon, F. 140, 150, 158, 162
Farber, B.A. 34
Faro, K. 160
Fenton, K. 63

Fernando, S. 146
Fishburne, L. 77, 84
Fisher, M. 42
Floyd, G. 5, 51, 65, 66, 67
Foley, T. 51
Forrest-Bank, S. 179
Freud, S. 40, 57, 96
Fryer, P. 52, 53
Furman, S.A. 39

G

Gelso, C.J. 138–139
Gendlin, E.T. 177
Gerhardt, S. 45
Geronimus, A.T. 73
Gibson, M.F. 34
Gilbert, P. 151
Ginsberg, E.K. 178
Giordano, A.L. 70
Goldfried, M.R. 133
Gorski, P. 185
Gov.uk 41, 116
Gramsci, A. 162
Greenberg, L.S. 183

H

Hahn, W.K. 110
Hardy, K.V. 99
Harper, P.B. 179
Harriott, A. 79
Hassan, M. 5
Hawkins, P. 181
Hayes, J. 139
Healing Justice London 56
Heimann, P. 150
Helms, J.E. 165
Henry, L. 79
Herman, J. 40
Hernandez, P. 111, 112, 113
Hersey, T. 169, 170, 171
Hirsch, A. 12
Hofstede, G.J. 18, 21
Holti, R. 131, 134
Hook, J. 189
hooks, b. 45, 158, 163, 171
Hope, S. 132, 133
Hubl, T. 164
Hycner, R. 181

I

Ikuenobe, P. 149
Ilga Europe 132
Irons, P. 18

J

Jackson, C. 79
Jackson, S.L. 77, 84
Jacobs, L. 181
Jana, T. 77, 79
Jenkins, B. ix
Jenkins, J. 74
Johnsen, C. 34
Johnson, M. 40
Johnson, R. 107, 108, 114
Johnson, V.E. 83
Johnstone, L. 116
Jolley, K.H. 34
Jones, B.A. 170
Jones, C. 45
Jones, K. 164
Jones-Nielsen, J.D. 63, 65
Joseph, B. 147
Judge, P.S. 149
Jung, C.G. 57

K

Kaleidoscope 133
Kareem, J. 73
Katz, J.H. 164
Kaur, J. 19–20
Kendi, I.X. 49, 52, 79
Kernberg, O. 139
King, D.K. 32
King, K.M. 140
King, M.L. ix
Kirby, J. ix
Klein, M. 139, 147
Kohli, R. 16, 17
Kuri 118
Kwarteng, K. 78

L

Lago, C. 73
Lambers, E. 176
Laszloffy, T.A. 99
Laungani, P. 140
Layton, L. 140
Leary, K. 140

Lee, S. ix
Leslie, P. ix
Levy, K.N. 139
Lewis, G. 181
Lichtman, R. 44
Lipscomb, A.E. 62
Lipsky, S. 162
Littlewood, R. 73
Livingston, R. 114
Loewenthal, D. 43
Lorde, A. 45, 171, 179

M

Malcolm X ix
Martín-Baró, I. 58
Martinez, E. 158
Mason-John, V. 168
Masson, J.M. 40, 44
Maté, D. 163
Maté, G. 163
McDowell, T. 111, 112, 113
McGoldrick, M. 143
Mckenzie-Mavinga, I. 5, 112, 160, 180
McLeod, J. 183
Mearns, D. 80, 177, 182
Menakem, R. 21–22, 49, 86, 100, 102
Mensah, B. 78
Merry, T. 175
Meyer, I.H. 140, 179
Michael, A. 17
Milton, D. 133
Miserandino, C. 33
Mitchell, S.A. 138
Miu, A.S. 69
Moore, J.R. 69
Morgan, H. 51
Morgan, L.M. 132
Morris, W. 177
Morrison, T. 64, 178
Mullan, J. 72, 161, 169

N

Nadal, K.L. 18
Nap Ministry 169
Natalya, D. 161
National Health Service (NHS) 30, 32, 35, 36, 42, 47, 94, 106, 113, 119
Nepo, M. 183
Neville, H.A. 185

Nichols, E.J. 154, 170
Nobles, W. 162, 169

O

Ocampo, C. 70
O'Connor, M. 51
Odafe, M.O. 63
Office for National Statistics 159
O'Keefe, V.M. 18
Ojelade, I. 160
Okun, T. 164
Olusoga, D. 74

P

Palsson, G. 18
Paradies, Y. 63, 141, 179
Phipps, A. 132–133
Pierce, C.M. 15, 79
Platt, L. 141
Porges, S.W. 39, 46
Powell, E. 158
Proctor, G. 186
Psychologists for Social Change 56
Psychotherapy and Counselling Union (PCU) 56

R

Race Equality Foundation 62
Radical Therapist Collective 44, 45
Radical Therapist Network (RTN) 56
Raghavan, R. 63, 65
Rape Crisis 92
Ratcliffe, S. 126
Rathod, S. 74
Reed, A. 53
Rogers, C.R. 57, 92, 176, 184, 185
Rowe, W. 165
Royal College of Obstetricians and Gynaecologists (RCOG) 159
Runyan, A.S. 160
Russell, C. ix
Rutherford, A. 52

S

Saad, L. 9, 51, 128, 130
Said, E.W. 141
Samaritans 92
Samra, R. 118
Samuels, A. 43

Sandler, J. 139
San Francisco Psychoanalytic Institute 95
Saunders, B. ix
Scala, J. 139
Schell, C.J. 158
Schultz, C.M. ix
Sears, M. 16
Sears, W. 16
Serano, J. 124–125, 134
Settles, I.H. 32
Shakespeare, W. 12
Shell, E.M. 63
Shohet, R. 181
Siegel, D.J. 85, 103
Singer, J. 34
Singh, R. 149
Smail, D. 45
Smith, J.A. 64
Smith, L.C. 98–99
Solórzano, D.G. 16, 17, 175–176
Some, L.M. 172
Some, M.P. 172
Soto, A. 126
Stallings, E. 71
Steiner, C. 95
Stern, D.N. 150–151
Stern, R. 185
Sue, D. 85
Sue, D.W. 15, 79, 87, 164, 178, 183, 184, 185, 186
Synergi Collaborative Collective 169

T

Tagouri, N. 78, 84
Tarakali, V. 163
Tasca, C. 40
Taylor, B. 5
Taylor-Muhammed, F. 178, 186
Taylor, S.N. 171
Thames, A.D. 63, 169
Thomas, L.K. 150–151
Thomas, R. 30
Thorne, B. 177, 182
Thunberg, G. 51
Tippett, K. 49
Torres Rivera, E. 58
Totton, N. 43
Towle, E.B. 132
Truth, S. 132

Tulshyan, R. 79
Turner, D. 27, 79, 85, 185
Tutu, D. 126
Tweedy, R. 43, 44

U
UKCP 2

V
van der Kolk, B. 40, 41, 82
Verdonk, P. 118

W
Walker, A. 45
Walley-Jean, J.C. 133
Walton, W.E. 18
Warwick, R. 141
Whelton, W. 183
White, A.I. 141
Williams, D.R. 185, 189
Williams, M.T. 179
Wilson, C. 40
Wilson Gilmore, R. 169
Winnicott, D.W. 150
Wirth-Cauchon, J. 40
Women's Aid 115
World Health Organisation (WHO) 134
Wright, W.D. 154
Wykes, E.J. 16

Y
Yalom, I. 57
Yellow Bird, M. 163
Yosso, T. 175–176

Z
Zahid, N. 77, 82
Zitkala-sa 18

Subject index

A

ableism 31, 134, 169, 170
   internalised, 125
abuse 2, 10, 118, 194
   childhood, 108
   childhood sexual, 32, 40
   as a form of coercive control 116
   cycle of, 2
   dual roles as, 117
   intraprofessional, 2
   of power 126
   power-motivated, 115–116
   racial, 1, 116, 156, 158
   racist, 49
acceptance 102, 103, 127, 131, 146, 166
   LGBTQA+, 124, 134
accreditation (therapist) 93, 94, 95, 97
ADHD 32, 40, 49, 133
adult ego state (TA) 101, 102
agency 4, 156, 183
ally/allies/allyship 25, 52, 70, 112, 114, 115, 116, 130–31, 189
anonymity (*see also* confidentiality) 2, 25, 80
anti-oppressive practice 7, 26–27, 55, 56, 57–58, 69, 84–87, 120, 128
   training in, 52
assimilation 180
authenticity (in therapeutic dyad) 148
autism 40, 49, 125,
   diagnosis of, 133

B

biomedical 35, 47, 48
black
   beauty 162
   deaths in custody 160
   as ethnic identity 175
   feminism 37, 45, 118
   Irish 51
   'not black enough' 95
   as 'other' 64, 68, 98
   as racial construct 41, 52, 53, 60,
   women, sexualisation of, 158
Black Lives Matter
   movement 5, 51, 62, 63
blackness ix, x, 53, 65, 68, 97
body/bodies 5, 15, 22, 26, 35, 36, 37, 47, 48, 67–68, 70, 82, 83, 86, 87, 100, 120, 121, 128, 155, 156, 162, 168, 170, 177, 180
   accrediting/professional, 4, 95, 96–97, 102
   'of culture' (Menakem) 49
boundaries (therapeutic) 3, 96, 106, 110, 117
   breach of, 113
   of ethical practice 186
   professional/managerial, 117
brown
   people, homogenisation of 12
   as racial identity 25, 53
   women and girls, stereotypes of, 19–21
brownness 177

C

capitalism 5, 30, 36, 39, 40–41, 45, 46, 48, 50, 51, 52, 169–170
   consumer, 31, 45
   as a dissociative state 46–54
   late-stage, 36
   therapy under, 38, 44

women participating in, 36–37
castration anxiety 150–151
Catholic 32–33, 90–91
childbirth 159
chronic fatigue syndrome (CFS) 32
cis- 33, 128
   heteronormativity 31, 43
   heterosexuality 165
   man/men 36–37, 39–40, 40–41, 44, 127, 141
   therapist 43, 131
   woman/women 105, 128, 132, 154, 166
class/classism 31, 34, 36, 39, 41, 45, 50, 53, 118, 162, 165, 180, 183–184
   -based hierarchies 54
   dominant, 178
   middle, 19, 32, 33, 34, 39–40, 44, 98, 105, 141, 185, 189
   mixed, 159
   'ruling hegemony' (Gramsci) 162
   working, 32
climate crisis/ecological emergency 30, 35, 51
coalition-building 54–55
coercive control 44, 82, 105, 115–116, 119
colonisation 131, 158, 160, 171
colour (*see also* homogenisation, misidentification, race, racism)
   awareness of difference 95, 190
   celebration of, 162, 182
   clients of, 43, 64, 65, 68, 69, 70, 71, 120
   invisibilisation of, 15–16, 18–19, 185–186, 187, 189
   and racism 14, 15, 52, 98, 101, 158
   of skin 1, 11, 19, 23, 52, 77, 82, 84, 99, 140, 148, 158, 162, 181, 182, 185, 187
   students of, 16, 87, 105, 110, 112, 113–114, 115, 120, 189
   supervisor of, 27, 103, 114–115, 176
   therapist/practitioner of, 4, 5, 6, 10, 27, 28, 62, 63, 64, 65, 68, 69, 70, 71, 72, 74, 105, 115, 116, 120, 176
   woman of, 19, 78, 80, 81, 82, 84, 105, 109
colour-blindness 9, 178, 184
competence/skills (*see also* training) 3, 115
   cultural, 37, 112, 126, 179
   supervision framework 110, 111, 113
complaints procedure 2

confidentiality 2, 4, 24, 80, 110
   breach of, 2
   client, 2
   and harm 4
conflict
   cultural, 166
   dual roles 110
   of interests for trainers 3
   of power in therapeutic relationship 185
congruence 181, 184, 187, 188, 189
   definitions of, 182
   ethics of, 186
   guidelines for, (Cain) 177
   in supervision 176–177
consumerism 5, 41
context(s) 13, 30, 39, 43, 44, 46, 48, 57, 74, 78, 109, 111, 145, 147, 179, 182, 188
   awareness of, 5
   of colonialism 131–132
   cultural, 132
   of educational organisation 28
   of forensic examination 82
   historical, 42
   of historical and continued racism 16
   of historical racial inequalities 159
   LBGTQA+, 128
   professional, 62
   racial, 183
   safe, 113
   social, 31, 56
   socio-economic/political, 141, 166
   of structural oppression 39
   training, 31
   UK, 165
continuous professional development (CPD) 2, 28, 80
conversation (*see also* dialogue) 68–69, 80, 101, 106, 108–09, 112, 113, 117, 128, 181
   about race 19, 21, 22, 23, 25, 67, 102
countertransference 139, 150, 151
crip theory 55
'critical/controlling parent' (TA) 96
cultural imperialism 169
   deconstructing, 164–165
culturally sensitive practice 70

D

decolonisation/decolonising 56–57, 161, 171

therapy 57, 72–73
dialogue (*see also* conversation) 66, 103, 183
   negative, 101
   peer, 70
   around race 70, 74, 87
   in supervision 111, 187
dissociative 'disorder' 32
diunital 154
   healing 170–172
diversity 28, 70, 95, 98, 100, 101, 102, 107, 119, 131, 146, 175, 178, 184
   of BIPOC culture 167–168
   gender, 129, 132
   law concerning, 3
   neuro-, 133
   in professional ethical frameworks 4
   within therapeutic practice 72, 98
dual roles 110, 117
dysregulation (*see also* emotional regulation) 98, 102, 103

E

embodiment/embodied 50, 98, 110
   abuses of power 116
emotional/nervous system regulation 39, 54
   skills 36
empathy/empathic 5, 103, 120, 130, 133, 151, 176, 181, 186, 103
   cultural, 183
epilepsy 32
equality (*see also* inequalities) x, 5, 93, 94, 98, 119, 186
   racial, between client and therapist 93–94, 98, 188,189
   as ethical principle 3–4
Equality Act (2010) 4
ethical framework 2, 4
   BACP 2
   UKCP 2
eurocentric 44, 47, 57, 58, 73, 140, 150
   curricula 113
'evidence-based practice' 47
exploitation 3, 7, 51, 52, 158
externalisation 169
extractivism 51

F

family matrix (systemic) 143
fear 73, 74, 128, 150
   amygdala and, 21
   of client's racism 98
   of congruence 188
   of criticism/exposure 7
   as defensive white reaction, 23
   of discrimination 94, 98
   of being invalidated 102
   of professional shaming 2, 4, 183
   of racial/cultural differences 177
   of racism 74, 98, 179
   silenced by, 2, 179
   of speaking out 121
   in the supervisory relationship 179
   white, 128, 150, 177, 181, 182, 184
feminist(ism) 140
   black, 37, 45, 118
   therapy 56
fostering
   transracial, 155, 159
fragmentation
   of therapist 150

G

gaslighting 2, 15, 82–83, 185
   cultural, 185
gender 21, 43, 49, 50, 71, 101, 118, 131, 162, 165, 180, 183
   -based trauma 167
   binary, 170
   diversity 129, 132, 135
   incongruence 123
   pay disparities 166
   race and, 135
   stereotypes 166
   'third', 128, 132
Global North 41, 46, 47, 53,
Global South 175
'Gotcha' game (Berne) 95–96
grief/loss 9, 30, 35, 65, 67, 69, 74, 84, 85, 94, 155
   anticipatory, 66
   loss of identity 84

H

harm
   from clients 2
   to clients 3, 120, 185
   of coercive control 113
   confidentiality and, 4

ethical value 72
iatrogenic, of therapy 42, 57, 134
caused by microaggressions 84, 85, 86
from peers/colleagues 2
psychological, 150
racially motivated/racialised, 120, 146
racist, 1, 2, 14, 16
self-, 162–163, 193
systemic, of oppression 42, 44, 74
of white defensiveness 85, 115
healing (*see also* diunital)
community/collective, 56, 57, 164
embodied, 170
indigenous traditions/rituals, 168–169
journalling as source of, 66
through narrative/story 5, 160
as neoliberal concept 41
practices 48
from racial harm/trauma xi, 4, 27, 87–88, 158, 160, 162, 165
self-care as, 70
self-regulation and, 39
social justice-allied, 169–170
as source of harm 46
space, therapy as 164, 165
supervision as, 187
therapy praxis 168–170
heritage 12, 19–20, 51, 128
British South Asian, 126
cultural, 20, 28, 99, 101, 166
dual, 175
English/white, 94
ethnic, 128
Jamaican, 37
mixed-, 32
mixed religious and class, 159
racial, 15, 20, 131,
South Asian, 134,
South Indian, 177
hijra 127, 128, 131, 132
history 13, 18, 38, 39, 40, 50, 51, 158
ancestral/heritage 15, 16, 19, 22, 24, 26, 28, 32, 37, 51, 94, 99, 126, 128, 129, 131, 134, 159, 164, 166, 168–169, 172, 182
British and North American, 158
colonial, 123, 131
of colonisation 118
of empire 158

Indian, 132
of oppression 58
of racism 132
homogenisation 81–82, 84
homosexuality
criminalisation of, 132
declassification as a mental illness 134
Human Rights Act (1998) 4
humility 84, 130
cultural, 189
hybridity 182–183
hysteria (Freud) 40, 49

I

identity/ies (*see also* misidentification)
and belonging 182
cultural/racial/ethnic, 15, 175, 178, 189
and difference 50
models of formation (racial/ethnic) 165–168, 170, 182
gender, 125, 129, 132–133
and 'hybridity' 182–183
importance of, 48, 49
and intersectionality 117–118, 119, 126, 160
LGBTQA+, 134
loss of, 84–85
marginalised, 32, 43
and misidentification 81, 82
multiple jeopardy and, 32
names and, 11, 12–13, 16, 18, 25, 28
pathologisation of, 134
personal narratives and, 48
racial/ised, 22, 25, 65, 66, 180–181,183, 185
and recognition trauma 180
shared (client–therapist) 127, 131
threat 73
imperialism 31, 39
cultural, 164–165, 169
inclusion/inclusive 3, 4, 12, 49, 62, 64, 77, 98, 119, 194
trans, 134
indentured labour/-ers 5, 18
Indian 25, 128, 129, 132, 182–183
South, 177, 178, 182, 184
Tamil, 175
inequality/-ies 5, 73, 74, 120, 160, 162
economic, 65

racial, 18
racial health, 159
social, 186
structural, 4, 124, 161
systemic, 189
inner/archaic child (TA) 96, 101, 102,
institutional racism 63, 116, 159, 160,
intergenerational trauma 63, 160, 168, 170,
interlocking oppressions 134–135
intersectional/-ality 19-21, 54, 56, 71, 73, 81, 111, 113, 117–119, 120, 135, 140, 159–160, 161, 180, 188, 190
   feminism 37, 56
   healing approach 169
   identity model 165–168, 183–184, 189
   justice 168
   theory of, 32
   violence 163
invalidation 189
Irish 8, 32–33, 34, 37, 51, 53, 95, 154

J

Jewish 12
judgement/judgemental 96, 124, 182
   non-, 102, 164, 170, 186

L

language 10, 32, 35, 39, 46, 48, 64, 68, 112, 133, 145, 182, 183,
   of capitalism 48
   of polyvagal and trauma theory 46
   of 'the science of safety' 46
   utilitarian, 48
lesbian 126–127
LGBTQA+ 124, 129, 131, 133, 134, 135
   and colonisation 126
   context in South Asia 128
   laws against, 131
   white, 124, 130, 134
liberation psychology 56, 58
lived experience 33, 38, 43, 71–72, 83, 84, 127, 128, 129, 131, 158, 167
   of black people 169
   narratives of, 48
   of oppression 162–163
   of practitioners of colour 115
   a therapist's, 64–69
love 9, 91, 172
   radical self-care and, 171

M

marginalisation/-ised 25, 33, 130, 189
   clients 131
   communities 56, 128, 164
   experiences 44
   groups 9, 163
   identities 32, 43, 167
   multiply, 135
   populations, 162–163
   stories 135
mental health/illness 18, 30, 35, 45, 47, 48, 49, 57, 63, 64, 71, 92, 96–97, 134, 189
   black therapists', 71
   effect of racism on, 73–74, 169
   of ethnic minorities 179
   inequality in systems 73
   pathologisation 32, 48, 129, 132
   professionals 72, 87
   racial disparities in, 74
   and racial trauma 74
   trans identities labelled as, 134
   worker 127
meta-awareness 187
microaggression(s) 2, 15–17, 27, 63, 77–78, 79, 82–83, 84–85, 86, 107, 114, 116, 125, 131, 157, 158, 185–186, 189
   effects of, 18, 49, 63, 79
   environmental, 185
   racial, 18, 79, 175–176, 178, 179, 183
   racist and transphobic, 133
microassault 15, 185
   racial, 185
microinsult 15
microinvalidation 16, 184, 185–186
migration 180
minimisation 63
minority development models 165–168
minority ethnic 5, 25, 175
   groups/peoples 106, 141, 148
   patient 140
   therapists 138, 140–141, 149, 151
   trainee 151
minority stress 133, 140, 194
   model (Myers) 179
misidentification 78, 79–81, 86, 87
misogynistic 40, 95, 157, 167
   abuse 156
misogynoir 55, *156*

mixed-heritage 32, 159
mixed-race 23, 41, 53, 95
multiculturalism 100
multiple jeopardy 32
multiple minority stress theory 140
Muslim
    journalist and activist 78
    psychotherapist 12
    women 19

N

name(s) 11, 12–13, 14, 16, 17, 25, 26–27, 77, 78, 80, 83 (*see also* misidentification)
    amnesia 18
    -calling 15, 65
    English/Western, 22, 28
    forgetting, 13–14, 16, 18, 19, 28
    gendered, 132
    mispronunciation of, 11, 12, 16–17, 28
    non-English, 11, 16
    power of, 17–18
    renaming 17
    shame around, 18
    of slaves 18
naming 135, 160, 165
    of culture 111, 112
    difference 118
    experience of the world 159
    experiences of racism 160
    feelings 144
    pain 181
neoliberal(ism) 31, 41, 57, 169–170, 194
    Western, 131–132
neurodivergence/neurodiversity 34, 124, 125, 126, 127, 135, 183–184, 194
    and racism and transmisogyny 133–134
neurotypical 33
Nigeria/Nigerian 32, 53, 93, 99, 100, 157, 162, 177

O

oppression
    capitalist, 45
    challenging systems of, 58, 72–74, 116, 135, 167
    and injustice 56
    within institutions 116–117, 169
    internalised, 28, 121, 162–164, 166, 168
    intersectional, 8, 9, 54, 55, 57, 117–119, 140, 160–161
    LGBTQA+, 131
    race-related 10, 23–24, 52, 71–72
    systemic, 36, 39, 42, 58, 134, 170
    therapy as palliative for, 44
    and 'tone policing' 130
    trauma of, 30, 63

P

pandemic/coronavirus/Covid-19 5, 30, 57, 62, 63, 65, 68, 69, 141
part-object (psychoanalysis) 147
passivity
    presumed, in Asian women, 134
patriarchy 31, 41, 162, 164, 166, 169, 172
    hierarchical, 118
    white, 97
peer group support 146
personal development 1, 3, 4
personality 'disorder' 41
    emotionally unstable, (EUPD) 32, 40, 125–126, 127, 129, 133–134
pharmaceutical industry 39
police 30, 156,
    custody 160
    station 155–156, 160
polyvagal theory 39, 46
post-traumatic stress disorder 179
    complex, 32
poverty 35, 36, 46, 58, 90
power 7, 16, 20, 21, 24, 50, 57–58, 97, 111, 112, 118, 119, 158, 159, 163, 166, 176, 186, 188
    abuse of, 126
    balance in therapy 5, 34, 110, 111, 184
    dynamics of, 8, 14, 74, 140, 187
    economic, 140
    hierarchy of, 42–43
    within institutions 116–117
    in knowledge 50
    -motivated abuse 115–116
    of names 17–18
    patriarchal, 166
    structures 47, 118
    teacher/supervisor over student 17–18, 21, 113, 114, 115, 116–117
    transformative, 171
    white, 184–185

premenstrual dysphoric disorder (PMDD) 32, 40, 49
presence 181
privilege 1, 8, 28, 42–43, 54, 57–58, 74, 160, 163, 176, 180, 188
  class 185
  educational, 36
  intersecting axes of, 161
  and power 58, 158
  professional, 69, 70–71
  systemic, 140
  white, 8, 23, 28, 101, 184–185, 186
projection 138, 147, 149
  of maleness onto trans women 125
  transference and, 138–140
prosody 46
psychoneuroendocrineimmunology (PNEI) 31
psychosocial
  mental health 49
  suffering 47
  wellbeing 35

Q

queer 8, 34, 43,
  people 166
  studies 55
  theory 57
  therapy 56

R

race 14, 16, 18–19, 24, 41, 42–43, 50, 64, 69–70, 71, 73, 74, 85, 86, 87, 88, 97, 101, 117–118, 127, 135, 138, 140, 144–145, 147, 148–149, 162, 163, 165, 178, 179, 183–184, 185, 189, 190
  -based hierarchies 54
  construct (Ellis) 22
  conversations about, 21–22, 23, 27, 67, 71, 102
  critical race theory 176
  and development of the other 140–142
  discrimination 65
  identity 180, 181
  minority, 25
  and multiple jeopardy 32
  'race reductionism' (Reed) 53
  -related stress and trauma 62, 63, 69, 71, 72, 74, 179

  -related violence 65
  as social construct 51–54
  as tool of oppression 64
'racial passing' (Ginsberg) 178
racial stress 23, 73
racial trauma 5, 6, 21, 22, 27, 62, 72, 73, 75, 110, 160–161
  effects of, 62–70, 74
  historical, 7, 62, 72, 108,
  pathologising, 114, 126
  repair/healing from, 5, 25–26
  self-care and, 70
racism (*see also* colour, harm, healing, microaggression, race, shame, white fragility, whiteness)
  anti-racist practice 72–74
  challenging, 1–2, 71, 87–88
  of clients 98–101, 148–149
  and colonialism 131–132
  coping mechanisms/strategies 63, 65, 163, 168, 178
  critiquing concept of, 52, 158, 159
  dehumanising impact of, 9
  effects of, 2, 17, 22, 64–66, 157, 169
  and ethical practice 4–5
  historical, 16, 18, 141, 159, 166, 167, 185
  institutionalised, 95, 97, 116
  internalised, 112, 121, 162–164
  invisibilising as, 185–187
  and neoliberalism 57
  normalising, 92
  'scientific', 52
  structural, 12
  and transmisogyny/transphobia 125, 126, 131, 132–134, 134–135
  and trauma 62–64
  unconscious, 24, 25, 130–131
recognition trauma 5, 112, 180
relational/relationality 27, 35, 37, 43, 80, 82–84, 87, 138, 147, 150–151, 188
  cultural theory 56
  safety 111–112
  trauma 1, 22
relationships 83, 86, 130–131, 138–139, 164, 166, 168
  dual, 3
  part-object, 147
  working, 109
reptilian (lizard) brain 21

respect 3, 9, 48, 72, 73, 92, 167, 177
risk 6, 13, 15, 25–26, 84, 87, 102, 106, 123, 132, 133, 156, 178, 179
    for therapists of colour 63, 72

S

safeguarding 110
    students/trainees of colour 113–115
safety 3, 9, 12, 24, 36, 39, 51, 55, 70, 97, 102, 108, 125, 130–131, 132, 146, 155, 160–161, 183
    emotional, 195
    relational, 111–112,
    science of, 46
self-awareness 12, 34, 159, 167–168, 172, 181, 184,
self-care 10, 36, 55, 189
    and racial trauma 70
    radical, 171
    and tools for anti-oppressive practice 84–87
self-compassion 127, 159, 168–169, 171
self-disclosure 34, 182, 184
self-image 44
sex 34, 50, 55
    binary, 131, 132
    work/worker 33, 39, 55
sex-critical 55
sexual abuse
    childhood (CSA), 32, 40
sexual harassment/assault 40
sexuality 49–50, 165, 183–184
    and discrimination 71, 117–118, 131
shame/shaming 2, 11, 18, 35, 36, 83–84, 98, 100, 101, 108, 110, 119, 121, 128, 129, 130, 155, 162, 176, 180, 181, 183
    cultural, 28
    professional, 148
slavery 5, 18, 169, 171
social justice 31, 34, 42, 55, 57, 70, 71, 109, 167, 186
    -allied approach/therapist 169
social media 37, 66, 87, 16
solidarity 1, 8, 9
South Asian
    clients 134
    culture 77, 149
    diaspora 16
    ethnicity 132
    heritage 126, 134
    man/men 15, 24, 195
    trans woman 129
    women 134
South Indian
    heritage 177
    immigrant diaspora 178
    roots 182
    second-generation, 182, 184
    therapist 184
splitting (Bion) 147
spoon theory 33
stereotype/-ing 124, 125, 162,
    gender, 166
    racial, 12, 19, 20, 21
stigma/stigmatised (*see also* mental health, hijra) 32, 40, 129, 132
    racial, 129
structural bias 114–115
structural racism 5, 12, 46, 185
supervision (clinical)
    competence framework (BACP) 110, 111, 113
    learning congruence in, 176
    cross-cultural', 175
    independent groups for students/trainees 189
    key questions/issues for, 26–27, 103–104, 129, 131, 139–140
    peer group, 27, 146
    person-centred, 183–184, 187
    placement, 106, 107, 117, 146
    racially-matched, 27, 109–110, 117
    as safe space to process/reflect 109, 146, 147, 148, 151, 181, 186
synaesthesia 34,
systemic privilege (in the therapy dyad) 140

T

Tamil Indian 175
therapy models
    CBT 31, 36,
    existential 31,
    focusing (Gendlin) 177
    Gestalt 31
    person-centred 31, 176, 183, 186
    pluralistic 183
    psychoanalysis 95, 140

psychodrama 183
psychodynamic 31, 56, 151
transactional analysis (TA) 95, 96
therapeutic relationship, 43, 71, 95
   difference/diversity in, 97–98, 98–99, 139, 140–141
   power imbalance in, 185, 186
   self-censorship in, 164
   transference in, 138–139
threat 21, 46, 116, 132, 138, 145, 146, 148, 151, 158, 163,
   identity, 73
   non-verbal, 108
   trauma as a, 160
tokenism 63
training/education (*see also* racism, white fragility)
   cultural competence, 52
   eurocentricity of, 73
   limitations of, with regard to minoritised/oppressed groups 39, 44, 64–65, 71, 189
   negative experiences of tutors of colour 99
   racism/discrimination in, x, 4, 8, 9, 18–19, 24–25, 120, 189
   reform of, 114, 119
   white fragility in, 23
trans 125, 130, 132, 133, 134, 135
   client 131
   therapist 128, 131
   woman/women 123, 125, 126, 127, 128, 129, 132–133,
transference 138, 146, 149, 151
   negative, 149
   and projection 138–140,
   total transference interpretation 147, 150
transmisogyny 124, 125
   and neurodiversity 133–134
   racialised, 129, 132–133, 134
transphobia/phobic 31, 39, 43, 123, 125, 126, 131–132, 134
   and misogyny 125, 126
transracial fostering 158, 159
trauma 10, 63 (*see also* racial trauma, post-traumatic stress disorder)
   in childbirth 159
   therapy (*see also* polyvagal theory) 39, 46,
   vicarious, 66
trauma porn 9

trauma-informed theory/practice 39, 56, 74

U

unconditional positive regard (UPR) 126, 176

V

validity 2, 38, 140, 156

W

wellbeing 63, 65, 68, 71, 108, 140, 149, 161, 162, 187
   of clients 3
   emotional, 18, 168
   material, 45
   of people of colour 9
   psychological, 45, 168, 179
   psychosocial, 35
   socioemotional, 35
   spiritual, 168
Western 40, 118, 151, 162, 182
   culture 98, 164, 165
   name 22
   neoliberalism and paternalism 131–132
   talking therapy 167
white (*see also* whiteness, colonisation, Western)
   fragility 22, 23-24, 115
   gaze 53
   privilege 8, 23, 28, 101, 186,
   silence 24
   supremacy x, 4, 5, 22, 23, 28, 31, 41, 56, 101, 127, 157–158, 159, 162, 165, 166, 169, 170
whiteness
   engaging with, 85–87
   as knowledge system 53
   as racial identity 53, 185
'window of tolerance' 46, 85, 98, 103

Y

Yoruba 53, 154

Z

Zoom/video 68, 78